From Recife to Manh

MW01600960

by
Daniela Levy

Translated by Victor Meadowcroft

Book Design by Todd Hester

BdMPublishing

www.amazon.com

ISBN: 9798828728251

Dedication

I dedicate this book to the great Anita Novinsky,
for the teachings of an entire lifetime.
To my husband, my companion in every moment,
and to my daughters, Sophia and Bruna.
- *Daniela Levy*

"He who was able to continue his task until nightfall – he who
believed in a better world, in the efficacy of good, in spite of the
skepticism of men and the lessons of history, he who did not
despair, who did not head for the cabaret to unburden himself of
man's responsibility to serve; he who did not seek distraction or
suicide, who did not flee from the strain of living with
responsibility, is the only one, perhaps, who truly deserves to be
called a revolutionary."
- *Emmanuel Levinas*

Table of Contents

.

List of Figures

Foreward

Just as the subjects of this book, I too am an immigrant from Recife to America. When I came to America, I took an airplane; the immigrants of the 1700s had no choice but to come by boat, a much more difficult journey. I am a U.S. citizen now, who lives in Los Angeles, and gets to meet and talk with many people from different backgrounds, religions, races and social classes. I was surprised how so few people knew the story of how America's first Jews came here. This is an adventure story, a triumphant tale of overcoming injustice, and a reminder of how we can change the present by understanding the past. I would love more Americans to know it.

When I found out about Daniela's insightful and significant work, I instantly decided to put all my efforts into releasing it to the entire world so everyone could learn about this forgotten but yet important piece of history. Recife is known as the Brazilian Venice, and in the timeframe this book covers, it had a direct trade route with Amsterdam with whom they traded sugar, the number one commodity of the age. Due to religious intolerance, the entire Jewish culture was driven away from the Recife region. The Portuguese colonizers were very unfair and so eventually paid a high economic price and tainted their human rights legacy.

I want to promote this story and turn it into a film or TV series or both, so this type of injustice doesn't happen again. All governments must understand their responsibilities and the impact their actions and decisions have on the welfare of the people of the world. Only then can different cultures and human beings learn to live together in peace and stop causing pain to each other. Our strength is in our differences, not our similarities.

Looking back, I wonder what would have become of Recife if the Jewish community had stayed there?

– Frederico Lapenda

Preface

Daniela Levy's book, which I have the satisfaction of introducing here, uncovers the poignant story of the Jewish people's tireless movement around the world. After the atrocities experienced in Portugal (forced conversions, massacres, inquisitorial surveillance) and the brief hope of freedom in Brazil – frustrated after only a few years – the New Christians found themselves once again on the move and, this time, with no fixed destination. They arrived in another America, known as New Amsterdam, where they would face the excesses of an antisemitic governor who made life difficult for them at every turn.

Authorized by the Dutch rulers, the small group of 23 Portuguese Jews who had arrived from Recife, indebted and with nowhere to turn, attempted gradually to begin a new life. And, it turns out, these converted Jews played a considerable role in every area they became involved with in New Amsterdam: the development of mercantilism, trade relations, culture, health, laws, etc.

At the beginning of this century, the work of Werner Sombart alerted researchers in economic history to a phenomenon that had until then remained ignored: the fundamental role that Portuguese and Spanish Jews, spread across the globe, had played in the development of European merchant and finance capitalism. Looking to enhance his work, Sombart inadvertently found himself confronting the Jewish question. Influenced by Max Weber's research into the relationship between capitalism and puritanism, Sombart delved more deeply into the study of the influence of religion over economic life, in an attempt to draw links between ideals and economic behavior. When trying to understand the reasons for the flourishing of commerce in Northern Europe and its decline in the south, the explanations Sombart uncovered, essentially attributing this to the discovery of new trade routes to the Indies, appeared insufficient to him. After endless research, he came to the conclusion that the expulsion of the Jews from Spain and Portugal and their dispersal across the globe were essential factors in the slide towards decadence of the Iberian nations and the prosperity of cities such as Amsterdam, Livorno, Hamburg, Frankfurt, Antwerp, etc. And, furthermore, that the Jewish presence in these cities had been a determinant factor in the development of European capitalism; much like the great discoveries, the mining and exploitation of gold and silver and the technical advancements of the age, the actions and enterprises of Iberian Jews had been decisive. Sombart's thesis was heavily disputed, both for its methodology and for his claims about the relatively moderate participation of Jews in financial and economic life in Northern Europe.

While we do not share Sombart's belief that the Jewish people were guided by "the capitalist spirit," there is, as Fernand Braudel has suggested, little doubt that they were able to adapt effectively to the geography and circumstances of trade. This adaptation appears to have been particularly fruitful in America, although there is still very little known about the extent of New Christian involvement in financial and mercantile life in the Portuguese and Spanish colonies. In response to investigations into his precarious claims, Sombart himself conceded the deficiency of the material at his disposal. One of the principal gaps in this material, and one which prevented the drawing of solid conclusions, was an ignorance of the "origins" of the men involved in the colonial trade.

Sadly, half a century on from Sombart's findings, we must acknowledge that scant progress has been made in this regard and little or nothing added to support or discredit his thesis on the economic activities of Portuguese New Christians in America. It is necessary to begin, first of all, by determining "who were" those men at the center of the commercial activity of the age – what was their background, their cultural heritage, their beliefs, their values and to whom were their economic and familial ties. Judicial records, a rich source for students of human sciences, can prove enormously helpful in this regard. They allow us to answer questions about genealogy, levels of education and employment, as well as to understand social groups: their solidarities, their rivalries, their disputes, their inclinations and their attitudes. The New Christians, both those who publicly declared themselves Jews and those who practiced Judaism in secret, as well as those still embedded within Catholicism following a number of generations mixing with Old Christians, present differing behaviors, and, as a result of the stereotypical interpretations of historiography, we are yet to fully understand the various ways in which they lived and thought.

In order to legitimize discrimination and violence against New Christians, the propaganda of the time focused on the Jews' own "worldview," with the concept of a "chosen people" being misrepresented, or perverted, as a position of privilege, a racial monopoly, when, in truth, there was no suggestion of favoritism in the bond between God and the Jewish people, but rather a choice that implied responsibility and constant betterment.[1]

But now a question rears its head, posed by the victims: what did the spokespeople for humanism do? Where were the Jewish spiritual leaders during the genocide of Portuguese New Christians or the destruction of Jewish communities in the 20th century?

Examining the anti-Jewish literature in Portugal and the propaganda against converted Jews in *Sermões* alongside the antisemitic writings of German authors, such as Abraham a Sancta Clara, a 17th century monk and spiritual model for Martin Heidegger, the destruction of the Jews at the beginning of the Modern Age, as with the 20th century, is unsurprising. This was a logical consequence, consistent with Western thinking. These are the words of Sancta Clara: "Aside from Satan, men have no greater enemy than the Jews. For their beliefs, they deserve not only the gallows, but also to be burned at the stake."[2]

Theodor Adorno, author of an exhaustive study into the antisemitic personality, demonstrates in his essay *Education After Auschwitz* that antisemitism is a pattern that is deeply rooted within civilization. Over centuries, and in numerous countries, Jews have been accused of ritual crimes. To paraphrase Adorno, I would argue that the *autos-de-fé* (ritual public penance) were the real ritual crimes, during which inquisitors spoke of the salvation of the soul just as Hitler spoke of salvation for the German nation.[3]

Adorno further suggests that the anti-Semite is less dependent on the object of his hatred than on his own subjective needs and psychological desires. Feelings of hostility toward Jews are a self-

---

[1] See KRISTEVA, JULIA. *Étrangers à Nouse-même*. Paris: Fayard, 1988. p. 95-111.

[2] "Abrahmishe Lauberhult"., 1921. Apud FARIAS, Victor. *Heidegger e o nazismo – moral e política*. Rio de Janeiro: Paz e Terra, 19988. p. 5-6.

[3] COHN, Gabriel (Org). *Theodor W. Adorno*. São Paulo: Ática, 1986. p. 33-35. See also ADORNO, Theodor. *La personalidad autoritária*. Buenos Aires: Proyección, 1965.

defense mechanism against personal failure. One who affirms that what occurred "was not all that bad already defends what took place and unquestionably would be prepared to look on or join in if it happens again." What is left for us to do, then, after the Inquisition, after Auschwitz? The author demonstrates the need for us to question our unconscious mechanisms, without which Auschwitz (and the Inquisition) could never have existed.

Adorno suggests that the issue of education is of primary importance. We live in a society captivated by objects, machines. That is the tendency, it is the spirit of the world. If men were not cold, if they were not profoundly indifferent to what happens to others, Auschwitz would not have been possible, because people would not have accepted it. For Adorno, the inability to identify with others was, without a doubt, the psychological condition that allowed something like Auschwitz to take place within a relatively civilized society. For Adorno, the failing all of us share today, without exception, is a lack of love. But in order for people to love, we would need a different kind of structure. One of the major drives of Christianity was to eliminate coldness, which penetrates everything. However, the experiment has failed. It is possible that the human warmth we so crave has never yet existed – or perhaps it only existed within some Pacific Island tribe. If anything were able to assist against coldness, as a tragic condition, it would not be the repression of human impulses, but rather an understanding of the very conditions that engender horror, and the battling against them, at the level of the individual first and foremost.[4]

It was antisemitism that forged, created and invented the Jew inside every Portuguese person. Perhaps the profound and insoluble anguish that inquisitorial repression produced in the souls of the Portuguese contributed to the fact that each one, every family, sought to forget the traces of their origin. With the exception of a small group of intellectuals, who kept a consciousness of Portugal's Jewish past alive, what imprinted itself upon the Portuguese masses was a forgetting of their dead, which, as Adorno points out, is the forgetting of oneself.

We must look for those "unconscious mechanisms" in the education that was imposed by Portuguese Catholicism, which

---

[4] ADORNO, Theodor, op. cit., p. 43-45.

repressed all of the most authentic human impulses. Education in Portugal abolished the love of fellow man in exchange for the love of God. To assess the sincerity of a confession, the Inquisition used as a yardstick the denunciation by children of their parents or by parents of their children.

The coldness with which the misfortune of "the other," of "the Jew," was witnessed was a result of an "education for death, not an education for living." The Portuguese were able to "live" through the horrors of *autos-de-fé* because all their love for fellow humans had been smothered, from childhood, by love of the greater good. And, as Adorno observes, as soon as the state is placed above the rights of the members of a society, the conditions for "horror" have been created.[5]

In relation to the identities of New Christians, Sombart set out from an affirmation which must be carefully clarified: not "all" New Christians found scattered around the Portuguese and Spanish territories or spread across Europe were Jewish. Faced with the challenge of establishing which of the enterprising New Christians were Jewish, the historian is presented with the requirement to define the term "Jewish." From the start, two interpretations become entangled: the religious and the socio-economic. From a religious point of view, despite the existence of New Christians in Catholic countries who kept up their Jewish faith for centuries – evidence of effective "Marranism" – the majority of the Portuguese population with remote Jewish ancestry, whether condemned by the Inquisition or not, could not be considered Jewish in the strict religious sense. From the broader point of view of "cultural heritage," the matter changes radically and becomes even more complicated. It can only be fully grasped with a deep understanding of the "phenomenon" of the Portuguese New Christian, without the simplistic definitions resulting from an acceptance of official sources, in this case the trials of the Inquisition, which lack the necessary degree of criticism.

It is also fundamental to understand how these trials functioned, as well as the fact that, in general terms, all suspects were considered guilty, and what the term "Judaizers" meant to the Inquisitors. An investigation into the psychology of the herd mentality could certainly provide huge insight into the behavior, values and

---

[5] Idem.

worldviews of such a large portion of the Portuguese population. Contrary to what is generally believed, the tragic "Jewish condition" of the Portuguese did not derive from the religious world, but was a result of problems within society.

Challenging conditions for survival, persecution and extermination all led New Christians back to Orthodox Judaism, but they also drove many to the verge of renouncing their beliefs. Like the Inquisitors, Sombart supposed that, one or two centuries after their conversion, as far as historical memory was concerned, all of the descendants of *conversos* should still be considered Jews.

Although we cannot speak in exact terms, we know that a significant number of New Christians lived in the New World and possessed excellent conditions, resulting from long experience, to take advantage of "the light that was offered." Without having invented Capitalism themselves ("did anybody invent it?" asks Fernand Braudel), they had an influence over it. They played an important role in the colonies in the West Indies, as traders and plantation owners in places such as Brazil, Surinam, Jamaica, Martinique, etc. Their strengths first became apparent in commercial and financial dealings in Holland and then England. Yet the wealth of the Jews of Amsterdam was insignificant in comparison to the city's Christian population, being, in the opinion of the Christians, a mere drop in the commercial budget of the great metropolis, though a significant and powerful drop.

The links between New Christians and those in other countries who shared their religion allowed them to have a sense of the pulse of the international market and to develop commercial relationships. In the 17th and 18th centuries, the expressions "New Christians" and "businessman" were synonymous. What we do not know, however, is the extent of participation New Christians from Brazil had in foreign commerce. Brazil, more than any other region, was the place where New Christians were able to fully develop their abilities. Despite Portuguese legislation relating to men of Jewish descent being frankly discriminatory, they were able to work around the situation and manage their businesses, acquiring positions of prestige and influence.

As the possibilities for development in their home country became more and more constrained, New Christians increasingly found themselves facing the challenge of having to survive at any cost, leading them to seek out and create new avenues and working methods. Some of the circumstances already in their possession, and which would prove essential in the early days of merchant capitalism, such as contacts and familial ties, a common language and a sense of trust, became increasingly important. New Christian merchants crossed the Atlantic tirelessly, carrying goods and ideas. They were men from different social backgrounds, consisting of as many merchants as graduates from Coimbra or even simple craftsmen. Despite inquisitorial persecution, some came across opportunities to enrich themselves and ascend socially, becoming a part of Brazil's upper classes.

The 17th century saw the precipitation of the crises of the Portuguese and Spanish empires. Confiscations by the Inquisition interfered in the economies of the Iberian countries and increasingly hindered trading activity, while Northern Europe presented ample opportunity to men with no pedigree or personal fortune. During the Habsburg reign over the peninsula, the persecution of New Christians in Portugal intensified, along with prejudice and myths of ethnic purity which hammered away inside the minds of the population, and rivalry between Old and New Christians became aggravated, leading to a rise in emigration. Whole regions became depopulated as a result of the lack of vision of the ruling classes, while, paradoxically, Brazil became a place of refuge and exile.

The economic upswing caused by the success of sugarcane cultivation, and the euphoria resulting from the discovery of gold, attracted large numbers of refugees. For two centuries, the Inquisition interfered in the behaviors and activities of these colonizers, periodically dragging large numbers of men and women down to the prisons of the Holy Office. This persecution, though still the subject of very little study, left marks, forcing many to abandon their lands and families in search of fresh exile. Braudel draws attention to the correlation between persecutions, massacres, expulsions and forced conversions of Jews and what he calls *conjuncture movements* (cycles or trends) in certain countries. He also highlights another important factor: the way these movements and struggles correlate not only with great historical events and extended periods of change, but also with smaller crises, over the years, during the day-to-day. It would be interesting to investigate

the persecutions carried out by the Inquisition in Brazil at determined periods and the local crises that followed in their wake.
  – *Anita Waingort Novinsky*

Introduction

In 1654, following twenty-four years of great economic prosperity, cultural development and huge opportunity experienced by Jews in Dutch Brazil, the Sephardim were forced to leave in search of a fresh start.

As with all summers, the days were not always filled with sunshine. There had been thunderstorms, floods and obstacles to overcome.

The peaceful relationship between Catholics, Calvinists and Jews is one of the myths constructed by official historical narratives, Dutch as well as Portuguese and Brazilian. While it was in the interests of the directors of the Dutch West India Company to favor religious coexistence, rivalry and professional competition often prevented Catholics, Protestants and Jews from living together in complete harmony. The Jews were, however, considered important political allies by the Dutch, and their role in helping overcome challenges in the new colony could not be overlooked. They had proven particularly important in establishing new commercial enterprises, primarily because they had mastered both Portuguese and Dutch, languages that benefited them in terms of trade.

Yet, once the Portuguese recovered the territory from the Dutch, the Inquisition, never having lost its hold over the rest of Brazil, restored its influence over Pernambuco. The Dutch returned to Holland, and the Jews were forced to leave the Northeast of Brazil and go in search of another land in which to rebuild their lives.

So began an arduous new pilgrimage. A fresh exile, following a brief interlude of freedom. Documents show that around 600 Jews left Dutch Brazil, abandoning assets and businesses. Their departure was turbulent, because the sixteen ships they set sail on lacked the space to accommodate all of the exiles.

After a tortuous journey, a group of Brazilians managed to reach Holland; others landed in the Guianas, Barbados and Martinique, and one small party, consisting of 23 people, arrived in New Amsterdam, now New York.

The group arrived in Manhattan in the Autumn of 1654, just days before the Jewish New Year. The new land, far colder than the one before, presented greater challenges. The frosty reception of the local governors, prejudice, discrimination and an attempt to prevent Jewish involvement in the local economy already hinted at the harshness of the coming winter. For the governor of New Amsterdam, Peter Stuyvesant, the Jews were "hateful enemies and blasphemers of the name of Christ." There were constant quarrels and confrontations between the Jews and the authorities, and religious difference served as an excellent pretext for social discrimination.

In Brazil, Jews and Calvinists had shared common interests, but this was not the case at the beginning in New Amsterdam. The region's society was affected by intense rivalries for economic survival, following the model of medieval guilds, and New Amsterdam was in fact characterized by a medievalism that had long since died out in Europe.

However, these challenges did not prevent a tiny group of Brazilian Jews and their ancestors from taking part in the development of the small colony of New Amsterdam, which would go on to become "the capital of the world": New York.

In Spring, the first victories took the form of developments within the community itself, such as the organizing of a cemetery, a place in which to commemorate religious traditions and the early stages of an aid network to help the neediest. As years went by, Jews gradually began engaging in various professions, working as butchers, bakers, and even becoming prominent businessmen.

Following their initial years of adaptation, Jews became involved in the development of commerce, then still incipient, the coordination of the early stages of the financial market, the construction of modern hospitals, the struggle for political emancipation, and the institution of renowned universities and cultural centers

Gradually, the Jewish population began to occupy a position within the colony's social hierarchy, demonstrated by elegant furniture and household items purchased from tradesmen and sales agents. Small European luxuries began arriving in Manhattan, such as damasks, saffron, quality paper, sassafras, sarsaparilla, medicines and medical equipment.

The Brazilian Jews brought with them enormous creativity, whether in the fields of medicine, literature, languages or human and natural sciences. The Christians took note of this spirit. On one occasion, a group of rebellious colonists challenging the impositions of the English metropolis sought out a Jewish community leader, Asser Levy, one of the twenty-three refugees from Brazil, for advice on the position they should adopt in response to English colonial policies.

Jewish women also contributed to local commerce, having had a long history of participation in this sector, a tradition that was resumed in New Amsterdam. As shopkeepers or influential merchants, widows would often take over the businesses of their deceased husbands, and even single and married women were allowed to manage small stores. One example of an influential merchant was Rachel Levy, sister of Asser Levy, who controlled the rum importation business for Boston and Rhode Island and sometimes brought in chocolate from Curaçao.

And when the new summer finally arrived, the struggle for the defense of democratic ideals was invigorated by the proclamation of American independence, and the Brazilian Jews and their descendants were granted equal rights and full citizenship, paving the way for them to achieve their dreams.

A line from Benjamin Franklin perfectly encapsulates the spirit and character of those pioneers: "Those who would give up essential Liberty, to purchase a little temporary Safety, deserve neither Liberty nor Safety."

1. Amsterdam: Return of the New Christians to Judaism

At the end of the 16th century and beginning of the 17th, Portuguese New Christians, fearing persecution by the Inquisition, fled to Amsterdam, Rotterdam, Hamburg, and Bordeaux – as well as leaving for Italy, North Africa and the Levant (now Turkey) – where they were able to resume the traditions of their ancestors and organize themselves into communities. The different branches of the diaspora maintained dynamic economic, social and cultural relationships and were characterized by a constant geographic mobility.

After 1609 came what is referred to as the "Twelve Years' Truce" between Spain and Holland, ending the Spanish embargo on maritime transport and on Dutch commerce with Portugal. New financial opportunities opened up in Holland for Portuguese New Christians. At the time, Portugal was governed by the Spanish crown, a fact that led to animosity between the Spanish and Portuguese, and vice versa.

Under Spanish dominion, religious intolerance in Portugal intensified, and Holland became a political and economic refuge for many Portuguese of Jewish descent. By 1952, some Portuguese New Christians were already living in the Netherlands, such as Rafael Cardozo Nemias, Manuel Rodrigues Veiga (who arrived from Antwerp in 1595) and Garcia Pimentel, who was born in Portugal, but had lived in Italy until 1595 when he left for Amsterdam.[1]

---

[1] PIETERSE, Wilhelmina C. *Livro de Bet Haim do Kahal Kadosh de Bet Yacoov*. Assen, 1970, 26. Banhos de Raphael Cardoso Nemias, of Lisbon, aged 23, resident of Amsterdam for 15 years. March, 1607. Apud SALAMON, H. P. The first Portuguese of Amsterdam. Documents from the National Archive of Torre do Tombo: 1595-1606. *Caminiana Revista de Cultura Histórica, Literária, Artística, Etnografia e Numismática*, n. 8, p. 34, Jun. 1983. PRINS, Izak, *De Vestiging der Marranen in Noord-Nederland in de Zestiende Eeuw*. Amsterdam: Menno Hertzberger, 1924. P. 161 – 171. On the date of 31st of March, 1957, Manuel Rodrigues Veiga was the first Portuguese immigrant to take the oath as a citizen of Amsterdam. Apud SALAMON, H. P., op. cit., p. 34. Garcia Pimentel was a member of the Garcia da Orta family. SALOMON, H. P., op. cit., p. 34 (notes).

After 1597, an increasing number of Portuguese New Christians began to arrive in Amsterdam. The arrival of the first group of *conversos* is mixed up in the personal tragedy of one family of Portuguese New Christians. When Gaspar Lopes Homem and Mor Ridrigues were taken to the Inquisitorial prisons in Lisbon, in 1594, accused of practicing Judaism, Mor Rodrigues, despairing over the fate of her children, asked her brother-in-law, Miguel Lopes, to flee Portugal with his niece and nephew, Maria Nunes and Manuel Lopes, then both 18 years old.[2]

The entire family, alarmed at the incarceration of Mor Rodrigues and Gaspar Lopes Homem, orchestrated the escape. The Inquisition worked on the basis of denunciations within the family network, and as soon as one member was imprisoned it became clear that it was only a matter of time until, like a house of cards, they all would be.

Miguel Lopes managed to strike a deal with two ships' captains who agreed to take them to Amsterdam. But the journey would not be a peaceful one for the Lopes Homem family. The ship carrying Maria Nunes, her brother Manuel Lopes and their uncle Miguel Lopes was intercepted by an English fleet, in the midst of the war being waged between England and Spain for maritime hegemony, and escorted to the port of London.[3] The ship's commander, an English duke, was captivated by the beauty of young Maria Nunes and eventually proposed to her. But the young lady declined his offer, asserting that she was already engaged to a cousin who had left Brazil on course for Amsterdam, where they were to be married – her future husband bore the same name as her brother, Manuel Lopes Homem.

The rejection of an English noble by a young Portuguese woman was communicated to Queen Elizabeth I, who was intrigued by the affair and ordered Maria Nunes to be brought before her. In order to discuss the matter, Elizabeth I invited the young lady on a ride through the streets of London in her carriage, where, according to the poet Daniel Barrios, the queen "exhibited Maria Nunes's beauty

---

[2] National Archive of Torre do Tombo – Inquisition of Lisbon. Trial of Gaspar Lopes Homem n. 8,543.

[3] There were numerous reasons for the conflict between England and Spain, among them the dispute over maritime hegemony. Spain were seeking to neutralise English influence in the Spanish Netherlands.

before the English people."[4] The conversation appears to have had a positive outcome for the Portuguese *conversos*, with Elizabeth I authorizing their ship to be released and escorted safely to Amsterdam.[5]

Maria Nunes, her brother and their uncle disembarked in Amsterdam in 1597. The next year, another section of the family also reached Amsterdam – their uncles Pedro Homem and Duarte Fernandes, their aunts Branca Nunes and Izabel Nunes, and their cousins. Young Maria Nunes's fiancé arrived in the same year, coming from Pernambuco, Brazil, and the wedding was celebrated on November 28, 1598.[6] In the meantime, her parents were undergoing torture in the prisons of the Holy Office. Her father, Gaspar Lopes, was sentenced to work as an oarsman on the galleys, and her mother, Mor Rodrigues, to exile in Africa. Because both were gravely ill, Mor Rodrigues was allowed to stay in the "penitential neighborhood" of Santa Marinha in Lisbon, and, after two months working on the galleys, Gaspar Lopes had his sentence commuted to exile in Brazil. In 1605, Mor Rodrigues and some of her children escaped to Antwerp, and, following a general pardon in 1605, Gonçalo Homem sailed from Brazil to Amsterdam, where he was reunited with a section of his family. His son, Antonio Lopes Pereira, who had been with his mother in Antwerp, arrived in Amsterdam in 1610 and took the surname Abendana – a surname that would also be adopted by his sister's husband, Francisco – because it was the name of a well-respected family within the community of Dutch Jews in Recife.[7]

Other New Christians arrived in Amsterdam from Portugal and Brazil, among them a businessman named Duarte Saraiva, a future

---

[4] Elizabeth I was the daughter of Henry VIII and Anne Boleyn. She was the last ruler of the Tudor dynasty.

[5] BARRIOS, Daniel Levi. *Triumph del gobierno popular en la casa de Jacob.* Amsterdam, 1683. P. 455-456. Volume B from the Bibliotheca Rosenthaliana (9G12), 5, 9. SALOMON, H. P., op. cit., p. 35-36.

[6] The story of Maria Nunes was recounted by the poet Daniel Levi de Barrios, op. cit., p. 455-456. The story is corroborated by a letter written by the Dutch ambassador in London on April 24, 1597, in which he relates the story of a Dutch ship carrying Portuguese passengers which was seized by the English. On this ship there was a young lady with an air of nobility about her who was travelling to Amsterdam to be married.

[7] There were five men living in Dutch Recife with the surname Abendana: two David Abendanas, Isaac Abendana, Manuel Abendana and Jacob Abendana.

benefactor of the Jewish community in Dutch Brazil. Duarte Saraiva was then 26 years old and had been living with his family in Olinda, where he owned property, since 1590.[8] Saraiva was the protagonist of the second marriage celebrated in Amsterdam – his bride, 19-year-old Maria Nunes de Sá, was a niece of Gaspar Lopes Homem and daughter of Pedro Nunes.[9]

The Jewish community of Amsterdam was therefore formed by the descendants of *conversos*, who had fled the Iberian Peninsula after spending several generations estranged from the Jewish world. The New Christian pioneers in Amsterdam had to face new kinds of existential challenges. The first of these was a redefining of their own Jewish identity and a delimitation of the contours of that identity. Because, at the same time as they had cultivated a profound critique of Christianity, they had also begun adopting some of the Christian symbols.[10]

There is a great deal of similarity between the Jewish Iberian society of Amsterdam and many other Sephardic communities. All considered the preservation of Halakha, the collection of Jewish laws, as an ideal that would afford legitimacy to the existence and functioning of their institutions. All harbored certainty of the common bond of a universal Jewish destiny. An attentive reading of the records of community protocols reveals a high degree of similarity in their rules and statutes, with the organizational structure of the community in Amsterdam principally characterized by an adherence to Jewish traditions.[11]

With the arrival of *converso* businessmen in Amsterdam, the Jewish community started to become organized. One section returned to Judaism, although with significant practical difficulty, since, after decades of living within a clandestine world in which Jewish customs and traditions inherited from their ancestors had mixed with Christian traditions, there was a great gulf in knowledge that would only be filled by the arrival of rabbis from Eastern Europe, whose mission it would be to instruct the new-arrivals in

---

[8] SALOMON, H. P., op. cit., p. 38.

[9] Idem.

[10] KAPLAN, Yosef. *Judios novos en Amsterdam:* estudio sobre la historia social e intelectual del judaismo sefardi en el siglo xviii. Barcelona: Gedisa, 1996. p. 45.

[11] Ibid, p. 48

their religion. Many New Christians would sign official documents including their Christian name alongside their Jewish one, demonstrating the cultural symbiosis existing at that time.

The new Jewish community built a cemetery in 1614, started its own printing press and set up institutions for the support of widows, the infirm and those orphaned by the Inquisition, called the Santa Companhia de Dotar Órfãs e Donzelas pobres [The Holy Company for the Adoption of Orphans and Poor Maidens], more commonly known as Dotar. Sometimes, the number of Inquisition refugees in need of assistance was so great that it overwhelmed the aid organizations. When this happened, the new-arrivals were sent on to other communities in Italy, Turkey or the Americas.

Construction of a great synagogue began in 1672, when the Jewish community made up 7,500 of the 200 thousand inhabitants of Amsterdam, representing a little more than 3.5% of the population. At its inauguration, in 1675, the Jews were able to enjoy an eloquent sermon delivered by Rabbi Isaac Aboab Fonseca, who had led the synagogue in Recife.[12] They also bore witness to the beauty and grandiosity of the structure in which the Jewish sacred texts, the Torah, were kept, known as the Holy Ark, or Aron Hakodesh, and crafted using jacaranda from Pernambuco – a gift from the New Christian Jerônimo Nunes da Costa, a prominent importer of Brazilian wood. Decorated with columns and obelisks, the structure has a raised central section on which the ten commandments are engraved in gold. The central pulpit, also jacaranda, is intricately carved.

The phoenix was chosen as the symbol for the synagogue, its image signifying the rebirth of the Portuguese New Christians within Judaism, following the example of the mythical phoenix that rises from its own ashes.

The synagogue's statutes centered around communal administration and were based upon laws adopted by the Jewish community of Venice. The council of elders, or Mahamad, was given authority to resolve all matters, and anyone ignoring their decisions could be penalized or, in some cases, even banished. Their

---

[12] WEITMAN, David Y. (Rabbi). *Bandeirantes espirituais do Brasil:* século xvii. São Paulo: Maayanot, 2003. p. 207.

responsibilities also included an investment in social well-being and education.

Politics in the Netherlands was centralized at the level of a provincial government. There was autonomy for the provinces, which were sovereign within the federation. The States General, a kind of parliament, was authorized to sanction only what had been approved by local provincial assemblies. Each province had its own *stadtolder*, a proxy to the king who combined the roles of governor and military commander and did not need to be a prince of the House of Orange or even a member of the dynastic lineage. Cities still contained church councils, but their power was limited by the secular government, a fact that favored a politics of religious tolerance.[13] For Jews to ensure their *status*, they were required to report to the magistrates of Amsterdam, representatives of the Dutch merchant class who acted as self-proclaimed regents.

These regents employed a policy of tolerance toward the Jews. There were tensions between Calvinists, Anabaptists and Lutherans, or Orthodox Calvinists and Liberals, and more opposition to Catholics than there was discrimination against Jews. When flooding or some other natural disaster occurred in the city, accusations were leveled against the Catholics rather than the Jews. The Catholics were associated with a demonized papacy, while the Jews were simply remembered as Hebraists.[14] But there were some who put up resistance to those they termed "foreigners," and medieval antisemitism was preserved in Christian traditions. Religion was used as a pretext for fear of the economic competition represented by Jews and New Christians.

The social structure of the Jewish community in Amsterdam was composed of learned rabbis, such as Joseph Pardo, Isaac Uziel and Saul Levi Mortera, who produced treatises, sermons, poetry and literary texts; a middle class consisting of doctors, lawyers and engineers; an underclass, which grew mostly from the arrival of

---

[13] SCHAMA, Simon. *O descomforto da riqueza:* cultura holandesa na época de ouro. São Paulo: Companhia das Letras, 1992. p. 102.

[14] BODIAN, Miriam. *Hebrews of the Portuguese Nation:* Conversos and Community in Early Modern Amsterdam.

illiterate Ashkenazi Jews fleeing the Thirty Years' War that had devastated the German states and their elite merchant classes.[15]

The Dutch economy was highly urbanized and primarily based on trade in cereals, wine, cod, ship-building materials and the maritime transport of these goods, as well as products required to stock the internal market.[16] The economy was left in the charge of those termed merchants, who were in fact the great mobilisers of commercial activity. They were involved in international trade, the land- and maritime-transportation of goods, the manufacture of products and also brokerage or, in many cases, a combination of all these activities. The principle commercial products were sugar, tobacco, spices and diamonds, sold almost exclusively to Lisbon, Porto and Madeira, despite these still being cut off from trading in essential products, such as cereals from the Baltics, hides from Moscow and iron and copper from Sweden.

The merchants were active participants in the multicultural Amsterdam Stock Exchange. Founded in 1602 by investors in the West India Company, the Stock Exchange counted several Sephardic Jews among its first brokers and investors, but it was only after 1604 that Jewish involvement became intensified, with the number of Jewish merchants who traded there eventually doubling. Two prominent businessmen involved in the Stock Exchange during the decade of the 1680s were the jewel merchant Jacob Athias, a relative of Isaac Athias, from Dutch Recife, and his partner Manuel Levy Duarte, with Rodrigo Dias Henriques acting as their broker. Brokering activity became so intense on the streets of the Jewish neighborhood, and even in the synagogue, that the Mahamad was forced to intervene and prohibit trading on the synagogue patio.[17]

The guilds, Amsterdam's associations of merchants and craftsmen until the end of the 17th century, tried to prevent Jewish involvement, limiting the number of Jews in each sector. The surgeons' and brokers' guilds, for example, admitted very few Jews, while the guilds for booksellers and fishermen did not impose any

---

[15] Idem.

[16] SCHAMA, Simon, op. cit., p. 580.

[17] PETRAM, L. O. The World's First Stock Exchange, 1602-1700. How the Amsterdam Market for Dutch East India Company Shares Became a Modern Security Market. Groninga: Istituut voor Cultuur en Gschiedenis, 2011. p. 42-46.

restrictions. These obstacles did not prevent there being a great diversity of trade within the Jewish economy. At the beginning of the 18th century, Jews could be found working in the textile and porcelain industries, in inns and taverns, as goldsmiths, and even in the production of cheeses.[18]

After 1609 and the Twelve Years' Truce between Spain and Holland, which ended the Spanish embargo on maritime transportation and on Dutch trade with Portugal, opportunities for expansion opened up for Holland's New Christians.

In Amsterdam, some Jews and New Christians dedicated themselves to the sugar trade, possessing an advantage in this area thanks to their international trade network. Through contact with relatives spread around the world, Jews in these communities had easy access to the production sites of Portugal's transatlantic colonies.

One example of such a network was the Milão family. The patriarch was a Portuguese New Christian based in Portugal, while two of his sons lived in Pernambuco, and his brother-in-law in Amsterdam. The sons sent sugar to their father in Portugal, who sent the product on to his brother-in-law in Amsterdam where it was refined and distributed to the rest of Europe.

Economically, Jews represented an important part of society, since 13% of deposits at the Bank of Amsterdam were made by members of this community. Trade was conducted in accordance with Dutch law, as the Jewish code of laws did not contain any articles regulating economic matters.

In the synagogues, issues relating to business were prohibited, and an environment limited to questions of morality was imposed. It was here that Sephardic society concerned itself with the upholding of Jewish traditions in response to tendencies being manifested in different spheres of the social lives of its members.[19]

The families of Jewish-Portuguese businessmen operated like clans. Marriage was generally kept within the Jewish community. Their way of life was captured by Dutch painters, such as Romeyn de Hooghe, who depicted Isaac Nunes, Jeronimo Nunes da Costa and the Pinto family.

---

[18] SCHAMA, Simon, op. cit., p. 583.

[19] KAPLAN, Yosef, op. cit., p. 80.

For Amsterdam's Sephardic Jews, adhering publicly to Judaism and remaining within the Jewish community allowed them to preserve the family capital, despite the distances over which members of the same family were often dispersed. The Jewish religion served as a unifying factor between distant branches of the family. Adherence to Judaism facilitated control over the family fortune and aimed at preventing its dissipation.[20]

Although Holland's Sephardic Jews played a vital role in the Dutch economy, laws were passed between 1614 and 1615 to regulate the ability of Jews to remain in the country. These laws were based upon three clauses:

- Jews could in no way calumniate or blaspheme against the Christian religion or its savior.
- Jews were prohibited from engaging in any form of proselytizing. (This measure would have little effect, as the rabbis themselves were reluctant to accept voluntary converts.)
- Jews were prohibited from any sexual or conjugal relations with a Christian woman. The transgressor could face violent punishment.

In 1651, Rabbi Measseh ben Israel, head of the Jewish community, received authorization from the church council of Amsterdam to publish texts in languages other than Dutch. Despite this show of tolerance, the Calvinist Church spared no effort in converting Jews. There was a professor at the University of Leiden whose specialty was entering into theological arguments with Jews, with the aim of convincing them of the superiority of the Christian faith.

The one exception to this intolerance were the studious humanists, committed to reinstating Hebrew as one of the three indispensable classical languages, and in a position to attenuate conflicts between the two religions in the interests of the academic community.[21]

The Jews of Amsterdam were committed to preventing themselves becoming absorbed by the society that had received

---

[20] Ibid, p. 89.

[21] SCHAMA, Simon, op. cit, p. 580-581

them. They preserved their fluency in Spanish and Portuguese and accepted both Jews and New Christians as members, in recognition of the fact that all shared a common social and ethnic heritage. However, all members of the community were required to comply with the precepts of Jewish law and also to identify intimately with the Torah.

According to Yosef Kaplan, there was, over time, a profound shift in the mentality, consciousness and sense of identity of Jews in Amsterdam. The New Christians were converted into "New Jews," and the community they founded reflected the paradoxical process of secularization that was taking place at the time, giving rise to the process of modernization of European Judaism.[22]

---

[22] KAPLAN, Yosef, op. cit., p. 48.

2. Brazil Invasion and Christian Collaboration

The Dutch always maintained a good economic relationship with the Portuguese, to whom they provided merchandise from the Far East that could be resold in other European countries. In return, the Dutch received sugar and brazilwood from the Portuguese.[23]

Between 1580 and 1640, or rather, within a sixty-year period, the kingdom of Portugal underwent considerable change, entering a phase known historically as the Iberian Union. When the king of Portugal, Dom Sebastião, disappeared during the battle of Alcácer-Quibir, it triggered a dynastic crisis for the Portuguese Crown because the king left no successor.[24] Until the impasse could be resolved, his great-uncle, Cardinal Dom Henrique, assumed the throne. Succession was disputed between Catherine de' Medici, queen of France and a supposed descendent of the old king, Dom João III; Duchess Catherine of Braganza, niece to Cardinal Dom Henrique (and the strongest claimant to the throne); Emmanuel Philibert, Duke of Savoy, and Dom António, Prior of Crato, both nephews of the Cardinal-King; and Ranuccio of Parma and Philip II of Spain, both great-grandsons of Manuel I, the Fortunate.

The Portuguese New Christians formed a strong and influential party in support of Dom António, Prior of Crato, who was the illegitimate son of Violante Gomes, a New Christian woman, and Dom Luís, second son of Manuel I, the Fortunate. Their marriage would have taken place in secret, explaining why Dom António was considered illegitimate. Although Dom António presented proof of the matrimony between his parents, his uncle, the cardinal, annulled a judicial decision to recognize the marriage. Despite strong opposition from his uncle, Dom António was able to move freely among the Portuguese nobility, whose support he attempted to

---

[23] SANTOS, João Henrique. "A Inquisição calvinista: o sínodo do Brasil e os Judeus no Brasil holandês". In: ASSIS, Angelo A. Faria de et al. (org). *Desvelando o poder – histórias de dominação: Estado, religião e sociedade*. Rio de Janeiro: Vício de Leitura, 2007. p. 107-124.

[2424] The disappearance of King Dom Sebastião's body led people to believe that one day he would return to rescue Portugal. The movement based on this messianic myth became known as Sebastianism.

secure while reminding them that the first king of Portugal, Dom João, Master of Aviz, had also been the illegitimate son of a king, Dom Pedro I. Dom António failed to receive the desired backing from the nobility, although he was the preferred candidate of Paulista *bandeirantes* (Portuguese settlers and fortune-hunters in Brazil) who were strongly in favor of his ascension to the throne.

Dom António did eventually succeed in being proclaimed king of Portugal by the people, at the Castle of Santarém, with his reign acknowledged in Lisbon, Setubal and the islands of the Azores and Madeira. However, a month later, on August 25, Dom António's forces were defeated at the Battle of Alcântara by those of the Duke of Alba. He sought refuge on Terceira Island, in the Azores, an active nucleus for crypto-Jews, who had taken his side, from where he would continue to govern until 1581, even managing to mint a coin displaying his effigy. However, his rule was only ever recognized locally, and in 1581 he was defeated by Spanish troops, leading him to seek exile in France.[25] In Continental Portugal and Madeira, power was transferred to Philip II of Spain, who invaded the kingdom with a powerful army to ensure his coronation.

In April 1581, the Spanish king held court in Tomar, where he would make his solemn Oath and be proclaimed king of Portugal, under the title of Philip I. With the kingdom debilitated and mired in confusion, the legitimate heirs to the throne were forgotten and the country fell under Spanish dominion.

Very soon, New Christians fears began to be realized, with Philip I adopting Spain's repressive policies towards Portuguese *conversos*, suspending emigration and ordering, by means of the law of September 6, 1583, that all New Christians be forced to wear a yellow cap. Anybody discovered wearing a cap of another color would be flogged publicly and forced to pay a fine of 100 *cruzados*.

In the political sphere, Portugal's subordinance to Spain transferred all the country's conflicts onto the Portuguese Crown. Animosity between Spain and Holland eventually hampered freedom of trade between the Dutch and Portuguese, with King

---

[25] PORTUGAL – DICIONÁRIO HISTÓRICO, COROGRÁFICO, HERÁLDICO, BIBLIOGRÁFICO, NUMISMÁTICO E ARTÍSTICO. Lisboa: João Romano Torres, 1904-1915. p. 603. v. 1. VERÍSSIMO, Joaquim Serrão, *O reinado de dom António, prior de Crato: 1531-1595*. 1956. Tese (Doutorados em Letras, Ciências Históricas) – Universidade de Coimbra, Lisboa.

Philip going as far as to order the confiscation of all Dutch ships lying in ports within his dominions in Europe, Africa, Asia and the Americas.

At that time, Portugal depended on the finances and technical assistance of the Dutch for the refinement and commercialization of Brazilian sugar. The Dutch occupation of Brazil's Northeast occurred within the context of the Netherlands' war of independence against Spain. Dutch colonial expansion was a vital tool in this effort, as it struck at the source of the wealth of the Iberian power.

The sale, refinement and distribution of sugar was of great importance to the Dutch economy during the 17th century, despite not being, in the opinion of Evaldo Cabral de Mello, a typically Dutch enterprise, but instead one carried out by the community of Portuguese Sephardic Jews established in Holland. At the time, it is estimated there were 29 refineries working in Amsterdam. Jews had been involved in the financing and operation of sugar mills from the start, as well as in trading of the product.[26]

During a relative cessation in hostilities between Spain and the Netherlands (1609-1621), around one million *arrobas* of sugar (ca. 32 million lbs) was able to reach Dutch refineries. As a result, the Dutch began a painstaking scrutiny of the Brazilian coastline and obtained important information about ports and the social and economic conditions of the American continent, factors which were crucial in the carrying out of attacks on Bahia and Pernambuco.[27]

In 1621, the West India Company was founded, and in the same year hostilities between the Netherlands and Spain were resumed. The company was principally comprised of Calvinist merchants, who came from the Spanish Netherlands, and whose goal was to

---

[26] Holland bought raw sugar from Portugal, which it then refined and distributed to the rest of Europe. The Jews, who were in contact with Portuguese New Christian relatives living in Portugal and Brazil, served as intermediaries in commercial transactions due to the readiness of their trading network. See MELLO, Evaldo Cabral de. O Brasil e os holandeses: 1630-1654. In: HERKENHOFF, Paulo (Org.). *O Brasil e os holandeses*. Rio de Janeiro: Sextante Artes, 1999. p. 32-40.

[27] This fact was principally due to the relationship between New Christian plantation owners in Brazil and Jewish businessmen in Holland, many of whom had spent time living with relatives in Brazil before returning to Amsterdam.

keep hold of the monopoly on trade with the Americas and parts of Africa, but in particular over control of trade with Brazil.[28]

In the wake of the Iberian Union, the invasion of Brazil's Northeast became inevitable, with Dutch ships finding themselves plagued by successive embargoes at Iberian-controlled ports. The conquest of northeastern Brazil was, therefore, planned in accordance with the commercial interests of the Netherlands.[29]

The choice of Brazil as the first region to invade can be explained by a number of factors. The country was the weak point in the Spanish Empire, since Spain was more concerned with its own colonies than those belonging to the Portuguese. In addition, the proximity of urban centers to the coastline meant they were relatively easy to access, and Brazil could then serve as a base for operations against Spanish fleets on the River Plate as well as Portuguese ships sailing to the Indies. It was also hoped there might be major profit to be made from sugar and brazilwood.[30]

From 1600, the Dutch maintained a presence within the colonial territory of Brazil, with two wooden fortifications on the east bank of the Xingu river, Fort Orange and Fort Nassau, erected by merchants from Amsterdam. Eventually, 150 Dutch immigrants founded a colony (1601-1622) on the Jenipapo river in order to trade with the natives.[31]

The first major attack and occupation of Brazil's Northeast took place on May 8, 1624, when an expedition from the West India Company arrived in Bahia with 26 ships and 3,300 men, under the command of the Dutch admiral, Jacob Willekens, the vice-admiral, Pieter Heyn, and Commander Jan van Dorth. The battle lasted only a few ours, with the Dutch capturing both main forts, an outcome

---

[28] MELLO, Evaldo Cabral de, op. cit., p. 24.

[29] It is customary to refer to the United Provinces of the Netherlands as Holland, the most important of the seven united provinces that make up the confederation. As a result, this book makes use of both terms: Netherlands when refering to the entire confederation, and Holland when specifying the most important province.

[30] MELLO, Evaldo Cabral de, op. cit., p. 24.

[31] SANTOS, João Henrique. A Inquisição calvinista: o sínodo do Brasil e os judeus no Brasil holandês. In: ASSIS, Angelo A. Faria de et al. (Org.). *Desvelando o poder – histórias de dominação: Estado, religião, sociedade.* Rio de Janeiro: Vício de Leitura, 2007. p. 111-113. The author based his work on the records of LAET historian, Johannes de. *Iaerlyck verhael van de verrichtinghen der Geoctroyeered West-Indosche Compagnie*, 2. Ed. Haia, 1931-1937.

that spread panic among the Portuguese troops in Bahia, who subsequently deserted.

The frightened population fled into the surrounding forests, along with Bishop Dom Marcos Teixeira, responsible for the activities of the Inquisition in the captaincy.[32]

Dutch rule over Bahia was short-lived, lasting approximately a year. Soon, the militias who had fled from the city on May 9 became organized under the leadership of Bishop Dom Marcos Teixeira and the city was surrounded on all sides, leading to guerrilla warfare.

On March 29, 1625, a Portuguese expedition, consisting of 52 ships and 16,566 men, joined forces with the local militia, and, on May 1, 1625, the Dutch surrendered.[33]

After only a year, the first Dutch expedition was over, ending in utter defeat and economic disaster. Expeditions in Paraíba, Rio Grande do Norte and Cabo de Santo Agostinho also ended in failure.[34]

The ambitions of the Dutch, however, had not reached their conclusion. Bahia had served as a lesson, meaning that the next incursion, in 1630, would prove far more successful.

---

[32] WIZNITZER, Arnold. *Os judeus no Brasil Colonial.* São Paulo: Pioneira, 1966. p. 10-20.

[33] Ibid, p. 30-36.

[34] Ibid, p. 43-48.

3. Myth of New Christian Collaboration

Once Dutch rule had been established in Bahia, one of its first commitments was the declaration of a policy of religious tolerance, offering protection to all those who wished to remain under its governance. This practice encouraged almost 200 refugees to return to the capital and has led historians to construct the myth of New Christian collaboration in the Dutch invasion of Northeast Brazil.

The concept of the "foreign Jew" as traitor to the homeland already existed within the Iberian mentality, a result of secular prejudice, and was revived in periods of crisis and transferred onto the descendants of *conversos*. Despite a great degree of coexistence between Jews, Christians and Muslims on the Iberian Peninsula during the medieval period, Jews had never stopped being regarded as "guests." Following the forced conversions in Portugal, New Christians were never considered equals and were stigmatized because of their "tainted blood."[35]

As Anita Novinsky's research demonstrates, during the Dutch invasion of Brazil many New Christians fought to the death to defend the Portuguese territory from the Reformed Protestants.[36] Integrated into the economic elite and society of Bahia, businessmen like Mateus Lopes Franco, Diogo Ulhoa and Domingos Alvarez de Serpa provided financial assistance for the reinforcement of the captaincy, helping with the construction of trenches and fortifications and participating in the committee responsible for the defense strategy.[37] These same men, responding to requests from the governor of Bahia, dipped into their own resources for the building of boats to defend plantations in the Recôncavo Baiano (a fertile region surrounding the bay of Bahia) and to transport provisions and slaves to the city. In 1638, a large loan was provided by the

---

[35] NOVINSKY, Anita. Antissemitismo, os marranos e a *fluctuactio animi*. In: CARNEIRO, Maria Luiza Tucci. (Org.). *Antissemitismo nas Américas.* São Paulo: Edusp, 2007. p. 30-31.

[36] Idem, *Cristãos-novos na Bahia: a Inquisição no Brasil.* 2. ed. São Paulo: Perspectiva, 1992. p. 126-127.

[37] Ibid, p. 126-127.

population with the aim of arming Luso-Brazilian soldiers for the resistance against Dutch troops – a register taken of all those involved in providing that sum of money shows that 50% were New Christians.[38]

The Portuguese New Christians living in the colony identified themselves with the mainland culture, the language, the lands of their ancestors, the customs and, most of all, the peculiar way the Portuguese had of externalizing the religious. This common culture provided the Portuguese, both Old Christians and New, with the strength to resist the Dutch. Aside from the economic factors acting upon these men, it is also necessary to consider the cultural ties to their Iberian roots.

Yet the attitude of Brazil's northeastern population was in no way homogenous. Political choices were made in accordance with personal interests. The Portuguese maintained a profound and long-standing antagonism towards Spain and, when they joined forces with Dutch invaders in Brazil, they were, in reality, just fighting against their traditional enemy, the Spanish.

This explains why many who would become formidable enemies of the Dutch by the end of the invasion had been their collaborators at the start, as in the cases of the chronicler Frei Manoel Calado and the businessman João Fernandes Vieira. Charles R. Boxer draws attention to the important contribution made by João Fernandes in the 1645 rebellion against the Dutch, despite Fernandes having been an active Dutch collaborator when the invasion began, even carrying out the role of municipal councilor in Dutch-controlled Cidade Maurícia.[39]

The emphasis placed by historians on New Christian cooperation with the Dutch is, therefore, part of a process of discrimination and deep-rooted prejudice against the Jewish people, which has been transferred onto their descendants. Contemporary

---

[38] Ibid, p. 128.

[39] BOXER, Charles R. *Os holandeses no Brasil: 1624-1654*. São Paulo: Companhia Editora Nacional, 1961. p. 391 and 394. Apud NOVINSKY, Anita. *Uma devassa do bispo dom Pedro da Silva: 1635-1637*. São Paulo: Paulista 1968, p. 217-285. n. XXII.

eyewitnesses, like Father António Vieira, for example, never included this theory in their writings.[40]

Documents from the time, such as investigations carried out by the Catholic Church to establish the names of those who had sided with the enemy during the occupation of Paraíba, demonstrate that, of the 80 people denounced, 8 were members of the Catholic clergy, 48 were Old Christians and only 24 were New Christians.

During the first Dutch invasion of Bahia, in 1624, once the Portuguese had managed to regain control and expel the Dutch, the civil authorities decreed prison sentences for all rebels who had collaborated with the enemy. Among the almost two thousand suspects questioned in the investigation, there were some New Christians, including Diogo Lopes de Abrantes, Manuel Rodriguez de Azevedo, Luis Martins, Francisco de Morin and Antônio de Matos, as well as Diniz Bravo, Pascoal Bravo, Manuel Rodrigues Sanches and Duarte Alvarez Ribeiro.

The defendants confessed under torture and received the following punishments: Diogo Lopes de Abrantes, Manuel Rodriguez de Azevedo, Luis Martins, Francisco de Morin and Antônio de Matos were sentenced to death by hanging. Diniz Bravo, Pascoal Bravo and their associates were found innocent. The properties of those condemned were confiscated.

In 1635, Bishop Dom Pedro da Silva carried out a grand inquest to investigate the local population's collaboration with the Dutch more rigorously. The majority of those denounced were members of the Catholic clergy. Witnesses attested that among the religious collaborators were the Augustinian friar António Caldeira, who had threatened those who refused to support the Dutch with excommunication, and Father Manuel de Morais, who had set aside his cassock to marry and go live in Holland. Until 1635, the friar had fought against the invaders, leading a band of indigenous fighters (he spoke fluent Tupi), but later became a political ally of the Dutch, converted to Calvinism and began urging the local population to follow the Reformed faith.

Another clergyman, friar Manoel de Beguíno, had helped the Flemish forces capture Porto Calvo. He would convince local

---

[40] NOVINSKY, Anita. Historical bias – the New Christian Collaboration with Dutch Invaders of Brazil. 5th Congress of Jewish Studies, Jerusalem, Aug. 1969.

populations to lay down their weapons by telling them they had no other option. He engaged in all kinds of behavior condemned by the Church, such as reading forbidden books, convening with heretics and openly disavowing the saints and the Virgin Mary.

The *licenciado*[41] João Gomes de Aguiar was accused of persuading the population to collaborate with the enemy and of failing to offer resistance on the grounds that "the Dutch were good Christians."[42]

The aforementioned Friar António Caldeira was denounced by Manuel Dias de Andrade, general of the captaincy of Pernambuco, as a causer of great confusion and the organizer of a plot to assassinate the governor of Bahia, Matias de Albuquerque. Like other denounced religious conspirators, he had "assembled and persuaded many honorable Portuguese men to flee into the hands of the enemy, which some did."[43] Before living in Pernambuco, Friar António Caldeira had been in Bahia, where he had come into conflict with the governor, Diogo Luiz de Oliveira. He had then remained in Pernambuco until the arrival of the Dutch, when he retreated with Matias de Albuquerque, later returning on the side of the enemy and threatening members of Bahia's elite with excommunication if they did not support the Dutch.[44]

There were economic interests, such as the waiving of debts, that influenced the clergy's decision to collaborate with the enemies of the Portuguese, but the reasons that led common people to assist the invaders were various and reflect a situation of crisis within the population.[45]

The grand inquest imposed by the bishop only served to spur on the collaboration of many Old Christians, who decided to embrace

---

[41] A *licenciado* was a priest who was also a teacher of theology.

[42] NOVINSKY, Anita, op. cit., p. 217-285.

[43] Denunciation by Garcia Lopes Calheiros. Transcript of some witness statements from the inquest conducted by "the illustrious Dom Pedro da Sylva, bishop of Brazil in the city of Salvador, All Saints' Bay" in June 1635. Handwritten. IAN/TT/IL, Notebook of the Prosecutor n. 19. Apud NOVINSKY, Anita, op. cit., p. 217-285.

[44] The culpability of Father António Caldeira, Augustinian friar and preacher... Denunciation by Belchior dos Reis, in Bahia on June 18, 1635, in the notebooks of the prosecutor of the Inquisition in Lisbon n. 19 [...] National Archive of Torre do Tombo, Lisbon.

[45] NOVINSKY, Anita, op. cit., p. 226-230.

Calvinism, and of some New Christians, who saw Dutch occupation as an opportunity to return to the religion of their ancestors.

The inquest uncovered the case of Bento Gozzo, who baptized his new-born son with the help of a Dutch pastor, following the baptism ceremony of the Reformed church. Afterwards, Gozzo had sought out priests from the Society of Jesus, neighbors in the town of Igarassu, and had his son rebaptized by the Catholic church.[46] Many colonists were clearly uncertain about which religion they were actually following.

The denunciations made during the inquest reveal that there may have been economic reasons driving members of the Catholic clergy to support the invaders, and that the behavior of the clergy would certainly have influenced the decisions of inhabitants, who, according to João Correia de Almeida's denunciation, would often state: "When the clergy sides with the enemy, what are we supposed to do...?"[47]

In relation to their adopted religion, the New Christians displayed some basic differences from Jews. The Jews who arrived in Brazil accompanying the Dutch, and who were responsible for organizing the Jewish community in Pernambuco, had been educated in the Judaism of Amsterdam; meanwhile, the New Christians born in Brazil, or newly arrived from Portugal, had been distanced from Judaism for over 100 years. Yet the behaviors of these New Christians were inconsistent and contradictory and resist broad generalization, as if they constituted a uniform group. There were those whose religious and political ideas were still ill-defined, as well as other more rebellious members who were restless and susceptible to the introduction of new ideas.

As a result of biased positions or a lack of thorough research, historians have tended to exaggerate the extent of New Christians involvement in the occupation of Brazil's Northeast. But more recent studies and examinations of handwritten documents demonstrate that this issue cannot be understood in isolation,

---

[46] Denunciation by Cosme Dias Massiel, Old Christian. Transcript of some witness statements from the inquest conducted by "the illustrious Dom Pedro da Sylva, bishop of Brazil in the city of Salvador, All Saints' Bay" on June 18, 1635. Handwritten. IAN/TT/IL, Notebook of the Prosecutor n. 19, op.cit.

[47] Denunciation of Garcia Lopes Calheiros ando f João de Sequeira. Customs clerk and bailiff on November 5, 1636. Apud NOVINSKY, Anita, op. Cit., p. 226-230.

detached from the social, religious and economic structures of Europe in the 17th century.

4. New Center of Attraction: The Dutch in Brazil

The Dutch army arrived in Recife on February 14, 1630. The expedition was comprised of 56 ships and 7,180 soldiers and sailors and was commanded by Admiral Hendrick Corneliszoon Lonck. The captures of Olinda, Recife and the island of Antônio Vaz happened quickly, within less than a month, and on March 3 the conquest was sealed.

The war for the conquest of the rest of Brazil's Northeast would continue for five more years and reach as far as Ceará and Rio Grande do Norte.

The battles disrupted the region's food supply, making life difficult for both sets of combatants. The hunger became so extreme that Dutch garrisons ended up eating mice and cats, and a daily ration for the Portuguese consisted of a single cob of corn.[48]

The government tried to raise funds to aid the Portuguese troops in Pernambuco, accumulating capital from both Spain and Portugal. Their eventual solution to acquiring the funds needed for the defense effort was to raise taxes on sugar, meat and wine, an approach that directly affected the Portuguese New Christian merchant class. A compulsory loan was also drawn from businessmen, the majority Portuguese New Christians. A list from 1632 indicates that men described as "people of the Nation" were the major contributors to the fund made up of compulsory loans.[49] Other attempts were made to resolve the situation, and Spain tried to negotiate a truce with the United Provinces, but their efforts proved fruitless, as neither side could reach an agreement.

The Dutch received substantial backing from bankers in Amsterdam. They also relied upon deserters from the Luso-Brazilian guerilla army, among them a *mulato* called Domingos Fernandes Calabar, remembered in history for his tactical contribution to the Dutch conquest. As a native of the region,

---

[48] BOXER, Charles R. *Os holandeses no Brasil: 1624-1654*. São Paulo: Companhia Editora Nacional, 1961. p. 58.

[49] AZEVEDO, João Lúcio. *História dos cristãos-novos portugueses*. Lisbon: Clássica, 1921. p. 211-212.

Calabar became the Dutch expedition's main guide, and his exceptional knowledge of local paths and trails meant he could plot strategic routes that placed Dutch troops in advantageous positions.

For the conquests of Ceará and Rio Grande do Norte, the Dutch made tactical alliances with the Tapuia Indians. It was an Amsterdam Jew, Samuel Cohen, adviser to the official in charge of the expedition to Rio Grande do Norte in 1631, who managed to enlist the support of the Tapuia in the conquest of the region.[50] As rivals of the Tapuia, the Tupi supported the Portuguese. Regional conflicts took on strategic significance in the dispute for Brazil's Northeast.

Portugal was at a clear disadvantage, with problems occurring both internally, including the great drought and famine which devastated the country between 1630 and 1633, and externally, including the loss of their largest shipment of silver in Mexico, the result of a hurricane.

In 1633 and 1634, the Dutch intensified their raids and consolidated their conquest of a large portion of the northeastern coastline, from the Cape of Santo Agostinho up through Sergipe, Paraíba, Ceará and Rio Grande do Norte.[51]

Among the Dutch troops there were soldiers of various nationalities, including Germans, Norwegians, Scots and Jews, who were contracted for a period of three years. Just like soldiers of other nationalities, Amsterdam's Jews were attracted by the Dutch occupation plan, which consisted in providing free passage to Brazil, as well as land (beginning from the third year on Northeastern soil and subject to a 10% tax on whatever was produced), with scope for economic growth and the attainment of positions in public office, not to mention religious tolerance and freedom of belief, which was necessary in order to guarantee the religious plurality of the troops.[52]

Some of the Jews within the Amsterdam community had already lived in the region, and were enlisted as guides to the new lands and

---

[50] MELLO, José Antônio Gonsalves de. *Gente da nação*. Recife: Massangana/Fundação Joaquim Nabuco, 1996. p. 211.

[51] BOXER, Charles R., op. cit., p. 76-79.

[52] WIZNITZER, Arnold. *Os judeus no Brasil colonial*. São Paulo: Pioneira, 1966. p. 49-50.

interpreters between the Dutch and the inhabitants of Pernambuco. These people had economic and familial connections in Recife. Antonio Dias Paparrobalos, a Jew who had been a merchant in Pernambuco, is proof of this, and, upon disembarking with the Dutch troops, he served as guide for their entry into the province. Others, like Moyses Navarro, Antônio Manuel and David Testa, were among the Jewish soldiers on the expedition, and were in fact the first Jewish soldiers recorded in the Americas.

At the end of their contracts, many of the soldiers asked permission to remain in Brazil as free citizens, independent of the West India Company. Among these, Moyses Navarro stands out for having obtained a license to trade in sugar, becoming a millowner and one of the richest and most important businessmen in Dutch Brazil. Navarro acquired his sugar plantation at auction, in the wake of the Dutch invasion. At the start of the occupation, numerous sugar plantations were auctioned off after having been abandoned by their original owners who had fled in fear of what could yet unfold.[53]

To allay the fears of the local population, the Dutch rulers published a manifesto "concerning the plantation owners and inhabitants of Pernambuco," in which they promised respect for property, the lowering of taxes and the allowing of freedom of thought.[54] Those who swore allegiance to the new government were granted freedom of faith and religious worship.

The only group to be denied freedom of faith were the Jesuits. Since the arrival of the Dutch, priests from the Society of Jesus had encouraged the Amerindians living under their protection to wage war on the invading troops.[55] The situation between the Dutch and the Jesuits worsened when the Dutch rulers intercepted a letter from the directors of the Jesuit College in Pernambuco and addressed to the Portuguese government in Bahia. The letter affirmed that the Jesuits were willing to do everything in their power to battle against the heresy in Pernambuco. Feeling threatened, one of the first undertakings of the recently-installed Dutch rulers was to expel the

---

[53] Ibid, p. 57.

[54] LAET-NABER, De. "Iaerlyck Verhael", III. *English Historical Review*, XV, p. 36. Apud BOXER, Charles R., op. cit., p. 81.

[55] BOXER, Charles R., op. cit., p. 81.

Jesuits, as well as to decree the shutting down of their convents.[56] In 1635, the Provincial Superior of the Society of Jesus himself issued an order instructing all Jesuits still within the occupied territory to leave.[57]

For the Jews, freedom of thought and worship were guaranteed from the start of the occupation. This presented considerable opportunity for trade, as, since the Dutch could still not speak Portuguese nor the Portuguese speak Dutch, the Sephardim, as well as translators, became intermediaries in negotiations, receiving a percentage on commercial transactions.

Within a few years of the arrival of the Dutch, Jewish involvement in the sugar trade of Pernambuco was growing. Jews achieved prominence as plantation owners and financiers of the sugar industry, increasing business between producers and exporters and becoming involved themselves in the exportation of sugar to Europe, as well as taking part in the building of infrastructure.

Trade was, without doubt, the most important activity for the Jewish people. According to a document from the Leadership Council of the Jewish community, as well as sugar, other products, such as tobacco, preserves, furs, slaves, credit notes, equipment for warships, interest loans, and all kinds of fresh and dry produce, became notable areas of trade. These goods were retailed, and even sold door-to-door.[58]

The figure of the Jewish peddler spread through the population of the Dutch Northeast, and became particularly active in the interior, reaching as far as the banks of the São Francisco river. As an example of Jewish involvement in this sector, we have João Nunes Velho (Samuel Velho), who used to wander the trails of the

---

[56] WÄTJEN, Hermann. O domínio colonial hollandez no Brasil: um capítulo da história colonial do século XVII. São Paulo: Companhia Editora Nacional, 1938. p. 340.

[57] Ibid, p. 346. According to the author, only priests and friars of the Jesuit and Franciscan orders were expelled from the occupied territory, for conspiring in favor of a return to Portuguese rulership. Other religious orders were given permission to remain in the region.

[58] List of products taken from the document "Tax on the nation," a tax the Leadership Council of the Jewish community levied on traded goods, with the objective of raising funds for the maintenance of the synagogue and the performance of other cultural activities. WIZNITZER, Arnold. Minute book of the Jewish congregations of Zur Israel in Recife and of Magen Abraham in Maurícia, Brazil. 1648-53. *Anais da Biblioteca Nacional*, Rio de Janeiro, v. 74, p. 228-229, 1953.

sertão (or back country) selling his wares to farms and smallholdings. He traded in everything from eyeglasses and pieces of fabric to slaves. João Nunes Velho was captured by Portuguese troops near the São Francisco river during their attempts to recover the territory, and was sent, along with others, to face the Portuguese Inquisition. From his Inquisitorial trial, we are able to obtain a sense of the extent of his business, mostly conducted among smallholders in the region along the São Francisco.[59]

Tax collection was a role often carried out by Jews, and 63% of businesses were handled by members of the community. This activity ended up provoking a certain amount of hostility within the various socio-religious groups.[60]

Jews and New Christians were also involved in the liberal professions. In the field of medicine, there was Dr Abraão de Mercado, who owned a private clinic and sold his own remedies; Dr Manuel Nunes; and Dr Musaphia, as well as another Portuguese-Jewish surgeon who treated some crew members from the ship he arrived on. There was also Jacob Moreno, who, while living in Amsterdam, applied for a license to open a surgery in Paraíba in 1635.[61] The Jewish community grew to such a point that its prosperity can be demonstrated by donations sent to charitable institutions in Amsterdam.

In keeping with traditions established in Holland, the Jews in Brazil became prominent jewelers and gemcutters, while two renowned goldsmiths, Jacob Henriques and Isaac Navarro, also lived in Recife.[62]

The only record of Jewish involvement in manufacturing, aside from goldsmithery, relates to a plant for the production of a whitening mineral called potash,[63] on the island of Itmaracá, which

---

[59] National Archive of Torre do Tombo – The Inquisition of Lisbon. Trial of João Nunes Velho n. 11,575. Inventory, June 6, 1647. Folio 72-75.

[60] WIZNITZER, Arnold. *Os judeus no Brasil Colonial*, op. cit., p. 60.

[61] MELLO, José Antônio Gonsalves de. *História dos cristãos-novos portugueses*, op. cit., p. 242.

[62] WIZNITZER, Arnold. *Os judeus no Brasil Colonial*, op. cit., p. 157. MELLO, José Antônio Gonsalves de. *História dos cristãos-novos portugueses*, op. cit., p. 226.

[63] Potash, a form of salt, is a powerful whitening agent obtained from plant ashes soaked in water, especially the trunks and branches of trees. See: CONCEIÇÃO, José Marianno (Frei). *Alographia dos Alkales fixos vegetal ou potassia mineral ou soda e dos*

was owned by Isaac Navarro and Jacob Henriques. In addition, there were Jews who earned a living making uniforms for the Dutch troops.

Jews also participated meaningfully within the justice system. Jacob Dorta, an attorney in Paraíba, worked alongside the Justice Committee, while Manuel Abendana, a Doctor of Law, acted on behalf of the Jewish community, and Miguel Cardozo dedicated himself to advocacy.[64]

On top of this, Jews were involved in all manner of trades, from the sale of sugar to everyday goods, as well as the vending of slaves. It is impossible to imagine the development of the Atlantic economy without the trafficking and labor of slaves. In relation to Jewish participation in these kinds of transactions, it is important to clarify a number of points. Anti-Semites in the United States have spread the notion that Jews were responsible for the introduction of slavery into America via their role in the financing and organization of the Atlantic slave trade and the system of slavery.[65] In Brazil, the same premise was put forward by José Gonçalves Salvador, in his book *Os magnatas do tráfico negreiro* [The Magnates of the Atlantic Slave Trade].[66]

When discussing this phenomenon, it is important to take into account the context of the Iberian Peninsula at that time. The whole economic system was propped up by slavery. The trafficking of slaves was a monopoly held by government agencies from which New Christians were barred, and various European governments were engaged in a tussle for control over this monopoly.

---

sues nitratos segundo as melhores memórias estrangeiras, que se tem escripto a este assumpto. Debaixo dos auspícios e de ordem de sua alteza real o príncipe do Brasil. Lisbon: Officina de Simão Thaddeo Ferreira, 1798.

[64] MELLO, José Antônio Gonsalves de. *História dos cristãos-novos portugueses*, op. cit., p. 242-243.

[65] JEFFRIES, Leonard. Speech made on July 20 at Empire State Black Arts and Culture Festival in Albany. Published by New York Post, "Account of vitriolic anti-semitism and racist speech". August, 1991.

[66] WIZNITZER, Arnold. *Os judeus no Brasil Colonial*, op. cit., p. 62. SALVADOR, José Gonçalves. *Os magnatas do tráfico negreiro*. São Paulo: Pioneira/Edusp, 1981. p. 4. "With much surprise we come to the conclusion that Iberian Jews were the main keepers of the slave trade and, furthermore, that a clan, connected by economic interests when not by ties of blood, exploited it widely."

For three centuries, the Spanish government prohibited *conversos* from any involvement in the trafficking of slaves, which was a lucrative business. During that period, Spain had a monopoly on the delivery of slaves to its own colonies and those of the Portuguese, as part of the contract agreed between the two territories.[67]

Sometimes, New Christians would work in parallel to official Portuguese agencies or act as intermediaries. This fact led Spain to refuse to renew the *asiento*, the contract providing them with a monopoly over the delivery of slaves to the Portuguese colonies.[68]

Holland's colony in Brazil required a great number of slaves to work on farms and sugar plantations. Jewish involvement was restricted to trading in slaves that had already arrived in the colony: the slaves were picked up at auction and then sold on to farmers.

The New Christian proprietors of sugar plantations were slaveowners. However, a rumor spread across the colony that slaves preferred their Jewish masters to Dutch or Portuguese ones, because the Jews allowed them two days of rest per week, while the Portuguese only gave them one day, and the Dutch (following their Calvinist doctrine on the value of work) did not allow any.[69]

Within the 129 inventories documenting the Inquisitorial trials of Brazilian New Christians scrutinized by Anita Novinsky in Portugal, only one New Christian was found to have owned a ship and participated in slave trafficking.[70]

During the second half of the 17th century, with the monopoly on slave trafficking having been disrupted by the West India Company, Jews managed to reap some of the profits of the trade.

---

[67] DAVIS, David Brion. The Slave Trade and the Jews: *The New York Review of Books*, p. 14=16, 22 Dec. 1994.

[68] KAYSERLING, Meyer. *A história dos judeus em Portugal*. São Paulo: Pioneira, 1971. DESCHER, Seymour. Jews and New Christians in the Atlantic Slave Trade. In: BERNARDINI, Paolo; FIERING, Norman (Eds.). *The Jews and the Expansion of Europe to the West*, 1450 to 1800 (European Expansion and Global Interaction, number 2). New York: Berghahn Books, 2001. p. 440-470. DRESCHER, Seymour. From Slavery to Freedom: Comparative Studies in the Rise and Fall of Atlantic Slavery. New York: New York University Press, 1991. p. 339-354.

[69] WIZNITZER, Arnold. *Os judeus no Brasil Colonial*, op. cit., p. 62.

[70] NOVINSKY, Anita. *Inquisição: inventários de bens confiscados a cristãos-novos*. Rio de Janeiro: Imprensa Nacional/Casa da Moeda/Livraria Camões, 1976. p. 154-158. 181 and 246.

Even so, this was only a small amount, as they were only ever passive participants (Jews retained a tiny portion of income, equal to 1.3% of the capital of the West India Company).[71]

---

[71] WÄTJEN, Hermann. *O domínio colonial hollandez no Brasil*, op. cit., p. 340. Using the West India Company's log of capital subscriptions, it can be demonstrated that, from 1623 to 1626, 18 Jews were shareholders in the company, and only one, Bento, had shares worth more than six thousand florins, the minimum amount required to join the board of directors. As such, Jews did not possess the means to influence the company's decision.

5. The Experience in the Tropics

At the beginning of the Dutch occupation, Jews used to gather in the homes of friends to hold religious ceremonies. Many of these gatherings took place at the home of Duarte Saraiva, an influential Portuguese Jew who bought the lands on which the Jewish street was established. Religious services officiated in private homes were common among Amsterdam's Jews and this practice was replicated in Brazil.[72]

The Jewish street became the main thoroughfare of an important commercial neighborhood. The most prosperous lived in two-story houses, with a business on the ground floor, its door opening onto the street, and a residence on the floor above.[73] Almost the entire area around the Jewish street was built by the Sephardim. According to an inventory carried out in 1654, there were 32 multi-story houses with 26 ground-floor shops, all owned by Jews. Another 36 buildings in the area had no listed owners, merely a note indicating they belonged to Jews.[74] Investment in the real estate market was regarded as important by businessmen, with many properties constructed as investments; others were simply built as homes, demonstrating that the Jews were intent on remaining for an extended period or even establishing themselves permanently in the region.[75] Some owners of properties on the Jewish street were Jacob Valverde, Moses Neto, Jacob Zacuto, João Lafará, Gil Correa, Gabriel Castanha, Gaspar Francisco da Costa, Avraham de Açevedo, Fernão Martins, David Atias and Benjamin de Pina. The

---

[72] SILVA, Leonardo Dantas. Zur Israel, uma comunidade judaica no Brasil. In: HERKENHOFF, Paulo (Org.). *O Brasil e os holandeses*. Rio de Janeiro: Sextante Arte, 1999. p. 89.

[73] Ibid, p. 88.

[74] INVENTORY of arms and munitions left in Pernambuco by the Dutch, as well as buildings constructed or repaired up to 1654. Recife: Imprensa Oficial, 1940. In: WOLFF, Egon; WOLFF, Frieda. *Quantos judeus estiveram no Brasil holandês*. Rio de Janeiro: s.n., 1991.

[75] For information on houses belonging to Jews in the vicinity of the Jewish street, see previous footnote. The inventory makes reference to numerous houses built by Jews, although the names of proprietors are unknown.

Pina family, in particular, achieved great prestige within the local society, and today one of the most affluent neighborhoods in Recife bears their name.

It was on the Jewish street, later renamed Rua do Bom Jesus, that Kahal Zur Israel, the first synagogue of the Americas, was built, with construction completed during the first half of 1636. Around 1642, Isaac Aboab da Fonseca, one of the four rabbis of the Talmud Torah congregation, was sent from Amsterdam to lead the synagogue. Aboab da Fonseca was born in Portugal, in 1605, and came from an illustrious line of men versed in Jewish law, including his great-grandfather, the last Gaon (the highest authority on the teaching and interpretation of Jewish law) of Castile.[76] Aboab da Fonseca completed his studies in Amsterdam, where, at 14 years old, as a sign of his erudition, he was elected to the role of rabbi's assistant by the Neveh Shalom Congregation. At 21, he became rabbi of the Beth Israel congregation in Amsterdam. As well as a rabbi, he was a thinker, writer and poet, and left behind America's first Hebrew poem, which makes reference to the expulsion of Recife's Jews. He settled in Brazil, and his daughter married a young scholar named Daniel Bellilos (who later became the official rabbi in Amsterdam), the son of sugar plantation owner Baltazar da Fonseca.

In 1637, the second synagogue, Kahal Kadosh Maguen Abraham, was founded on the island of Antônio Vaz (where it operated out of a private home). The synagogue's spiritual leader was rabbi Mosseh Rephael d'Aguilar, a renowned teacher, poet and dedicated student of the Talmud, with exemplary knowledge of the Hebrew language and 22 books to his name.[77] Rephael d'Aguilar, who was born between 1615 and 1620, received his Jewish and secular education in Amsterdam and arrived in Brazil when he was still very young in the group led by Aboab da Fonseca. From his manuscripts, we can tell that he dedicated part of his time to convincing New Christians to return to Judaism. He corresponded

---

[76] RAMOS, Frank dos Santos. *O paradoxo da América católica: Kahul Zur Israel – a primeira comunidade judaica legal no Novo Mundo*. In: ASSIS, Angelo A. Faria de et al. (Org.). *Desvelando o poder – histórias da dominação: Estado, religião, sociedade.* Rio de Janeiro: Vício de Leitura, 2007. p. 96.

[77] WEITMAN, David Y. (Rabbi) *Bandeirantes espirituais do Brasil: século XVII.* São Paulo: Maayanot, 2003. p. 83.

with Marranos in other parts of Europe, who would question him about the Jewish faith. Rephael d'Aguilar accused the Inquisition of being an institution that purported to be concerned with the battle against Judaism, while in reality displaying far more interest in the assets of New Christians.[78]

In June, 1633, some years before the founding of the synagogues, Isaac Franco purchased a Torah (the religious text containing the Old Testament) in Amsterdam, which he sent to Duarte Rodrigues Mendes, in Recife. This information proves the existence of an assembly that had been enacting the role of a synagogue before an official place of worship was established in Recife. When those in the tropics needed to clarify some liturgical doubt, they would send letters to the rabbis in Amsterdam.

In Recife there were a number of experts and eminent scholars of the Talmud who became responsible for the education of children. Two religious schools, the Talmud Torá and the Etz Hayim, operated within the premises of the Zur Israel synagogue.[79] On the advice of the Mahamad, the rabbinical council of Amsterdam, the two synagogues were eventually unified during the final years of Dutch rule, in 1648, and served around 600 Jews in the area.

The moment the Jews were allowed to exist as a community, they returned to the humanist traditions of Judaism. There was great concern with the needier members of the Jewish population, and those associated with the synagogue contributed monthly donations intended to help orphans, widows, the sick and the elderly. There were also plans to build a hospital, which actually functioned for a short time and was recorded in the Community Statutes of 1648.[80]

Dietary laws were adhered to, including the presence of a slaughterer, Benjamin Levy, who received a monthly salary from the synagogue for inspecting and slaughtering animals in accordance with Jewish law.[81]

---

[78] Ibid, p. 84.

[79] Ibid, p. 15.

[80] Ibid, p. XXIII.

[81] WIZNITZER, Arnold. *Os judeus no Brasil colonial*, op. cit., p. 121. WEITMAN, David Y. (Rabbi) *Bandeirantes espirituais do Brasil*, op. cit., p. XXII.

Off the Jewish street, was the Jewish square[82] and, near this, the Jewish beach.[83] Further away from the city, on the banks of the Capibaribe river, in a clearing called "rabbit place," was the Jewish cemetery.[84] There was no dirt path to the cemetery, which had to be reached by boat across the river.[85] According to Ronaldo Vainfas, the first document to mention the location of this cemetery is a Dutch map from 1639 with the label: *De Joods Bergraafplaats* (meaning "place of the Jewish cemetery").

In 1645, the size of Recife's Jewish population reached its peak. Using a census carried out by the Dutch, we can estimate there were 1,450 Jews living in the Dutch Northeast – representing around half the white civilian population, which totaled 2,899 people. The minute book of Recife's Zur Israel congregation shows that this population soon fell into decline, and in 1648 there are only 180 signatures of heads of families belonging to the congregation (supposing an average of three members per family, this gives approximately 720 people).[86]

Recently, a new archeological site was discovered near the Jewish Guard House, also called Forte João de Albuquerque and described as *Excubiae Iudaeorum*, or Jewish Guard, in a famous account by the Dutch humanist, Caspar Barlaeus. Today, it is known as Marin d'Olinda de Pernambuco. Beside this fort, a cemetery was discovered that all signs indicate was Jewish. This discovery leads to the following question: why was there a need for a second cemetery? After 1645, the fighting between Portuguese militias and Dutch troops intensified to the point where the population of Recife and Maurícia became confined to the area. In order to reach the first cemetery, a boat would have had to be taken across the river, which had by that point been blocked off by Portuguese militias. During

---

[82] MELLO, José Antônio Gonsalves de. *História dos cistãos-novos portugueses*, op. cit., p. 275.

[83] WOLFF, Egonl WOLFF, Frieda. *A odisseia dos judeus do Recife*. São Paulo: Edusp, 1979. p. 11.

[84] WEITMAN, David Y. (Rabbi) *Bandeirantes espirituais do Brasil*, op. cit., p. XXII. MELLO, José Antônio Gonsalves de. *História dos cistãos-novos portugueses*, op. cit., p. 280.

[85] VAINFAS, Ronaldo. *Jerusalém colonial. Judeus portugueses no Brasil holandês*. Rio de Janeiro: Civilização Brasileira, 2010. p. 173.

[86] WIZNITZER, Arnold. *Os judeus no Brasil colonial*, op. cit., p. 115.

the conflict, the Jewish Guard House may have been used as a hospital, in order to attend to the wounded and care for the isolated population. Nothing could be more obvious, then, than the founding of a cemetery nearby where the dead could be buried. At this site, skeletons were found buried directly in the earth, without a coffin, and with no evidence of buttons on their clothing, only traces of linen. All of the dead lay with their arms by their sides and were turned to face the east. These features are in accordance with the traditions of a Jewish funeral: following religious law, or Halacha, Jews must be buried directly in the ground, have had their bodies cleaned, be free of any adornments, and wear a shroud – a kind of white linen shirt, stitched without any fastenings or buttons. Jews must also always be buried facing in the direction of Jerusalem and may never have their arms crossed over their body, but instead lying by their sides.[87] At the same site, a candelabra was discovered, decorated with the star of David. The menorah, or seven-branched candelabra, is the oldest Jewish symbol.

The human genetics laboratory at the Federal University of Pernambuco has carried out mitochondrial DNA tests, and the Museum Foundation for the American Man and the Seridó Foundation will carry out biomolecular analysis to establish the origins of the unearthed remains. The only information verified so far is that these were European men living in the 17th century. Professor Tânia Kaufman, from Pernambuco, has investigated the new find in order to establish whether these men belonged to a troop of Jewish soldiers. This is just one more piece of the puzzle that is Brazilian colonial history.

---

[87] KAUFMAN, Tânia. Um cemitério em arrecife dos navios. *Revistas de Arqueologia*, Recife, UFPE, n. 28, 2013.

6. New Christian Identity in Recife

Not all New Christians who had been living in Recife before the arrival of the Dutch shared the same opinion of the nascent Jewish community. According to Anita Novinsky, a deeper analysis of the relationship between New Christians and Jews shows that, in terms of their upbringing, culture and psychology, the *conversos* were Portuguese and still felt emotionally attached to Portugal. Legal discrimination singled them out among the Portuguese, but it did not eliminate their condition as men sharing the same origin, language and customs. This fact led New Christians to display fluctuating behavior: they became torn between the Catholic faith of their Portuguese countrymen and their Jewish heritage. After various generations living under Catholicism, they now found themselves swaying from one religion to the other.[88]

There are numerous examples of this condition, such as the case of Manuel da Costa (in Paraíba) who described himself as Jewish when he spoke to Jews, but as Catholic when he spoke to Catholics. When he found himself among the Dutch, he said he was a Calvinist. This behavior was common among the families of New Christians: they called themselves Catholics on the Iberian Peninsula, Jews when they could and Calvinists when they had to. Many *conversos* felt a strong sense of pride, on one hand repeating that they would rather be flies or go to hell than be Old Christians, while on the other boasting about their New Christians status and attributing it to "the grace of God."[89]

Long coexistence with Catholicism had conditioned New Christians towards syncretic behaviors, such as the concept of individual salvation which does not exist within Judaism, whose practitioners only acknowledge collective salvation. The Old

---

[88] NOVINSKY, Anita. *Cristãos-novos na Bahia: a Inquisição no Brasil.* 2. ed. São Paulo: Perspectiva, 1992. p. 141.

[89] Idem. Avatar du marranisme au Brésil. In: *Les marranismes: de la religiosité cacheé a la societé ouverte.* Paris: Demopolis, 2014. Idem. Sur le marranisme au Brésil et la *fluctuatio animi.* In: *Miroir de l'anthropologie historique.* Rennes: Press Universitaires de Rennes, 2013.

Christian notion of salvation was repeated among New Christians, with the difference being that this would be in accordance with the laws of Moses, not the laws of Christ.[90]

There were also those who cared little for the salvation of the soul or divine redemption and were only concerned with the present. Theirs was a paradoxical existence and, despite living within an organized community, they kept up the tradition of practicing Judaism in secret among their close family. Following their long experience with Catholicism, many New Christians could not adapt to either religion.[91] Miguel Abensour, who practiced the Marrano spiritual state known as *fluctuatio animi*, reminds us that Spinoza referred to this feeling, stating that Marranos found it very difficult to adapt to Rabbinic Judaism but were at the same time unable to position themselves within Christian dogma, which to them resembled superstition. This division produced a sense of deep unease within the soul of the Marrano, as well as a search for "belonging," for a "place in the world."[92] This mental upheaval led the Marrano to fluctuate between one religion and the other, giving rise to restlessness.

This search to define themselves led some *conversos* back to Judaism, and, despite the difficult adaptation and adjustment to the practices of the synagogue, they were able to find their true identity within the Jewish religion.[93] Some were circumcised by the hand of Rabbi Isaac Aboab da Fonseca – who also performed the role of *mohel* (circumcizor) – including the men from Gaspar Francisco da Costa's family, Baltazar da Fonseca and his son, Vasco Fernandes Brandão and sons, Miguel Rodrigues Mendes, Simão do Vale Fonseca and Simão Drago.[94]

---

[90] Idem. Ser marrano em Minas colonial. *Revista Brasileira de História*, São Paulo, v. 21, n. 40, p. 167, 2001.

[91] Damasio, Antonio. *Looking for Spinoza: Joy, Sorrow and the Feeling Brain*. New York: Harvest, 2003. p. 246-247.

[92] ABENSOUR, Miguel. Au-delá de la fluctuatio animi marrane. Spinosa en quête de l'universel. In: *tumultes. Le Paria. Une figure de la modernité*. Paris: Kimé, 2003. n. 22-23. GEBHARD, Carl. *Spinoza*. Buenos Aires: Losada, 1940. p. 18.

[93] NOVINSKY, Anita. *Cristãos-novos na Bahia*, op. Cit., p. 141-162.

[94] SILVA, Leonardo Dantas. *Zur Israel, uma comunidade judaica no Brasil*, op. Cit., p. 82.

In the 17th century, each individual was placed within a defined category: you were either a Catholic or a Lutheran or a Calvinist. And those who did not define themselves within one of these categories lived on the margins of society, like pariahs.[95] The Dutch rulers permitted the practicing of Judaism, but it would not be true to say that the majority of inhabitants of Jewish descent returned to the religion. The Marrano mentality was still divided; in accordance with the concept developed by Novinsky, their mental universe had transformed, and neither the answers provided by Orthodox Jewish wisemen or Christian priests and pastors could satisfy them.

---

[95] NOVINSKY, Anita. Avatars du marranisme au Brésil, op. Cit., p, 119-134.

7. Jewish Institutes and Tzur Israel Statutes

Since the Middle Ages, the Jews of the Iberian Peninsula had existed in self-governed communities embedded within and subordinate to the regional government. Self-regulation allowed Jews to organize and maintain their synagogues and cemeteries, mediate legal disputes between members in the rabbinical courts, collect tribute, fine and punish members of the congregation and obtain taxes for the state.

Over time, many similarities developed in terms of the structures and communal behaviors of the congregations of the Sephardic diaspora. Each new congregation had its own regulations, directors, council and leaders, who were elected from among the most learned. The congregation also included a number of paid officiants, such as the rabbi, the judge, the cantor and the teacher.

The first step when organizing the Jewish community of the Dutch colony of Recife was to compose the statutes that would regulate the running of the synagogues and serve as moral parameters for the population.

In 1648, the Jewish council, comprised of Dr Abraão de Mercado, Jacob Drago, Abraão de Azevedo, Jacob Navarro and David Dias, assembled to elect four more members of the congregation to form a responsible team entrusted with composing the statutes for the two working synagogues. They elected Isaac Atias, Abraão Israel Dias, Jacob Valverde and Benjamin de Pina.

The 28-page manuscript of statutes was written in 17th century Portuguese and Ladino (the mixture of Spanish and Hebrew used by Sephardic Jews in prayer). It focused on four main areas: the administration, justice, financing and revenue of the community.

It was decided that administration would be left in the hands of a council, or Mahamad, consisting of four councilors and a treasurer. Each council would be elected by the previous council and receive a mandate for one year, in a system of rotation that allowed two or three members to be removed every six months so that successors could be elected. Members could not run for consecutive reelection, but would have to wait the one-year period of a mandate. Those wishing to run for election were required to live in the colony, be practicing Jews, and have been circumcised for longer than a year. Those responsible for reading the Pentateuch and any other treasurers would also be elected by the council.[96]

The Mahamad were entrusted with overseeing the needs and safety of the community. For a new member to be accepted, they would need to receive the council's permission for circumcision, or the ritual bath in the case of women. Crypto-Jews returning to Judaism – those who, for fear of being persecuted, had kept their traditions secret and adhered publicly to Christianity – had to wait a year before applying to the directorship, which differed from the practice in Holland, where the wait was three years. In relation to slaves, only those who had been freed could be accepted as members.

It was the role of the trustees of the congregation (the Mahamad) to nominate the directors of Chevra Kadisha, the organization overseeing the Jewish cemetery, as well as the directors of the Jewish schools (Talmud Torá and Etz Hayim). The schools were run by the elected directors and a treasurer. Religious instruction was left in the hands of Rabbi Isaac Aboab da Fonseca, while teachers Samuel Frasão, Isaac Nahimas and Abraham Azuby took charge of secular education.

The powers of the Mahamad also extended to the synagogues and could not be overruled. As well as matters concerning the running of the synagogues, the council had a judicial role within the community, or, in other words, they were tasked with avoiding conflicts between Jews and resolving any legal disputes. They had the authority to issue fines to anyone found guilty of verbal or physical assault, disrespecting the synagogue, behaving immorally or causing public scandal.

If there was a matter relating to money or a crime, those involved would be called before the council, who would adjudicate and issue an appropriate fine. Any funds received from fines were given to charity. If there was any suspicion of favoritism by a member of the Jewish council in relation to one of the parties, the council could be replaced by a special audience of "good men" drawn from the town

---

[96] MELLO, José Antônio Gonsalves de. *Gente da nação*. Recife: Massangana/Fundação Joaquim Nabuco, 1996. p. 338.

council, or else special permission could be requested to have the case redirected straight to the Dutch justice system.[97]

The statutes forbade the construction of any further synagogues, and the Maurícia synagogue was declared subordinate to the one in Recife. Any form of dispute with other religions was also forbidden.[98]

In relation to the community's revenue, taxes were collected twice a year, which would cover the cost of maintenance on the synagogue, schools and cemetery. Various levies were brought together within an overall taxation system: the so-called "tax of the nation." This included a percentage taken from all commercial transactions and services rendered; an emigration tribute, meaning anyone emigrating to another region would pay a determined amount to the council; a contribution towards alms and charity; and fines for troublemakers. Article 28 states that part of the money drawn from fines should be given to the poor, and the other part used for the upkeep of the Jewish hospital. There was a common solidarity fund, that paid for everything from trousseaus for poor and orphaned brides to emergency voyages to Holland. This fund was also intended to provide monthly or weekly financial support for the neediest.[99]

All Jews living in Dutch Brazil were bound by these statutes and were required to sign their names in the minute book. These signatures facilitated control over the payment of taxes.

Conflicts with Christians regarding religion were forbidden, in accordance with article 27 of the statutes. There was fear that controversy of this nature could end up jeopardizing the Jewish community and lead to misunderstandings and problems with the local population and authorities.[100] Despite religious tolerance, opposition to Christian dogma was still considered blasphemy by

---

[97] The "good men" were members of the town council, people with great political influence – usually rich farmers – who in the 17th century held the status of regional leaders and were required to have "pure blood." On the "purity of blood", see CARNEIRO, Maria Luiza Tucci. *Preconceito racial em Portugal e Brasil Colônial: os cristãos-novos e o mito da pureza de sangue.* São Paulo: Perspectiva, 2005.

[98] MELLO, José Antônio Gonsalves de. *Gente da nação.* Recife, op. cit., p. 339.

[99] WEITMAN, David Y. (Rabbi) *Bandeirantes espirituais do Brasil: século XVII.* São Paulo: Maayanot, 2003. p. 15.

[100] Ibid, p. 14.

the Dutch and punished with harsh prison sentences and, in extreme cases, death.

The book of minutes and statutes of the Zur Israel synagogue of Recife has made it possible to achieve a better understanding of the organization and workings of the Jewish community in Dutch Brazil. The first person to mention the existence of the book was J. Mendes dos Remédios, in 1911. Later, in 1925, Dutch-Jewish historian Jacob da Silva Rosa carried out an analysis of the document, associating the name Zur Israel (meaning "Rock of Israel") with the reef formations of Recife. The entire document was translated into English and analyzed by Arnold Wiznitzer, in 1954, before being translated into Portuguese by Rabbi David Weitman, in 2003, and published in his book, *Bandeirantes espirituais* [Spiritual Pioneers].[101]

The only moment of light during three hundred years of religious and political darkness in Brazil, when it was possible for Jews to live in relative freedom and practice their religion, was the twenty-four-year period of Dutch rule in Brazil's Northeast.

Holland's politics of tolerance in Brazil brought rich economic and cultural rewards and paved the way, for the first time in the Brazilian colony, for developments in scientific research, literature and the arts. The Jews of Dutch Brazil were actively involved in these intellectual developments until their definitive departure in 1654.

During the final decade of the 16th century, which witnessed a fast-growing middle class in Northern Europe and an intensification of repression in Portugal, Holland offered its citizens relative religious freedom, which attracted Portuguese nationals of Jewish ancestry to Amsterdam.

Despite the relative freedom Holland afforded to New Christians who had already converted back to Judaism, life was challenging for the Portuguese refugees, who, attracted by the economic

---

[101] REMÉDIOS, Mendes. *Os judeus portugueses em Amsterdã*. Coimbra: França Pinto Amado, 1911; ROSA, J. S. Silva. *Geschiedenis der Portugeesche joden te Amsterdam 1593-1925*. Amsterdam: M. Hertzberger, 1925. WIZNITZER, Arnold. *The Members of the Brazilian Jewish Community (1648-1653). Publications of the American Jewish Historical Society,* Philadelphia, V. II. March and June, 1953; Idem. *Os judeus no Brasil Colonial,* São Paulo: Pioneira, p. 121-122. WEITMAN, David Y. (Rabbi). *Bandeirantes espirituais do Brasil: século XVII,* op. cit., p. 43-51.

opportunities offered by the New World after 1630, gradually made their way to the Dutch colony in Brazil.

The Dutch Northeast developed economically and financially because of the international sugar trade and also as a result of genuine cultural dynamism.

Jews, Catholics and Calvinists were able to coexist within this climate of tolerance for many years and build extensive trading relationships.

In Pernambuco, the Jews created a community inspired by the Jewish model in Amsterdam. They demonstrated enormous creativity in the field of medicine, as well as in literature, languages, the sciences, grammar and architecture.

A century before the European Age of Enlightenment, the Jews in Dutch Brazil (1630-1654) were already proposing a politics of democracy, with foundations in justice and liberty, and very similar to modern human rights. These principles guided the organization of the Jewish community in Recife.

In the statutes of the congregation of Zur Israel, the first synagogue of the Americas, we can highlight the defense of democratic ideals by means of representation, elections and the alternation of officials.[102]

During a period when European discrimination differentiated between Sephardic and Ashkenazi Jews, in the Ascamot – the set of laws and regulations devised by the Mahamat – no differentiation existed between these two groups, which was a significant innovation for the time. In 18th century France, for example, Sephardic Jews were afforded certain privileges for belonging to the wealthy classes and for assimilating more readily than the Ashkenazim, who locked themselves away behind their traditions.

Within the Jewish community of Recife, all members received the same treatment. Men summoned to read the Torah in the synagogue (a practice conferring honor and privilege upon those chosen) were selected by a draw and not as a result of any social distinction. However, recent converts to Judaism and new arrivals

---

[102] WEITMAN, David Y. (Rabbi). Estatutos da Sinagoga Tzur Israel. In: *Bandeirantes espirituais do Brasil: século XVII*. São Paulo: Maayanot, 2003. p. 25-80.

from Holland were afforded a degree of priority, as a kind of welcoming.[103]

The Jewish council, the governing body, exercised rigorous control over legal aspects of the community. Any litigation between its members was first analyzed by the council, and only taken to the official courts after being given their assent. Without this permission, no Jew in Dutch Brazil could testify against another Jew. There was concern with keeping the community united in order to strengthen its defenses against Catholics and Calvinists.[104]

In Dutch Recife, there were two religious stances: firstly, the one of Jews coming from Holland and concerned with the rigid practice of their religion; secondly, the stance of Brazilian New Christians, who had already been living in Brazil for a number of generations and knew little about the Jewish faith. With the arrival of Jews from Amsterdam, many New Christians converted back to Judaism, which led to conflicted emotions.[105]

One of the greatest contributions made by Brazilian New Christians to 18th century Enlightenment thinking was their critique of religion, expressed in defense of freedom of thought and of belief. This critique can largely be interpreted as a result of the repression of Judaism, which had been required to exist in secrecy for centuries.[106]

Since antiquity, Jews have distinguished themselves from other peoples by defending that all men are free, equal and possess the right to criticize power.[107] These precepts were inadmissible under the Roman Empire, just as they were during the modern period, when the theory of the divine right proclaimed that power was

---

[103] These converts were returned New Christians. WEITMAN, David Y. (Rabbi) *Bandeirantes espirituais do Brasil*, op. cit., p. XXXII.

[104] Ibid. p. XXXIII

[105] NOVINSKY, Anita. *Cristãos-novos na Bahia: a Inquisação no Brasil*, 2. ed. São Paulo: Perspectiva, 1992. p. 140-162.

[106] Idem. Marranos e a Inquisição: sobre a rota o ouro em Minas Gerais. In. GRINBERG, Keila. (org.) *Judeus no Brasil: Inquisição, imigração e identidade.* Rio de Janeiro: Civilização Brasileira, 2005. p. 161-183. Apud BAUER, Yehuda. Anti-Semitism as European and World Problem. In: *Patterns of Prejudice.* London: The Institute of Jewish Affairs, 1993. v. 2. p. 14-15.

[107] NOVINSKY, Anita. "A sobrevivência do judeus na visão de Baruch Spinosa: o exemplo da Paraíba" (to be published). Apud BAUER, Yehuda, Anti-Semitism as European and World Problem, op. cit., p. 15-24.

absolute and indisputable, with men classified according to their origins and social class. Nevertheless, under Dutch governance in Brazil, Jews were given the opportunity to develop their democratic ideas.

The freedom afforded in Pernambuco under the Dutch rulership of Count Maurice of Nassau made it possible for Jews to develop in a wide range of fields. The renowned calligrapher Yehuda Machabeu and the rabbi Mosseh Rephael d'Aguilar left behind writings in defense of the equality of men and the freedom of the soul in accordance with Aristotle's conception.

During this period, there were numerous scholars living in Brazil, among them the Jewish convert Isaac de Castro, whose tragic story has been documented by Elias Lipner.[108] Isaac de Castro was versed in Greek and Latin literature – the height of erudition at the time – and spoke Hebrew, French, Portuguese, Dutch and Spanish. He was arrested by agents of the Inquisition in Bahia and sent to stand trial in Portugal. In prison, he would argue with the clergy about the veracity of passages of the New Testament. When debating a French diplomat, a representative of the chief minister, Mazarin, he was urged to adopt the Christian faith. Isaac responded that, while he was free to do anything based upon human motivations, he would do nothing that offended the principles of his own conscience.[109]

Daniel Levy, also known as Dom Miguel de Barrios, was a poet of Portuguese descent living in Holland who based his writings on the lives of Jews in the Brazilian colony. He dedicated a poem to Abraham Cohen, an important businessman in Dutch Recife. In this poem, he highlighted Cohen's powerful intellect and generosity, as well as his sense of solidarity and social responsibility, given that he offered assistance to Jews and Christians equally. It was only a century later that Cohen's attitudes and writings in defense of fraternity would begin to be debated within intellectual circles.

Jews also achieved prominence as engineers and architects. A large urban project carried out in Recife under the rulership of Maurice of Nassau was responsible for transforming this sugar

---

[108] LIPNER, Elias. *Izaque de Castro, o mancebo que veio para Brasil.* Recife: Massangana/Fundação Joaquim Nabuco, 1992. p. 10-20.

[109] Ibid, p. 26.

distribution center into a modern city, expediting economic growth with the construction of bridges and sanitation facilities. One of the key figures in this development was a Jew named Baltazar da Fonseca. Da Fonseca was a member of Pieter Post's team during the construction of the bridge between Recife and the island of Antônio Vaz, which simplified the journey between the center of Recife and the periphery – the bridge is now known as the Maurício de Nassau. This construction allowed for the expansion of the city, which was considered densely populated at the time, towards the periphery, in addition to connecting Old and New Maurícia, important business centers.[110] This connectedness reflected the new ideas of the urban middle classes and contrasted with older conceptions which envisioned a town as the hub for a rural area, in the service of large farms and sugar plantations.

Naturalists began to study Brazilian flora and fauna. Philosophers debated theoretical questions in the field of natural sciences, among them the nature and origins of the fauna, flora and inhabitants of the Americas. During their fieldwork, scholars came into contact with an increasing number of living species previously unknown to Europeans. These new discoveries raised speculation regarding the plurality of creation. Within this field, José da Costa, an Amsterdam Jew living in Recife during the period of West India Company investment, achieved prominence. In his spare time, Da Costa engaged in philosophical enquiry prompted by the discovery of new plant and animal species in Brazil's Northeast. As a result of his research, doubts began to surface in relation to the story of Noah's Ark: Da Costa queried whether it would have been possible to build an ark large enough to hold all living creatures, supposing that all animals were saved by a single vessel, and also asked why certain animals could be found in some parts of the world but not others. Could there have been, at some point in the past, a single origin for all this diversity? The prominent businessman was the most eloquent articulator of these questions.[111]

---

[110] MENEZES, José Luís Mota. A cidade de Maurício: observações sobre a história urbana de Recife. In: *A presença holandesa no Brasil: memória e imaginário.* Rio de Janeiro: Museu Histórico Nacional, 2004. p. 185-194.

[111] TEIXEIRA, Dante Martins. O mito da natureza intocada: a história natural no Brasil holandês (1624-1654) e a sua contribuição para o conhecimento da história recente

In the field of law, the outstanding figure was Miguel/Michael Cardozo, the first lawyer and public prosecutor in Brazil, and a descendent of Portuguese converted Jews. In August 1646, Cardozo was given authorization to practice his profession in the city. Cardozo can be regarded as the patriarch of a well-known family of North American lawmen: his descendant, Benjamin Cardozo, was an important merchant in New York in the late 17th and early 18th centuries, and another apparent relative, also Benjamin Cardozo, would become an Associate Justice of the Supreme Court of the United States in the 1930s. There is no concrete evidence of kinship between Miguel and Benjamin Cardozo, only indications.

Another renowned and illustrious figure living in Dutch Brazil was Isaac Aboab da Fonseca, the rabbi responsible for the Zur Israel synagogue. One of the most recognizable personalities of the 17th century Jewish world, he had a deep knowledge of Hebrew grammar and was a popular preacher, as well as a poet. What stands out among his body of work, and should be considered a historical document, is the poem "Zekher asit leniflaot El," in which he describes events of the war between the Dutch and Portuguese for the recovery of Pernambuco. Aboab de Fonseca also wrote a preface to the translation of *Casa de Dios y puerta del cielo* [House of God and Door to Heaven], in which he narrates the vicissitudes and sufferings of Jews during the years of war between 1645 and 1654, as well as his departure from the territory.[112] A great theologian, Aboab da Fonseca defended the thesis that the Jewish sinner, no matter how great his sins, would never be punished with eternal extinction. This belief chimed perfectly with the Marranos, who had fled Portugal and returned to Judaism in Holland, as well as with New Christians who had adapted to their new faith.

Aboab's ideas were also recognized and admired by non-Jewish intellectuals, such as Father Antônio Vieira, who used to say that "Aboab knew of what he spoke."[113]

---

da fauna no Novo Mundo. In: *A presença holandesa no Brasil: memória e imaginário*. Rio de Janeiro: Museu Histórico Nacional, 2004. p. 279-280.

[112]WEITMAN, David Y. (Rabbi) *Bandeirantes espirituais do Brasil*, op. cit., p. 171. Aboab de Fonseca's poem is transcribed in the chapter which refers to the invasion of Pernambuco and the expulsion of the Jews from Recife.

[113] Ibid, p. 163.

Another prominent figure was Mosseh Rephael d'Aguilar, rabbi of the Maurícia synagogue, who established a pioneering system of study in the medieval liberal arts (grammar, rhetoric and logic). He wrote a treatise on Aristotelian logic and Greco-Roman rhetoric, which was intended to provide students and teachers at the Recife Jewish school with a thorough understanding of rhetorical devices. He became personally involved in the students' early lessons in oratory, guiding them in their development of debating skills (a common practice in Dutch literary society).[114]

It might be said that Luso-Brazilian Jews and their descendants are remarkable for having managed to achieve a stable life anywhere they found themselves, and, fundamentally, for the ideas they left etched into the traditions of democracy, a century before Voltaire and Rousseau proclaimed their defense of the freedoms of religion and of thought.

---

[114] Ibid, p. 83. Greek and Roman culture and the ancient philosophers were a part of the intellectual life of Marranos in Spain and Portugal.

8. Fragile Coexistence of Catholics, Protestants and Jews

The fact that Jews were deemed necessary as interpreters meant they were protected by the directors of the West India Company. However, despite relative freedom and opportunities for economic and cultural development, antisemitism was ever-present, on the part of Calvinists as much as Old Christians. Uncovered documents confirm that this attitude was a reality.

There was a range of accusations. Calvinists complained about the "arrogance" of the Jews, claiming they usurped trade and married Christian women – or, worse, lived with them outside of wedlock.[115]

The West India Company received yearly reports on trade in the colonies, and the report from 1641 accused the Jews of dominating the entire sugar trade and professing their faith openly in public places. These reports requested that Jews be banned from participating in auctions, from working as public servants and from collecting taxes.[116]

These complaints were recurrent. It was argued that in other countries Jews were forced to wear identifying markers – red caps or yellow insignias on their chests – so everyone might know their origins and avoid being cheated or robbed, "for all were aware of the means used by these sons of Judas, who lie, cheat, provide false measurements and impede the competition of Christians, who do not resort to such chicanery. Due to their extortionate moneylending to farmers, they are an authentic plague on the land of Brazil. Brazil belongs to Christians and not to the accursed sons of Israel, who profane the name of Jesus. The Israelites are not needed here, Christians can do everything they can!"[117]

---

[115] WÄTJEN, Hermann. A egreja no Brasil holandês. In: *O domínio hollandez no Brasil: um capítulo da história colonial do século XVIII.* São Paulo: Companhia Editora Nacional, 1938. p. 349.

[116] WIZNITZER, Arnold. *Os judeus no Brasil Colonial*, São Paulo: Pioneira, 1966. p. 64.

[117] WÄTJEN, Hermann, op. cit., p. 350-353.

But for the West India Company, the Jews were important political allies, and the same could not be said of Portuguese Christians. And, whatever pressure might be mounting, there was an interest in consolidating the business of imports and exports. The company, therefore, could not adopt any drastic measures towards the Jews, such as granting Christians exclusivity within the retail market; Jewish investors had influence within the company. Following Maurice of Nassau's return to Holland, the only action taken against the Jews was the prohibition of the construction of a new synagogue and the resolution that, from that point forwards, two-thirds of all brokers should be Christians.

Maurice of Nassau drew attention to Christian merchants' increasing hatred towards the Jews. He defended religious tolerance, believing it would lead the colonists to pledge fidelity to their Dutch rulers, and suggested that hardening their stance toward either Jews or Catholics would only increase the risk of a revolt. He also believed the Jews were more faithful than the Catholics, but feared that if the Portuguese government were to grant freedom of religion the Jews might side with the enemy. Occasionally, under pressure from Calvinist ministers, Maurice of Nassau found himself forced, in the interest of relieving tensions, to make a declaration or take a stance against the Jews.[118]

His humanist spirit, however, was acknowledged by the Jewish community, when, in 1642, upon learning of the count's intention to return to Amsterdam, the Jewish leaders offered him an annual payment throughout his time in power if he would remain as governor.

The concerns of the Jewish leaders in Amsterdam can be justified by the fact that, since 1642, a Calvinist synod – a kind of Inquisition of the Reformed Church – had begun operating in Recife. The synod had deliberative and executive power over matters relating to the internal organization as well as the moral behavior of the population living in Dutch Brazil, and was able to recommend corrective and punitive measures to the governors in cases deemed scandalous or deserving of censure or punishment. Trial and punishment were regulated by a civil tribunal, established

---

[118] WIZNITZER, Arnold. *Judeus no Brasil Colonial*, op. cit., p. 66.

at the request of civil or religious authorities, and not ecclesiastical ones, as was the case with the Catholic Inquisition.[119]

The synod's concern with moral behavior focused upon five points: the marital situation of couples living together outside of wedlock; prostitution; Catholic practices, such as blessings, blasphemy, heresy and apostasies; the disregarding of Sundays on the part of blacks and Jews; and the religious freedom of Jews and Catholics.

Despite the synod only having been officially installed in Brazil in 1641, from 1637, class assemblies – as meetings between the Dutch colonial government and representatives of the Reformed Church were known – had been dedicated to discussing issues involving Jews, primarily in relation to complaints contained in documents like the ones considered at the beginning of this chapter, such as the excessive freedom of Jewish worshipers, "scandalous" Jewish practices and dishonest competition. The only case involving a Jew to be judged by the synod was that of a Jewish woman in Paraíba, who stood accused of profaning the name "of Jesus Our Savior and the Holy Baptism." The synod concluded that the woman was a regular church attendee and offered hope of being converted, and, therefore, should be treated with kindness by the priests.[120]

The year the synod was installed in Pernambuco saw the beginning of restrictive regulations on the social and religious activities of Jews. Jews were prevented from marrying Christians, and it was decreed that the children of mixed couples, in cases where the mother was Jewish, should be entrusted into the care of Christian relatives.

On one occasion, a Jewish sugar merchant, Moisés Abendana, ran up debts with Dutch creditors that totaled 12 florins. Abendana was found hanged, with the authorities concluding he had committed suicide. The *schepens*, or town councilors, of Maurícia, directed by the *schout* (a kind of public prosecutor), Paulo António Daems, prohibited burial and determined that Abendana's body

---

[119] SANTOS, João Henrique. A Inquisição calvinista: o sínodo do Brasil e os judeus no Brasil holandês. In: ASSIS, Angelo A. Faria de et al. (Org.). *Desvelando o poder – histórias de dominação: Estado, religião e sociedade*. Rio de Janeiro: Vício de Leitura, 2007. p. 107-124.

[120] Idem.

should be displayed on a gallows as an example, as was the practice in Holland. The leaders of the Jewish community in Recife approached Maurice of Nassau, offering to take on Abendana's debt, as well as pay a bonus for the inconvenience, in order to avoid a scandal. Since Nassau declined this offer, the leaders went to the creditors, who accepted payment of the debt and authorized Abendana's burial.[121]

One of the most ferocious attacks on the Jews came from a protestant pastor, Vicente Joaquim Soler, who provided services to the West India Company in Recife. Soler wrote numerous letters in which he insulted the Jews, accusing them of "sucking the blood of the people," "stealing from the company" and enjoying "privileges that jeopardized Christian merchants."[122] In these letters, it is possible to observe great concern on the part of the Calvinists with the growth of the Jewish population. The uninterrupted arrival of Jews from Holland and the increasing birthrate led to apprehension among Calvinists, who feared Jews might eventually become the dominant population in the region.

In 1641, *schout* Daems requested that a wealthy New Christian, Gaspar Francisco da Costa, be expelled from the colony and have his assets confiscated for having returned to Judaism and submitted to circumcision.[123]

Another example of the antisemitism of this period occurred when a Jew accused of blasphemy was tortured to death by a crowd instigated by the speeches of priests and pastors. The Jewish community of Amsterdam reacted indignantly and accused Recife's Dutch rulers of supporting the persecution of Jews. They also insisted that the *schepens* of Maurícia turn the case over to the justice council for trial, as was standard practice in Holland in cases

---

[121] WIZNITZER, Arnold. *Judeus no Brasil Colonial*, op. cit., p. 76, SANTOS, João Henrique. A Inquisação calvinista, op. cit., p. 120-122.

[122] Brasil holandês. Ezasete cartas de Vicente Joaquim Soler. Rio de Janeiro: Index, 1999.

[123] A *schout* is a public servant. Daems was, also, over a number of years, Maurice of Nassau's secretary-general and was able, on numerous occasions, to display his dislike of the Jewish people.

of blasphemy, claiming that the *schepens* were not competent to rule in this matter.[124]

The most emphatic anti-Semite of this period was a priest, Friar Manuel Calado, who left behind a text containing the most violent accusations against Jews. Calado describes Recife as a paradise, and stated that with the arrival of the Jews, "usury, illicit gains, corruption, rape and all kinds of crime had spread across the territory." In his sermons, and by taking advantage of grievances passed on by word-of-mouth, Friar Calado led an anti-Jewish moment.[125]

Numerous attempts were made to prevent Jews from practicing their religion freely. In one of these attempts, the Calvinist ecclesiastic council decided that both of the synagogues should be closed down. The Jewish community of Recife reacted, contacting the Jewish leaders in Amsterdam, who, in 1645, organized a petition intended to ensure no distinction would be made between Jews and Christians in the Dutch colonies. The response to this petition was a document known as the "Patente Honorosa" [Honorable Patent], addressed to the Supreme Council of Brazil and to the governor. By means of this document, the Jews were able to defy their enemies and keep the synagogues open.[126]

A large part of the hostility towards Jews was the result of competition for trade. Yet, even with this increase in animosity, Dutch Pernambuco was one of the few places in the 17th century world where Jews could work and practice their faith, if not publicly, then at least protected from the greatest evil of the age, the Inquisition.

---

[124] MELLO, José Antônio Gonsalves de. *Gente da nação*. Recife: Massangana/Fundação Joaquim Nabuco, 1996. p. 269.

[125] CALADO, Frei Manuel. *O valoroso Lucideno e o triunfo da liberdade.* Belo Horizonte, Itatiaia and São Paulo: Edusp, 1987. v. 1.

[126] MELLO, José Antônio Gonsalves de. *Gente da nação*, op. cit., p. 254.

9. The Holy Office and its Influence on Dutch Territory

The Inquisition could not operate within Dutch Brazil. However, this did not prevent it from inflicting distress and anguish upon some Portuguese living within the region and its environs.

It was during the war waged by the Portuguese against the Dutch for recovery of the occupied territory that "Judeophobia," previously widespread, was ratcheted up again. On September 18, 1645, the rebels took control of Fort Maurício, at the mouth of the São Francisco river, built in honor of Maurice of Nassau. Around two-hundred Dutch and Portuguese soldiers were taken prisoner. Protestants and Catholics made up the majority of these prisoners, but ten Jews were also taken captive and sent to Bahia, where they were transferred to the prisons of the Holy Office of the Inquisition in Portugal. Those ten Jews have become known in history as the "prisoners of the São Francisco river."[127]

Of these prisoners, four were able to evade the Inquisition because they came originally from Germany and Poland and spoke no Portuguese. These were Jacob Polaco, David Michel, Isaac Johannis and Salomão Jacob.

The other six remained confined in the prisons of the Inquisition in Lisbon, while the inquisitors ordered investigations into their origins and the extent of their fidelity to Catholicism. Only Portuguese who had been baptized were considered within the jurisdiction of the Tribunal of the Holy Office of the Inquisition. Jews were not officially allowed to live within territories belonging to the Portuguese Empire and, if a prisoner were able to prove he had never received the sacrament of Baptism, he could not be punished by the tribunal.

Because they spoke fluent Portuguese, suspicions were raised about the origins of Samuel Israel, Samuel Velho, David Shalom,

---

[127] LIPNER, Elias. *Izaque de Castro, o mancebo que veio preso ao Brasil.* Recife: Massangana/Fundação Joaquim Nabuco, 1992. VAINFAS, Ronaldo. Inquisição e judeus novos no contexto das guerras holandesas. Available at: <periodicos.unb.br/index.php/textos/article/download/6056/5014>. Accessed on: Nov. 20, 2017.

Abraão Bueno, Isaac de Carvalho and Abraão Mendes, and the inquisitors decided to investigate their lives and beliefs.[128]

Numerous witnesses were called upon to provide statements about the Brazilian prisoners, among them a secretary of the Inquisition, charged with evaluating the familiarity of those accused with the Portuguese language. Using the criteria of language, the inquisitors sought out those who had been born in Portugal. The New Christians who raised the strongest suspicions were Samuel Velho and David Shalom, because both spoke very bad Dutch and perfect Portuguese, and Abraão Bueno, who came originally from France.

Dutch soldiers, who had been companions of the Portuguese New Christians at Fort Maurício, were also called upon to provide statements. One soldier, Martim Crama, a Dutch Jew of Ashkenazi descent, reported that Samuel Velho and Abraão Mendes were originally from the city of Porto, and that Abraão Bueno came from a village near Coimbra. The Holy Office ordered that the birthplaces of the defendants be investigated, and managed to acquire baptismal certificates for Gabriel Mendes and João Nunes Velho.[129]

In order to ensure their safety, New Christians frequently adopted two names, and sometimes even three. The penitents were João Nunes Velho (or Samuel Velho), Diogo Henriques (or Abraão Bueno) and Gabriel Mendes (or Abraão Mendes). The inquisitors learned that these men were all baptized Portuguese who had fled from Portugal during childhood, becoming Jews in France and Holland. All three confessed before the inquisitors to being "Jews of the Jewish faith", and also "public," meaning that in Pernambuco they had professed their religion openly. At 11 years old, Gabriel Mendes had arrived in Hamburg, where he was instructed in the Jewish faith and submitted to circumcision. João Nunes Velho was circumcised at the home of his uncle, Jerônimo de Souza (or Samuel Barbanel), during a religious ceremony. Diogo Henriques, or Abraão, as he was known to the Jews – or Jacques, to the French –

---

[128] VAINFAS, Ronaldo. Inquisição e judeus novos no contexto das guerras holandesas, op. cit.

[129] LIPNER, Elias. Izaque de Castro, o macebo que veio preso ao Brasil, op. cit., p. 25.

was circumcised as a ten-month-old baby, at the home of his parents.[130]

The story of these three Jews is similar to that of many other Marranos who had relied on the help of friends and relatives to escape from Portugal. In the 17th century, there was a strong international network in Europe focused on helping fleeing New Christians by connecting the Pernambuco-Portugal-Holland axis. This network, unprecedented in world history, was established with the help of wealthy Jewish merchants, and was similar to a network that had existed in the 16th century, with the aid of Dona Gracia Mendes, one of the most remarkable and influential women of her era. Dona Gracia had lived in Italy and Turkey, where she was a friend of Sultan Suleiman, the Magnificent, and was able to use her fortune and economic prestige to create an international communications network that served as an escape route for Marranos persecuted by the Inquisition.[131]

As soon as the Portuguese were captured beside the São Francisco river and handed over to the Inquisition in Portugal, the Jewish community of Amsterdam and the States General interceded with the Portuguese king, demanding their release. They invoked article 25 of the treaty of June 12, 1641, according to which all peoples from the United Provinces living within the Dutch colony, independent of their professed religion, would be free from inquisitorial persecution.[132]

At the time of his ascension to the Portuguese throne in 1640, Dom João IV had as his adviser a Jesuit named Father Antônio Vieira, an enthusiastic defender of Jews and New Christians. Following the advice of his confessor, and keen to form a political alliance with Holland, the Portuguese king intervened with the Inquisition on behalf of the prisoners.[133]

---

[130] VAINFAS, Ronaldo. Inquisição e judeus novos no contexto das guerras holandesas, op. cit.

[131] ROTH, Cecil. *Dona Gracia of the House of Nasi*. Philadelphia: The Jewish Publication Society of America, 1948.

[132] MELLO, Evaldo Cabral de. O Brasil e os holandeses: 1630-1654. In: HERKENHOFF, Paulo (org.). *O Brasil e os holandeses*. Rio de Janeiro: Sextante Artes, 1999. p. 42.

[133] NOVINSKY, Anita. Padre Antônio Vieira, A Inquisição e os judeus. *Revista Novos Estudos Cebrap*, São Paulo, n. 29, p. 172-181, Mar. 1991.

Three Jews were released due to a lack of evidence: Samuel Israel, the oldest, who had served as rabbi at a small synagogue on the São Francisco; David Shalom, who spoke the worst Dutch; and Isaac Carvalho.

During this period, tensions between the Inquisition and the Portuguese monarchy were at their peak. The Inquisition was powerful and could limit royal involvement in religious matters.

Under pressure from the Inquisition, the prisoners were forced to confess offences relating to Judaism. While attempting to devise a way of entangling their inquisitors, the prisoners pretended to be repentant and willing to reconcile with the Church. Gabriel Mendes, João Nunes Velho and Diogo Henriques received sentencing at an *auto-de-fé* on December 15, 1647. The majority of New Christians received sentences of imprisonment, confiscation of assets and the wearing of a penitential tunic depicting flames over their clothes for the rest of their lives. Years later, the penitential garment was abandoned by the Inquisition as "an act of mercy."[134]

The three New Christians mentioned above were not the last "Brazilians" to be punished by the Inquisition of Lisbon during the period of war between the Dutch and the Portuguese. A number of others were arrested in various regions of Brazil, and one of those with the most tragic fate was young Isaac de Castro, captured and burned alive during the same *auto-de-fé* at which the "prisoners of the São Francisco" received their punishments.

Isaac de Castro arrived in Brazil in 1641 as a 19-year-old. Some historians claim he came to the country on the run because of a minor offence he had committed while studying sciences in Leiden, where he is said to have injured a young man during a duel in defense of his honor.[135] Other historians claim the youth arrived in Brazil with the aim of spreading the Jewish faith among New Christians. With this intention in mind, he made for Recife, accompanied by his uncle, Mosseh Rephael d'Aguilar, the learned rabbi responsible for founding the second synagogue in Recife.

Isaac de Castro was a teacher of Judaism, and travelled to Paraíba, Rio de Janeiro and Bahia looking to contact New

---

[134] VAINFAS, Ronaldo. *Jerusalém colonial. Judeus portugueses no Brasil holandês.* Rio de Janeiro: Civilização Brasileira, 2010. p. 285-294.

[135] LIPNER, Elias. Izaque de Castro, o mancebo que veio preso ao Brasil, op. cit.

Christians, who could also be found spread across the *sertão*, and bring them the message of Judaism. He was a peddler, and used these journeys to conduct business as well. After twenty months in Pernambuco, the legal authorities learned of his situation as a fugitive from justice, and Isaac de Castro was forced to flee to Salvador.

In Bahia, conscious of the threat of the Inquisition, De Castro presented himself before the bishop of the city as a Jew seeking conversion. However, his plan backfired, and he was arrested in Bahia before being transported to the prisons of the Inquisition in Portugal. Accused of proselytizing, among his possessions the inquisitors discovered a *Thesouro dos Dinim*, a ritual compendium written by a famous Amsterdam rabbi, Menasseh ben Israel, which served Marranos as a guide to their religion.

Although still young, Isaac de Castro had a deep knowledge of Jewish culture. He did not renounce his faith before his inquisitors, but tried instead to convince them that the one true law was the law of Moses. He was condemned and burned alive. It is written that on the day of his death the winds blew so hard that it took hours for the defendant to become reduced to ashes. His screams reverberated around the square, and, as he died, he recited the most famous Jewish prayer, the Shema Yisrael.[136] It is said that the inquisitors were so impressed by the young man's suffering that they decided to renounce the use of the death penalty – a decision that was never carried through.

In the first book to be written about Isaac de Castro in Brazil, Elias Lipner reinforces the idea of this young man as a martyr for Judaism. Recently, Ronaldo Vainfas has provided a new reading of this character, highlighting, among his many facets, the violent character who chose to resolve personal disputes with the sword attached to his belt. Vainfas dismisses Isaac's journeys across various regions of Brazil as a simple consequence of his work as a peddler.[137]

The financial difficulties and explosive temperament described by Vainfas do not necessarily preclude Isaac de Castro's interest in

---

[136] Shema Yisrael (Listen Israel]. The prayer says "Shemá Israel!/ Adonai Elôhenu!/ Adonai Echad!" ["Hear, O Israel! Adonai is our God! Adonai is One"].

[137] VAINFAS, Ronaldo. *Jerusalém colonial*, op. cit., p. 293-294.

Judaism and its teaching. Living with his uncle, Rabbi Rephael d'Aguilar, and his uncle's millenarianist beliefs – which affirmed that the advent of the messianic era would only be possible once Jews had spread to all parts of the world – may have influenced De Castro's personality, which only serves to demonstrate the extent of human complexity.[138]

The fact is that Isaac de Castro did travel on business, as Vainfas puts forward. Yet it is also true that he always carried the *Thesouro dos Dinim* with him. If De Castro had not been concerned with spreading the Jewish faith, why risk carrying a manual on Judaism through Portuguese colonial territory? It is also a fact that the young man held in the prisons of the Holy Office was able to debate on philosophy and theology while attempting to convince the priests and inquisitors of the superiority of the Jewish faith. Isaac de Castro's dramatic death provided a moment of reflection with regard to the "Church's mercy."

There were other Jews and New Christians imprisoned in Recife by the Luso-Brazilian troops. On January 28, 1649, two young men, Samuel Nehemias and Arão Moreno, whose parents had lived in Amsterdam for more than fifty years, were arrested and sent to the Inquisition in Lisbon. The Jews appealed to the States General to intercede with the king of Portugal, but the king responded that there was nothing he could do. It has not been possible to discover how this trial was concluded, as the Hebrew names of the accused have impeded identification of the appropriate file at the Torre do Tombo in Portugal.[139]

On January 26, 1649, another New Christian, Pedro de Almeida, was held in the prisons of the Estaus Palace. The 31-year-old was arrested in Paraíba, where he worked as a merchant and where he claimed to have been living for sixteen years. Pedro de Almeida had been denounced by his cousin, Samuel Velho, one of the "prisoners of the São Francisco," who exposed him as a resident of Amsterdam and a professed Jew. The accused attempted to defend himself by claiming that, following the Dutch invasion, he had been arrested by

---

[138] In 1666, Rephael d'Aguilar even signed a manifesto supporting the purported messiah, Sabbatai Zevi.

[139] MELLO, José Antônio Gonsalves de. *Gente da nação*. Recife: Massangana/Fundação Joaquim Nabuco, 1996. p. 323.

Dutch authorities while escaping on a Portuguese caravel and had then been sent to Recife, where he was convinced by a Jew named Simão de Leão to return to Judaism. Pedro de Almeida was reconciled with the Holy Office during an *auto-de-fé* on June 10, 1650, at which he was sentenced to imprisonment and the wearing of a penitential garment, as well as having his assets confiscated.[140]

As with Pedro de Almeida, many of those who had been denounced by the "prisoners of the São Francisco" were arrested in transit, either travelling on business or during battles. The imprisonment of those ten men proved a fruitful collaboration for the Portuguese Inquisition, who, despite being distanced from Pernambuco for political reasons, still kept an attentive eye on the population of the region.

An intriguing case, and one that differed somewhat from the others, was that of Miguel Francês, a prominent figure in Pernambuco society who was arrested in the region in 1645 by order of the chief magistrate of the captaincy, a representative of the Portuguese government who had probably found refuge in Bahia or Paraíba. This event was unprecedented because the region was still under Dutch rule, so the Inquisition had no jurisdiction over the territory.[141]

Miguel Francês was taken to Lisbon on a caravel that had docked at a port in Pernambuco. The captain of the ship delivered Miguel Francês, along with a letter of unknown content (the faintness of the handwriting made it impossible to be read out during the trial), to an associate of the Holy Office in Lisbon, who escorted him to the Inquisition Tribunal.

---

[140] National Archive of Torre do Tombo – Inquisition of Lisbon. Trial of Pedro Almeida n. 11,562.

[141] MELLO, Evaldo Cabral de. *O negócio do Brasi-Portugal, os Países Baixos e o Nordeste 1641-1669*. Rio de Janeiro: Topbooks, 2003. p. 20. According to Wätjen, with the arrival of the Dutch, all members of the Portuguese government in Pernambuco fled to the *sertão* or Bahia, or returned to court. Even during the years of Portuguese guerrilla resistance, the captain-general and the governor remained in hiding in the *sertão*. In 1645, the Pernambucan revolt broke out, and the Portuguese crown began organizing the administrative structure of the Captaincy of Pernambuco. Paraíba and Maranhão were reconquered and were considered a strategic region for Portugal in the process of recovering its territory. Since 1642, there had been a "deputy of Pernambuco" in Lisbon, Friar Estevão de Jesus, who was tasked with negotiating an alternative plan for the rebellion: the buying back of the Dutch Northeast for the sum of 2 million cruzados.

In his statement, Miguel Francês declared himself a professed Jew. He had been baptized in the city of Abrantes, Portugal, where he had been born, but at 12 years old had moved with his family to live in Flanders, where he received a Jewish education. His trial featured a great number of denunciations. These were mostly of acquaintances in Pernambuco, although he did also denounce all of his friends and relatives living in European countries, far beyond the limits of the Portuguese Inquisition's jurisdiction which reached only as far as the south-west of France. These facts can be confirmed by comparing the names of those denounced to the list of members of the Jewish congregation in Recife.

Miguel Francês provided detailed accounts of the Jewish ceremonies he had performed and the liturgical rituals he was aware of. He knew the prayer used by Jews to praise the unity of God and of bread, which is said before dinner on Friday evenings, when the Shabbat, the Jewish sacred day, begins. He also demonstrated a thorough knowledge of the Old Testament. Prayers were recounted in Ladino, a mixture of Spanish and Hebrew, the language used by the Sephardim when they pray.[142]

The defendant's *auto-de-fé* took place on May 4, 1645. Due to his extensive collaboration, he was only sentenced to wearing a penitential garment, which was removed during the *auto-de-fé*. In 1647, Miguel Francês requested permission to return to Brazil, where he promised to live among Catholics. His assets were never confiscated, because they all fell within Dutch territory, and by 1648 Miguel Francês had already arrived back in Recife, where he was considered the wealthiest Jew in the region.[143]

---

[142] National Archive of Torre do Tombo – Inquisition of Lisbon. Trial of Miguel Frances n. 7,276.

[143] The claim that Miguel Francês was the wealthiest Jew in the region comes from Gonsalves de Mello.

10. War: The Beginning of a New Exile for the Jews

Since 1640, the Portuguese had been trying to recover the territory conquered by the Dutch, but without any success. In 1639, Governor-General Fernando de Mascarenhas, the Count of the Tower, ordered the governor of Rio de Janeiro, Salvador Correia de Sá e Benevides, to assemble a regiment from the captaincies of the South to help with the recovery of the Northeast. As an incentive, the governor-general decreed that all those enlisting on the mission would be pardoned of the crime of capturing and enslaving Amerindians, a clear enticement to the *sertanistas* (farmers of the *sertão*) and Paulista *bandeirantes* (settlers or fortune hunters from São Paulo).

At the same time, Salvador's town council sent a letter to Captain-General Raposo Tavares, asking him to replace Dom Francisco Rendon in enlisting soldiers in São Paulo for the recovery effort against the Dutch.[144] For leading this undertaking, Raposo Tavares received the title of "governor of recruitment" and set sail from Bahia with 150 men, who soon joined the infantry division of the Count of the Tower's army.[145] In November of that year, the Count of the Tower's troops began a long naval assault against the Dutch along the Brazilian coastline, with the aim of recovering control over Pernambuco. Four battles took place in less than two months, and the Luso-Brazilian forces were defeated on all fronts. Only a single ship, commanded by the Pernambucano colonel, Luís Barbalho Bezerra, and also carrying Raposo Tavares and his regiment, managed to escape and proceed to Rio Grande do Norte. Disembarking at the port of Touro, they once again faced Dutch troops before fleeing in the direction of Bahia. Contemporary accounts tell of soldiers being reduced to a wretched state. The lack

---

[144] CORTESÃO, Jaime. *Raposo Tavares e a formação territorial do Brasil*. Rio de Janeiro: Ministério de Educação e Cultura. – Serviço de documentação, Departamento de Imprensa Nacional, 1958. p. 92.

[145] The New Christians and Jews always fought on the side of their homelands. If the Jews of Amsterdam fought alongside the Dutch, the Portuguese New Christians, such as Raposo Tavares (Trial of the Inquisition in Lisbon n. de Maria de Costa), were on the side of Portugal.

of arms, munitions, clothing and food drove the troops, in their struggle for survival, to butcher their own horses to avoid starving to death. [146]

Alongside the military effort, the Portuguese employed diplomacy through the figure of Father Antônio Vieira, who negotiated with Holland, offering financial incentives and a sum of money in exchange for the ceding of the Northeast. [147]

Three years passed, and the colonists' discontent with the Dutch administration was growing. On October 13, 1644, a group of Jews living in the Pernambuco interior informed the directors of the West India Company of reports of the beginnings of a plot by the Portuguese to recapture the Northeastern territory. [148]

A number of armed Portuguese civilians and soldiers had been circulating in Pernambuco. The conspirators, with the informal backing of King Dom João IV, began seeking support for their movement, promising to pardon debts that had been run up with the Dutch and Jews. [149]

Upon being invited to join the rebellion, Sebastião do Carvalho and Antônio de Oliveira were advised by a Jew named Fernão do Vale, owner of the Guararapes sugar plantation, to inform on the insurgents. The denunciation reached the Dutch rulers via Abraão de Mercado, a Jewish doctor. On October 14, 1644, Moisés da Cunha revealed that a New Christian named João Fernandes Vieira had sent jewels and silver articles to Bahia and, along with Portuguese based in Várzea, was planning a surprise attack on the governor during a slave auction in Recife. [150]

As soon the first reports of the rebellion came in, the Dutch and Jews began collecting on debts owed by the owners of small

---

[146] ELLIS, Miriam. A presença de Raposo Tavares na expansão paulista. *Revista do Instituto de Estudos Brasileiros*, São Paulo, Universidade de São Paulo, p. 40-41, 1970.

[147] MELLO, Evaldo Cabral de. *O negócio do Brasil-Portugal, os Países Baixos e o Nordeste 1641-1669*, Rio de Janeiro: Topbooks, 2003. p. 20 and 253.

[148] MELLO, José Antônio Gonsalves de. *Gente da nação*. Recife: Massangana/Fundação Joaquim Nabuco, 1996. p. 297. The group of Jews who presented information about the plot to the Dutch rulers was led by Fernão do Vale, Sebastião de Carvalho and Dr Abraão de Mercado in. Secrete Notulen, October 13, 1644.

[149] Idem.

[150] Idem.

properties and sugar plantations. Part of this payment was made in sugar, which was shipped directly to Europe.

Many Jews living in the Pernambuco interior took refuge in Recife, as reports were circulating that the military campaign had begun. In June, 1645, the Portuguese had attacked Jews in Ipojuca who were transporting Dutch ships carrying cassava flower and sugar, a confrontation which left two Jews dead. In December of the same year, a regiment of forty soldiers was ordered to confront Portuguese troops approaching the island of Itamaracá, enlisting the aid of a group of Amerindians who lived there, but were surprised when a large Portuguese fleet attacked the island, set fire to three Dutch ships and captured three Jewish prisoners at the port of Pau Amarelo.[151] These Jewish prisoners were questioned by the local Catholic clergy about their family histories. The interrogation was carried out by Friar Manuel Calado, the man responsible for leading the anti-Jewish movement at the time. Calado claimed that two of the Jews were New Christians who had been born in Lisbon and had later returned to Judaism. For unknown reasons, the baptized Jews, Moses Mendes and Isaac Rusten, were not delivered to the Inquisition of Lisbon, but were instead tried by the magistrate of Bahia, before being indoctrinated by the friar and sentenced to death by hanging. The third prisoner managed to escape and reach Recife. This news was received very badly by the Dutch rulers, who began preparing their defenses.[152] The Jewish community of Amsterdam also expressed its disapproval, reminding the Dutch authorities about Jewish loyalty in this moment of crisis.

When the rebellion broke out on June 13, 1645, many Jews were caught off guard and found themselves cut off deep inside the captaincy. Fearing for the safety of these people, on July 1, 1646, a group of Jews consisting of Arão Navarro, David de Torres and Fernão Martins da Silva asked the Dutch directors to allow for the Jews living in Paraíba to be transferred to Recife.

---

[151] WIZNITZER, Arnold. Jewish Soldiers in Dutch Brazil (1630-1654). *Publications of the American Jewish Historical Society*, Baltimore, v. 46, p. 3, 1956.

[152] CALADO, Frei Manuel. *O valoroso Lucideno e o triunfo da liberdade.* Belo Horizonte, Itataia and São Paulo: Edusp, 1987. v. 1. p. 48. WIZNITZER, Arnold. *Os judeus no Brasil Colonial.* São Paulo: Pioneira, 1966. p. 82-83.

The need to defend Recife meant that Jews in the civil guard lost the privilege of being able to rest on Saturdays, especially after September 12, 1645, when the Jewish Guard (Jewish militias who guarded the fort and protected Recife's north entrance) came under cannon fire.[153]

With the surrender of the fort, Luso-Brazilian forces took more than 200 prisoners, 180 of whom consisted of Dutch, French, German, Polish, Scottish and English soldiers. Also taken were the Jews known as the "ten captives of the river São Francisco," or the "prisoners of the São Francisco."

On November 13, 1645, a unit of forty Jewish soldiers was tasked with a special mission: to sail in the direction of the Portuguese fleet and ascertain the number of ships in the attacking force. On November 21, after completing their mission, the soldiers disembarked in Recife with the news that there were many Portuguese ships, and that the island of Itamaracá had already been taken.[154]

By November 28, the situation in Recife had become so challenging that the Dutch were considering surrender. The Jewish leaders were aware that, if this came to pass, they would need to negotiate the safety of their people. As a result, a document was sent, requesting that the Jewish question be handled with the sensitivity demanded of the situation, insofar as it was clear that the Jews would have no place within the Portuguese empire.[155]

In response, an honorable document was drawn up in support of the Jewish people, in which the maximum Dutch authority, the States General, recognized them as having the same rights as all other Dutch subjects.[156]

As the rebellion wore on, however, a wave of religious fervor took hold of the Dutch rulers, who renewed the public notice prohibiting blasphemy and the profanation of Sundays. The Jews

---

[153] Idem. Jewish Soldiers in Dutch Brazil, op. cit., p. 2. MELLO, José Antônio Gonsalves de. *Gente da nação*, op. cit., p. 300. This was a small fortification that protected the entrance via Recife's northern isthmus and was known by the Dutch as Judenwacht or Steene reduit ["Jewish guard" or "stone keep"].

[154] WIZNITZER, Arnold. Jewish Soldiers in Dutch Brazil, op. cit., p. 3.

[155] MELLO, José Antônio Gonsalves de. *Gente da nação*, op. cit., p. 302.

[156] The document known as the "Patente honrosa" [honorable patent] was cited in the chapter referring to the difficult coexistence of Catholics, Protestants and Jews.

were accused of disrespecting the day of rest by continuing to open their schools and go to work, behavior that scandalized the Christians.

1646 was a particularly difficult year. The Dutch and the Jews found themselves besieged inside Recife. Meanwhile, the Luso-Brazilian forces achieved a number of important victories, at Mount Tabocas, Casa Forte (a large fortified sugar plantation) and Cabo de Santo Agostinho, which cut Recife off from rural areas and prevented access to the agricultural region.

Supplies of food became scarce. As well as being blockaded by land, Dutch ships carrying goods began finding it difficult to reach the port. Around eight thousand people spent months living under strict rationing, and also found themselves having to share supplies with the troops at Itamaracá, where shortages were even more severe. There are reports from this period of a great number of deaths caused by starvation.[157] The situation became so drastic that domestic animals began to be regarded as a means of sustenance. Among slaves, who were normally left with only scraps, the wretchedness was felt even more acutely. In the statutes of the synagogue, a considerable lowering of the wages of officials is apparent in response to the crisis.

Rabbi Isaac Aboab da Fonseca left an account of these days of hardship in the form of a poem: the Hebrew poem "Mi Kamocha," or "Who is like you," makes reference to the alliance between the king of Portugal, Dom João IV, and João Fernandes Vieira, who assisted Portugal's reconquest of the Brazilian territory and is characterized as an arrogant, perverse and condescending man. It also describes the great hunger experienced by inhabitants, and the traitors who were holed up inside Dutch Recife and in communication with the besieging Portuguese forces.[158]

Here is the version of the account of that fateful period cited by Gonsalves de Mello:

[...] The traitorous Portuguese intended to exterminate those in Brazil, led by a villain who had risen up from the muck, the son of an unknown father and a black woman; news of the conspiracy was

---

[157] MELLO, José Antônio Gonsalves de. *Gente da nação*, op. cit., p. 310.

[158] WEITMAN, David Y. (Rabbi). *Bandeirantes espirituais do Brasil: século XVII.* São Paulo: Maayanot, 2003. p. 173.

scoffed at by the Dutch rulers, but when the truth was revealed, the man fled to the safety of the woods, to await the arrival of regiments sent by the king. He intended the sacking and extermination of the people of Israel, but was unable to achieve this. However, the challenges have weakened this people, for outside the sword sowed death while inside terror reigned, because the conspiracy was both internal and external [...] It was then the hunger began, yet rations were distributed to the needy. Bodies were reduced to almost nothing but bones, and our people began to substitute bread for fish. And the stomach felt the effects. This was the moment the enemy had been waiting for to take possession of the house and belongings of the people of Israel. Yet God allowed his people to be saved by means of two ships arriving from Holland. Remember and keep this, my brothers: that day was a miracle from God.[159]

During 1647, illness, hunger and military operations led citizens to their deaths. The Jews had further cause for concern: they feared being captured by the Portuguese, for, ever since the start of the uprising, those taken prisoner were being condemned and hanged as traitors. This is exactly what took place in 1645, when thirteen Jews were captured by the Luso-Brazilian rebels and executed.[160]

From 1649 onwards, the Jews of Recife were offered some opportunities for survival. Contracts were agreed for the provision of clothing for Dutch troops, and some Jews, such as Arão Pina and Abraham Cohen, dedicated themselves to making uniforms, which provided them with the means to pay their rent.[161]

Not all Jews remained in Recife after the beginning of the uprising. Starting in 1646, many of those who did not have assets or vested interests in the region began returning to Holland, taking shipments of sugar and brazilwood with them.

The Dutch experienced their first taste of defeat when, in 1648, their territory was reduced to just the coastline – Recife, Maurícia, Paraíba, Itamaracá – as Rio Grande, Maranhão, Ceará, the Pernambuco interior, Alagoas and Sergipe were all reconquered. A

---

[159] KAYSERLING, Meyer. Isaac Abaob, the First Jewish Author in America. *Publications of the American Jewish Historical Society,* Baltimore, v. 5, p. 125-136, 1897.

[160] WIZNITZER, Arnold. Jewish Soldiers in Dutch Brazil, op. cit., p. 2.

[161] Ibid, p. 96-97.

great battle was waged in Guararapes, near Recife, in which the Dutch suffered defeat, signalling the approaching of the end.

In 1653, the people of Recife sighted a large Portuguese fleet consisting of sixty vessels, which would anchor outside the city, meaning that the assault could now be conducted by land and sea.

At the beginning of 1654, the city descended into chaos as soldiers gave up on the war, with many redirecting their efforts to sacking and pillaging. Gonsalves de Mello suggests there was a large appetite for the sacking of houses, particularly the residence of the merchant José Francês, the richest Jew in the city. Discussions of this topic were overheard by Abraham Cohen, who arranged a meeting with the council of Jewish elders, consisting at the time of Jacob de Lemos, Benjamin de Pina and Fernão Martins. The council contacted the Dutch rulers, who had already assembled the civil and military authorities, to suggest that an agreement should be reached with the Portuguese.[162]

The Dutch could no longer hold out, primarily due to the fact that their efforts were now being focused on Europe and the parallel war that Holland was waging against the English (1652-1654).[163] The battle was lost.

A commission was sent to negotiate the surrender, with discussions beginning on December 23, 1653. By the 25th, the terms of surrender had been drafted. The agreement was signed on January 26, 1654, and on the 27th, Portuguese troops took possession of Recife's forts.[164]

---

[162] DAG NOTULE, 22 Jan. 1654. Algemeen Rijksachief, The Hague, Holland, Criminele Papieren, n. 22, 1624, Portefeuillevan. ERICEIRA, Conde. *História de Portugal restaurada.* Porto: Livraria Civilizaçã, 1945-1946. 4 v. WIZNITZER, Arnold. *Judeus no Brasil Colonial*, op. cit., p. 111.

[163] In 1651, Oliver Cromwell proclaimed the Navigation Act, aiming to deliver a fatal blow to Dutch seafaring and strengthen the English fleet. Holland called upon its maritime fleet to defend its coastline from English ships. Brazil went many months without seeing the arrival of a single Dutch ship, and, in 1652, English ships began capturing Brazilian vessels.

[164] WIZNITZER, Arnold. *Judeus no Brasil Colonial*, op. cit., p. 114.

11. The Expulsion, A New Approach

An analysis of the events of the final period of the Jewish presence in Brazil suggests the need for historical revision. The document signed by the Dutch and Portuguese made specific reference to the Jews, but the clause in question is open to a variety of interpretations.[165] In the interests of a deeper analysis, here are the principle terms of the agreement:[166]

Article 2 – This agreement shall pertain to all peoples, regardless of their origin or religion; all shall be forgiven, though they have rebelled against the Portuguese crown, with the same being extended, as far as possible, to all Jews situated in Arrecife and Cidade Maurícia.

Article 3 – To the subjects and peoples showing obedience to the Lords of the States General are conceded all assets deemed moveable and currently found in their possession.

Article 8 – To the subjects of the Lords of the States General, who are residents of Arrecife and Cidade Maurícia, is granted permission to remain in said cities during a period of three months; it is also conceded that they may purchase within said cities all supplies necessary for their sustenance and their journey.

Article 10 – [...] but assures that the subjects of the Lords of the States General shall be free from harassment or persecution by any Portuguese person, and shall instead be treated with great respect and courtesy; and concedes that, during the three months in which they remain in this land, they may settle any outstanding claims and differences, between themselves, before the minister of justice.

---

[165] The clause referring to the Jews had been under negotiation since 1645, and the beginning of the Pernambuco rebellion. The Jewish leaders in Recife sent word of the war to the Jews of Amsterdam, who addressed a letter to the burgomasters of that city, who, in turn, sent a request to the States General. On December 7, 1645, the States General dispatched an order to the Dutch governors in Brazil, underlining their loyalty to the Jewish people and stating that, in the case of surrender, the Brazilian Jews should be included in any agreement, to ensure they could be "protected and defended as equals." MELLO, José Antônio Gonsalves de. *Gente da nação*, op. cit., p. 303.

[166] Terms of surrender of the Dutch-Portuguese war. In: MELO, Francisco Manoel de. *Restauração de Pernambuco: enáfora triunfante e outros escritos*. Recife: Secretaria do Interior, 1994. p. 55-57.

Article 12 – Upon embarkation, said moveable assets, intended for sale, may be left in the care of attorneys nominated from any nation, provided these display obedience to the Portuguese armed forces.

Article 13 – It further places at their disposal all produce, both wet and dry, stored within the warehouses and fortresses of Arrecife, so that they may make use of these and prepare for their journey; releases to soldiers that which they require for their sustenance and their journey; but does not grant them use of rigging for ships, instead promising to provide said ships fully equipped, on the occasion of their departure for Holland.

General Barreto further includes:

[…] Foreigners remaining within the territory following the deadline, as a result of the delayed arrival of ships, shall receive the same honorable treatment dispensed until that time; with the exception of Jews originally baptized under the Catholic faith, who shall be considered heretics and delivered to the Portuguese Inquisition.[167]

When analyzing the terms of the surrender agreement, it is worth raising a number of questions: were members of the Jewish congregation given the option of leaving or remaining? If the Jews had been allowed to stay in Brazil, why would they have wanted to leave? Were the Jews expelled or not?

Traditionally, historians have used the word "expulsion" to describe the departure of the Dutch and Jews from Brazil. Wiznitzer claimed "[…] Portugal had declared a war of liberation against invaders from other religions, that is, the Calvinists and the Jews […]. The Dutch departure from Recife signaled the start of a national sentiment." He concluded: "[…] any Jew who had not been baptized as a Catholic was able to remain in Brazil without the risk of harassment or persecution." Gonsalves de Mello writes that "the idea of expelling the Dutch from the Northeast was never far from the minds of the Portuguese statesmen and officers of the metropolis or the colony." More recently, Rabbi David Weitman expressed this even more clearly, stating, in "1654, the Jews are expelled from the

---

[167] WIZNITZER, Arnold. *Judeus no Brasil Colonial*, op. cit., p. 124.

Northeast and either return to Holland or make for the Caribbean and North America."[168]

Upon careful examination of the words of these authors, we come away with the sense of a supposed expulsion. However, it is important to understand the nature of the international politics being applied by Holland at the time. According to Evaldo Cabral de Mello, the two defeats in Guararapes and internal problems facing the States General – resulting from a coup d'etat organized by the *stadtholder*, William II – forced Holland to abandon the idea of fighting to keep possession of the territory in Northeastern Brazil, instead adopting a diplomatic stance towards Portugal.[169] At the end of the Pernambuco rebellion, therefore, there was no expulsion, but rather an agreement between parties, under which the Dutch army would leave Brazil within a period of three months. Yet, according to the terms of the agreement, anyone who wished to remain in the territory definitively would receive permission to do so. In the case of the Jews, there was an aggravating factor: the majority had New Christian backgrounds and their decision to remain in Portuguese-held territories could be interpreted as a death sentence.[170] General Barreto, the Portuguese officer responsible for recapturing the territory, confirmed that, if "[...] the vicar general decided to persecute Jews who had once been Christians, there was nothing he could do to stop him."[171] Despite not being expelled from Brazil, the majority of Sephardic Jews had no choice but to leave the region.

The surrender in 1654 did not signal the end of the impasse between Portugal and Holland; between 1657 and 1661, the conflict developed into naval warfare, near Portugal, but also in the Indies. In 1661, a settlement was reached in which Holland recognized Portuguese sovereignty in the Brazilian Northeast and, in return,

---

[168] Ibid. p. 111. MELLO, José Antônio Gonsalves de. *Gente da nação*, op. cit., p. 295.

[169] MELLO, Evaldo Cabral de. "Os holandeses no Brasil", op. cit., p. 62-68.

[170] The origins of the members of Recife's Jewish community are provided by WIZNITZER, Arnold. *Judeus no Brasil Colonial*, op. cit., p. 149-158; and MELLO, José Antônio Gonsalves de. *Gente da nação*, op. cit., p. 369-522.

[171] WIZNITZER, Arnold. *Judeus no Brasil Colonial*, op. cit., p. 124.

Portugal paid them a sum of 4 million cruzados, as well as agreeing commercial incentives.[172]

It is worth highlighting the relative tolerance shown by the Portuguese rulers towards the Jewish community. In contrast to other periods in history, when Jews had been forced to abandon their homes and were reduced to misery, in 1654 the Portuguese demonstrated respect for Jewish dignity. Jews were given permission to close down their businesses, gather their assets and personal belongings, and were provided with ships, stocked with medicines and supplies, for their crossings to other territories. Following their return to Amsterdam, many of those who had been unable to liquidate their businesses presented a petition to the States General, requesting compensation for the loss of infrastructure. The court ruled in favor of the petitioners, and included a clause stating Portugal should provide compensation for this infrastructure in the Peace Treaty of 1661. The decision of the States General was reaffirmed in 1663 and, later, in 1669, in a commercial treaty between Portugal and Holland.[173]

Charles R. Boxer has already drawn attention to the integrity of General Francisco Barreto in his treatment of the Jewish community of Recife.[174] Anita Novinsky reminds us that, from 1497, Portugal had not allowed the presence of any Jews within its territories, which limited General Barreto's options, and demonstrates the extent to which state power had submitted to the Church. General Barreto's benevolent position, therefore, challenged ecclesiastical power by allowing equal treatment of Jews within the agreement signed at the end of the Dutch-Portuguese war.[175]

---

[172] MELLO, Evaldo Cabral de. O negócio do Brasil-Portugal, os Países Baixos e o Nordeste 1641-1669, op. cit., p. 13 and 253.

[173] Inventory of claims made by inhabitants of the United Provinces, in the name of the West India Company and other parties, in relation to properties, mortgages and personal debts in Brazil under the rulership of the king of Portugal. Composed by order of the high and mighty States General, in accordance with article 25 of the Peace Treaty. Indemnity Claims – Recife, 1663. Apud WOLFF, Egon; WOLFF, Frieda. Quantos judeus estiveram no Brasil holandês. Rio de Janeiro: s.n., 1991. p. 100.

[174] BOXER, Charles R. Os holandeses no Brasil: 1624-1654. São Paulo: Companhia Editora Nacional, 1961. P. 340.

[175] This statement by the historian was made during an interview in which she explained that she likes to take up positions, granting permission for her position to be referred to in the aforementioned interview.

One occasion, in particular, demonstrated the general's close relationship with the Jews, and this was when he granted José Francês, a Sephardic Jew, permission to send a shipment of brazilwood to Holland. Despite the transportation of moveable assets being included in the terms of surrender, the dispatching of such a large consignment was unusual. Barreto justified his decision by stating that it was fair to grant this privilege to the "foreigner," as José Francês had done the general "some favors" during his own imprisonment in Recife, in 1647.[176]

A historical account from 1662, left by Yehuda Machabeu and recorded by the chronicler Saul Levi Morteira, acknowledges the positive stance of the Portuguese rulers towards the Jews in the wake of the Dutch-Portuguese war, and also highlights the role General Barreto played in protecting the Jewish people, by issuing an order, unprecedented within the context of 17th century Portuguese politics, that they be left alone, under pain of severe punishment. What follows is Machabeu's account:[177]

Firstly, in relation to the soul, it is plain for all to see what happened when Brazil was captured by the Portuguese, natural enemies of the Jewish people, and particularly of those who they forced to become Christians, accustomed to cruel autos-de-fé in which, with much ostentation and enjoyment, as if performing a sacrifice, they would turn them into the human victims of this persecuted people, and alongside these Portuguese, at least by inclination, is an army of soldiers made up of blacks, mulattoes, the poor, the starving and the barefoot, all hoping to improve their fortunes by putting an end to the nation that is so hateful to them. And almighty God, in his infinite power, prevented this and saved his people from all of these grave dangers, infusing within Governor Barreto's spirit reasons which led him to proclaim severe

---

[176] The favors to which Barreto is referring concern a sum of money that was loaned to the general by José Francês. MELLO, José Antônio Gonsalves de. *Gente da nação*, op. cit., p. 356.

[177] MORTERA, Saul Levi, *Tratado da verdade da lei de Moisés* (facsimile edition). Coimbra: Universidade Coimbra, 1988, p. 72-81. Yehuda Machabeu's manuscript is included in a book by Saul Levi Mortera and was published in 1784 by Franco Mendes in the Jewish journal *Há-Measeph*. The manuscript is kept in the Oxford library. MENDES, David Franco; REMÉDIOS, J. Mendes dos. *Os judeus portugueses em Amsterdão*. Lisbon: Edições Távola Redonda, 1990.

punishments for any who touched or harassed any person of the Jewish faith. And not only this, but he also agreed to allow them sell their goods and provided passage to Holland for over 600 of our people, and then, in the absence of Dutch vessels, he provided Portuguese ones, so that they were able to set sail on 16 ships, many of them terribly old, and all, by grace and divine providence, reached safety. And though on this journey they would face great dangers, the Lord rescued them from every one, such as when a Spanish ship was transporting Jews to the Inquisition yet, before it could put its evil plan into effect, He carried them to safety in Florida and New Netherland, from where they were able to travel in peace to Holland. It would require a long and convoluted story to relate in detail what each man tells about what occurred on that sea journey. Suffice it to say that all arrived safely, and that the Lord rescued their souls and consciences from the hands of those who, with so much deceit and cruelty, seek to attack them daily.[178]

Following a period of three months, the Dutch and Jews were preparing to leave Recife. It was at this point that General Barreto requested a report including the names of every Jew living within the district.[179] Wiznitzer writes that, although the original document has been lost, it was cited in another document, from February 21, 1654.[180] The loss of the original document prevents us from verifying how many Jews actually left Brazil at the end of the war, and who they were, since many had succumbed during the rebellion.

There is documentation that can tell us the exact number of Jews killed in action, in the struggle to defend Recife. We know that the militia included approximately 350 Jews in 1645, which corresponds to about half the men in the regiment. A document signed by Abraão Azevedo, one of the most important Jewish men in the city, in 1653, confirms that Jews were on guard day and night

---

[178] OPPENHEIM, Samuel. A Contemporary Account of How the Jews Came to Arrive in New Netherland. Publications of the American Jewish Historical Society, Philadelphia, p. 4, Oct. 1926.

[179] DAG NOTULE, 21 Feb. 1654. Algemeen Rijksarchief, The Hague, Holland, Oude West Indische Compagnie, collection of manuscripts (codices and scrolls), 75.

[180] Notulen van Brasilien, 21 Feb. 1654.

in the region's forts, and that many were struck down by Portuguese bullets while on duty.[181]

Most of the Jews who had been living in Dutch Brazil returned to Holland and, sometime later, moved on to other regions, like the Antilles, where a sugar-producing industry developed. This was made possible by knowledge gained on the sugar plantations of Pernambuco. Other groups of Jews settled in Guiana, Barbados, Martinique, New Amsterdam, North America and, later, in Curaçao.

Despite being Portuguese, and even though many had fought alongside their compatriots, the Jews were forced to leave territories which were now an extension of their Portuguese homeland. Once again, they were given no choice but to depart in search of their much longed-for liberty. After facing terrible dangers and setbacks, twenty-three Jews managed to reach New Amsterdam, today's New York, having been "rescued by God."[182]

---

[181] There were around 720 Jews in Recife in 1645, according to Wiznitzer, with only 600 remaining at the end of the war. In: original petition at the Rijksarchief, The Hague, O.W.I.C., n. 3, fol. 1720. Apud WIZNITZER, Arnold. *Jewish Soldiers in Dutch Brazil*, op. cit., p. 3.

[182] MORTERA, Saul Levi. *Tratado da verdade da lei de Moisés*, op. cit., p. 24.

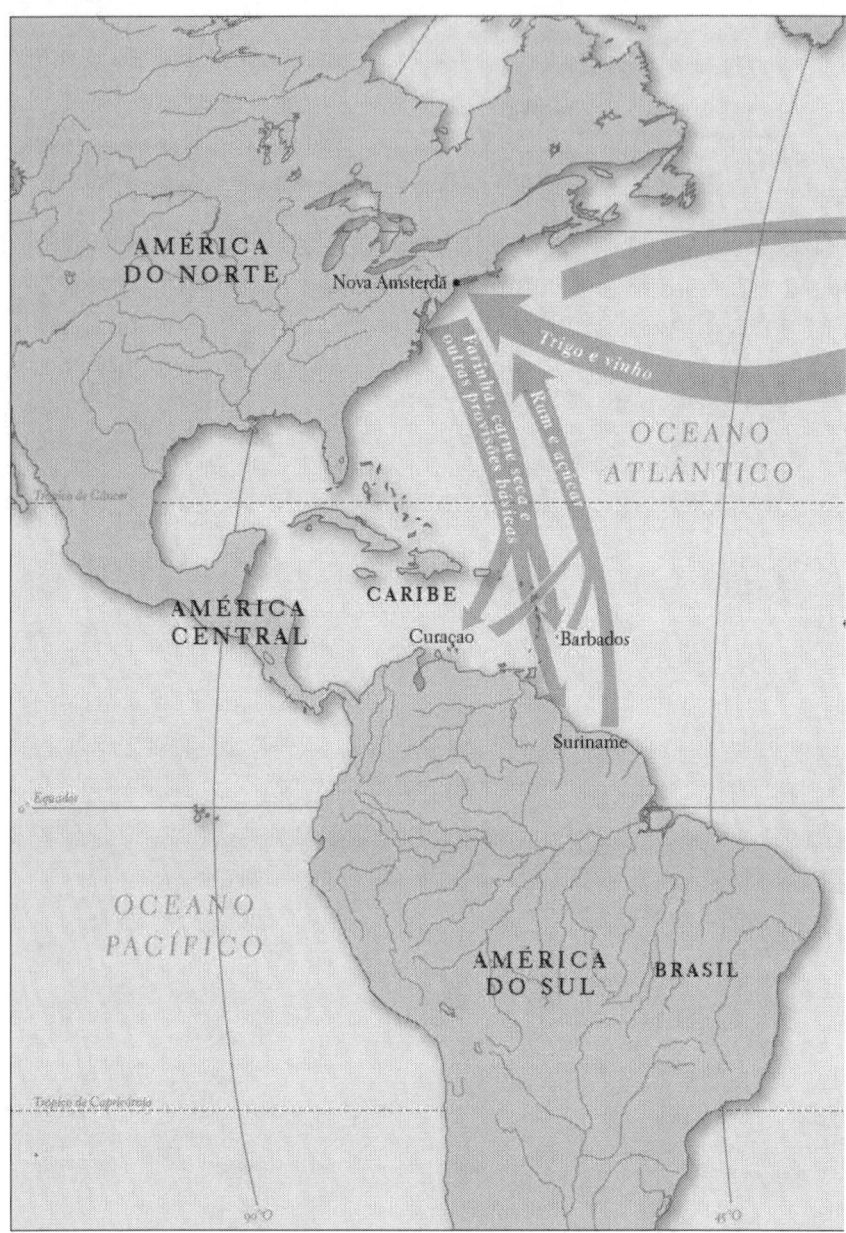

Figure 1. Map of North and South America

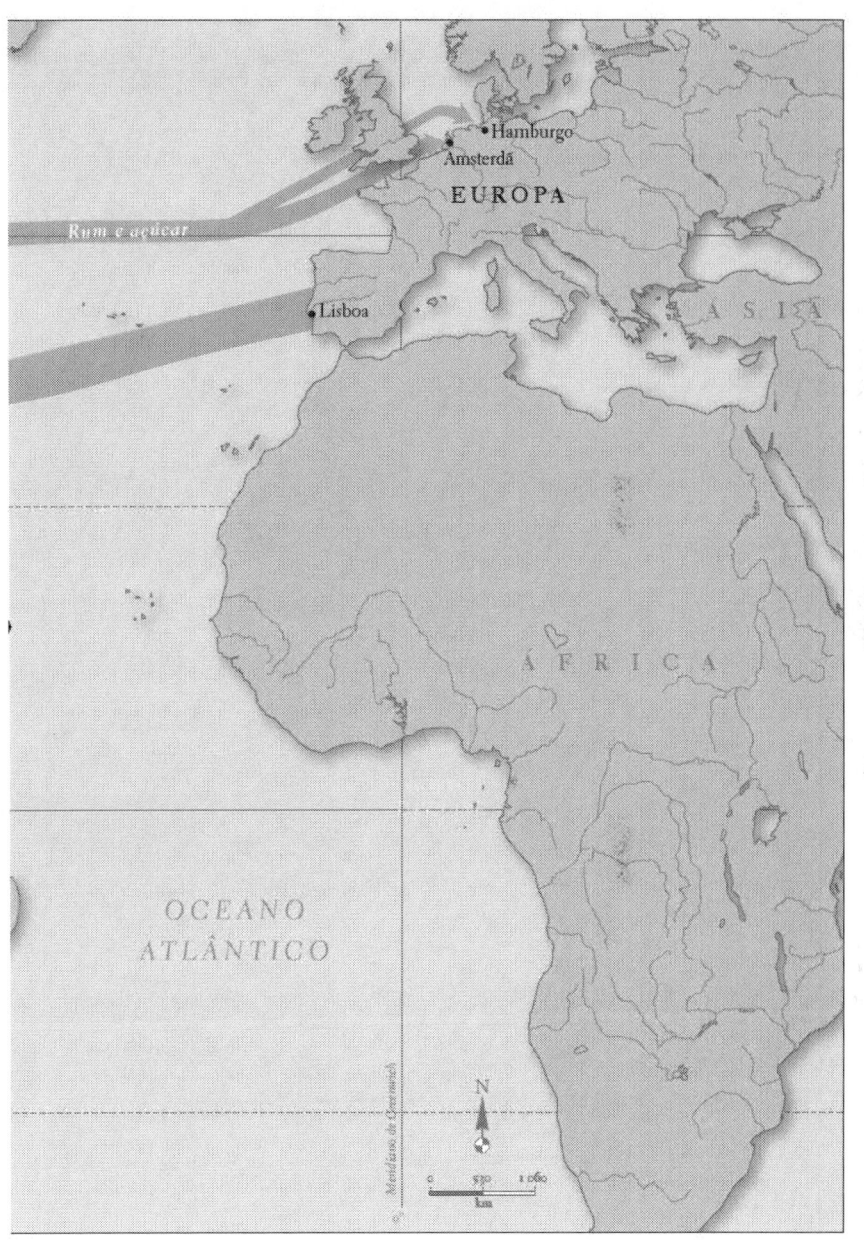

Figure 2. Map of Europe and Africa

12. A New Port, a New Hope

The Portuguese Reconquest of 1654 signaled the end of Dutch occupation of Brazil. Jews living in Recife were forced to leave the region, abandoning property, businesses, family and friends.

The Portuguese general, Francisco Barreto de Menezes, put sixteen ships at the disposal of the expelled Jews. According to some authors, approximately 600 people boarded these ships; others say 150 families made the voyages to Amsterdam and the Dutch colonies in the Caribbean.[183] The terms of the agreement allowed the Jews to depart with all their moveable assets, personal belongings and merchandise, such as brazilwood and crates of sugar.[184]

In the 17th century, the standards of hygiene and comfort on sea voyages were minimal. Contemporary accounts tell of terrified screams in the night coming from children assailed by "ship fever," measles and lice epidemics.[185]

On April 26, 1654, three groups of Jews departed from Recife. The first group returned to Holland, the second made for the Caribbean, and a third group, the focus of this book, sailed onboard the *Valk*, a Dutch ship commanded by Captain Jan Craeck and owned by two Dutchmen, Paulus and Jacob de Sweert.[186]

Numerous documents, often contradictory in their accounts, recount the challenges faced by the Jews and Portuguese while onboard the *Valk*.

---

[183] WIZNITZER, Arnold. *Os judeus no Brasil Colonial*. São Paulo: Pioneira, 1966, p. 125. OPPENHEIM, Samuel. A Contemporary Account of How the Jews Came to Arrive in New Netherland. Publications of the American Jewish Historical Society, Philadelphia, p. 4, Oct. 1926.

[184] OPPENHEIM, Samuel. A Contemporary Account of How the Jews Came to Arrive in New Netherland, op. cit., p. 5. WIZNITZER, Arnold. *Os judeus no Brasil Colonial*, op. cit., p. 123-124. MELLO, José Antônio Gonsalves de. *Gente da nação*. Recife: Massangana/ Fundação Joaquim Nabuco, 1996. p. 354-355.

[185] SOLA POOL, David; SOLA POOL, Tamar de. *An Old Faith in the New World. Portrait of Shearith Israel*, 1654-1954. New York: Colombia University Press, 1955. p. 4.

[186] WIZNITZER, Arnold. *Os judeus no Brasil Colonial*, op. cit., p. 183-184.

One of the first historians to reconstruct the voyage made by the Jews after leaving Brazil was Samuel Oppenheim, at the beginning of the 20th century. Oppenheim based his work upon an article by David Franco Mendes, entitled "Toledot Gedolei Yisrael," published a century after the Brazilians arrived in New Amsterdam.[187] In his writing, Franco Mendes related details drawn from an unpublished manuscript, "Providencia de Dios com Israel" [God's Providence with Israel], penned by the famous Saul Levi Morteira. Morteira's manuscript was written between 1655 and 1662, and includes a preface by Yehuda Machabeu, describing the vicissitudes of the journey in a text entitled "Account of the judgements and redemption of Brazil in 1654." Both Machabeu and Morteira were in Brazil during the years of the Dutch occupation. Morteira left the country in the company of Recife's rabbi, Isaac Aboab da Fonseca, in 1654, and his manuscript was discovered by Oppenheim in the catalogue of the J. W. Six de Vromade Library. Initially, Oppenheim was unable to gain access to the document, but eventually he found copies at the Bodleian Library, in Oxford, the Royal Library of the Hague, and also in Hamburg. The text consists of 237 pages.[188]

Oppenheim narrates that a heavy storm blew the *Valk*, which had been heading for Holland, off course, towards Martinique. Upon resuming their journey, the Jews were attacked by Spanish pirates, who looted and took control of the ship; the Jews were then rescued by the captain of a French frigate, who fought off the pirates. Upon docking in Jamaica – then in the possession of Spain – to restock supplies and negotiate further protection from the captain who had rescued them, the passengers were all arrested by the Spanish

---

[187] OPPENHEIM, Samuel. The Early History of the Jews in New York, 1654-1664. *American Jewish Historical Quarterly*, Philadelphia, v. 18, p. 16, 1909.

[188] OPPENHEIM, Samuel. The Early History of the Jews in New York, *1654-1664*, op. cit., p. 13. The Bodleian Library is located in Oxford, England. The Royal Library of the Hague is in Holland; Saul Levi Mortera was a rabbi who collaborated with Menasseh ben Israel, chief of the rabbinate of the Amsterdam community. Yehuda Machabeu was a celebrated calligrapher and Jewish writer, who was a member the Amsterdam community and lived in Recife during Dutch occupation.

Inquisition, who suspected them of being Jews; or rather, New Christians.[189]

The prisoners were divided into two groups, with those raising the strongest suspicions of being New Christians forced to remain in Jamaica until November of 1654. These prisoners were only released following the intervention of the Dutch government, which invoked the surrender agreement reached with the Portuguese in Brazil that guaranteed the freedom and safety of Dutch subjects, independent of their origins or faith. Portugal had separated from Spain in 1640, yet failing to honor a treaty signed between the Portuguese and Dutch governments would certainly lead to an international conflict.

The other group of prisoners was released after interrogation. These were Sephardic Jews from Holland and Italy, as well as some Ashkenazi Jews and Dutch Calvinists. The group also included a Protestant pastor called Dominus Johannes Polhemius, who came from the island of Itamaracá, near Bahia, which had belonged to Dutch Brazil.[190] Polhemius disembarked in New Amsterdam, in North America, along with the twenty-three Jewish refugees from Brazil and was placed in charge of the Protestant congregation of Midwout (now Midwood), Long Island.

In all, the group of Jews disembarking on Manhattan Island consisted of six families – six married men and two who were single, two widows, and thirteen children of various ages.[191]

Leon Hühner disputes Oppenheim's account of where the pirate attack took place, suggesting instead that it happened near Cuba. He agrees that the ship was looted by pirates, who stole most of the passengers' belongings, but concludes that the passengers were actually rescued by the French frigate near Cape San Antonio, Cuba, with the vessel then docking in Jamaica before continuing its

---

[189] OPPENHEIM, Samuel. The Early History of the Jews in New York, *1654-1664*, op. cit., p. 5. Only New Christians, baptized as Christians, would be within the Inquisition's jurisdiction.

[190] WIZNITZER, Arnold. The Exodus from Brazil and Arrival in New Netherland of the Jewish Pilgrim Fathers, 1654. *Publications of the American Jewish Historical Society*, Philadelphia, v. 44, p. 4, 1954. The Sephardim are the Jews of the Iberian Peninsula; the Ashkenazim originate in Eastern Europe.

[191] Ibid, p. 5.

journey to New Amsterdam, adding that it was at this moment that some of the passengers were stopped by agents of the Inquisition.[192]

Arnold Wiznitzer presents yet another version of the misadventures of the Sephardic Jews: upon leaving Recife, three groups of Jews faced difficulties. The first group, which was the one mentioned by Saul Levi Morteira and revisited by Oppenheim, were shipwrecked near Martinique. The second and third groups were passengers on the *Valk*, some of whom had been born in Holland and others in Portugal.[193] When attacked by Spanish pirates and taken to Jamaica, those born in Holland were freed by the Inquisition, while the Jews born in Portugal, and therefore baptized, were considered heretics and kept in the prisons of the Holy Office in Jamaica until the intervention of the Dutch government.[194]

The three historians agree that, upon reaching Cape San Antonio, the Jews negotiated with the captain of the *Saint Catherine*, Jacques de La Motte, who charged them an exorbitant fee for the time: 2,500 guilders for the transportation of all cargo, food and moveable assets that their ship had been carrying.

There is some disagreement in relation to the name of the frigate: *Saint Charles* or *Saint Catherine*. On the document upon which the name appears there is an ink stain, which is why Samuel Oppenheim claims it was the *Saint Catherine*. Officially, English historians acknowledge Oppenheim's claim, but Dutch historians support the *Saint Charles* theory. There is, however, evidence suggesting that the ship really was called the *Saint Charles*: a bill of sale from November 7, 1654, on which the owner, Symon Fell, transfers possession of the frigate to Captain James Mills.[195]

Following extensive research, we can, therefore, conclude that the *Valk* was thrown off course by a storm while sailing on the Caribbean Sea, near Jamaica. Before coming into port, the boat was attacked by pirates, who stole the Jews' possessions, took them prisoner and negotiated their release with the Spanish, in exchange for silver. Spanish merchants then handed the Jews over to the

---

[192] HÜHNER, Leon. *Whence Came the First Jewish Settlers of New York? Publications of the American Jewish Historical Society*, Philadelphia, v. 9, p. 75-85, 1909.

[193] WIZNITZER, Arnold. *Os judeus no Brasil Colonial*, op. cit., p. 10.

[194] Ibid, p. 11.

[195] In this book I shall refer to the ship as the *Saint Charles*.

ecclesiastical authorities on the island of Jamaica, where they were held until a part of the group was released and transported to the port of Cape San Antonio, Cuba. There, they encountered the captain of the *Saint Charles*, who they already knew from Recife, and with whom they negotiated their voyage to New Amsterdam.[196]

The entire voyage, including the imprisonment in Jamaica, took over six months. Documents reveal that the Jews had departed during Passover and arrived in New Amsterdam a few days before Rosh Hashanah.[197]

According to Wiznitzer, among the twenty-three Jews that left Brazil were Abraham Israel, David Israel, Assar Leeven, Moses Ambrosius, Judicq de Mereda and Ricke Nunes. These names were identified within the register of the Zur Israel synagogue of Recife as Abraham Ysrael, David Israel, Asher Levy, Mose Lumbroso, Judith Mercado (widow of Rafael, or Moseh, de Mercado) and Ricke Nunes (widow of Moseh Nunes).[198] Abraham Israel travelled with his wife and two children; David Israel, Abraham's brother, with his wife and three children; and Mose Lumbroso also travelled in the company of his wife and two children.[199]

However, Egon and Frieda Wolff question the research on which Wiznitzer bases these names. The Wolffs allege that, in the minute book of the Zur Israel congregation of Recife, the signatures have been spelled differently, and that the author's argument relies on deduction rather than concrete evidence.[200]

Wiznitzer deduces that Moses Ambrosius is a corruption of Mose Lumbroso, while Judite de Mereda's surname is a corruption of Mercado. Asser Levy could be Benjamin Levy's son, and would have arrived in Brazil at a very young age; David Israel Faro is identified as David Israel; Abraham Israel could be either Abraham

---

[196] The captain of the *Saint Charles* conducted trade between Recife, the Caribbean and Holland, presenting the likelihood that he was already acquainted with the stranded group.

[197] Passover, or Pesach, is the Jewish Easter; Rosh Hashanah is the Jewish New Year.

[198] WIZNITZER, Arnold. The Exodus from Brazil and Arrival in New Netherland of the Jewish Pilgrim Fathers, 1654, op. cit., p. 15.

[199] BEL BRAVO, Maria Antônia. *Diaspora sefardi*. Madrid: Mapfre, 1992.

[200] WOLFF, Egon; WOLFF, Frieda. *Quantos judeus estiveram no Brasil holandês*. Rio de Janeiro: s.n., 1991. p. 91-107.

Israel Dias or Abraham Israel Pisa; and Ricke Nunes would be the widow of Moseh, or Mose, Nunes.[201]

The Wolffs point out that Abraham Israel Dias was recorded as having paid his *finta* in Holland just two days before the twenty-three Jews arrived in New Amsterdam.[202] Therefore, Abraham Israel Dias could not be the same person as Abraham Israel – it was a mistake to associate them. While the name Abraham Israel appears on petitions in New Amsterdam from 1654 onwards, it is worth remembering that, when dealing with New Christians during the time of the Inquisition, it is common to find one name used by multiple people, or one person using multiple names.

Egon and Frieda also criticize a theory presented by Oppenheim, and partially endorsed by other historians, which identifies a place called Gamoniké as Jamaica; according to Wiznitzer, Gamoniké was the name used for Jamaica in old documents. However, the Wolffs suggest that Gamoniké could be Tamariké, a version of Itamaracá in Bahia, and that Santo Antônio could also be a place in Bahia, and not Cuba, as the Jews would have departed from this region, given that Itamaracá had belonged to the Dutch until their surrender.

The history of the Jewish departure from Recife is shrouded in legends and hypotheses that have yet to be fully investigated. What is known for certain is that a group of Jews left Recife on the *Valk*, were shipwrecked near Martinique, imprisoned by the Spanish on Jamaica, taken before the Inquisition, and that only a few of them arrived in New Amsterdam. In 1655, two more ships carrying Jews who had been living in Recife reached the Dutch colony in North America. Onboard were José da Costa, Jacob Henriques Cohen, Abraham de Lucena, Salvador d'Andrada, Benjamin Bueno de Mesquita, Isaac Israel (Isaque Izarael), David de Ferera and Benjamin Cardozo.[203] Their names appear in the minute book of the

---

[201] WIZNITZER, Arnold. The Members of the Brazilian Jewish Community (1648-1653). Publications of the American Jewish Historical Society, Philadelphia, v. 42, p. 1-5, 1953.

[202] The *finta* was a tax that specifically targeted Jews.

[203] HERSHKOWITZ, Leo. New Amsterdam's Twenty-Three Jews – Myth or Reality? In: *Hebrew and the Bible in America: The First Two Centuries*. Hannover/London: Shalon Goldman/University Press of New England, 1993. p. 169-183.

Zur Israel synagogue of Recife and a year later they can be found conducting business in New Amsterdam.

The newly arrived Jews from Brazil faced a number of challenging situations. In May of 1665, William Thomasson, captain of the *Great Christopher*, sued David Ferera, Abraham de Lucena and Salvador d'Andrada for failing to provide payment for a consignment that had been shipped from Amsterdam to New Amsterdam.[204]

The businessman José da Costa, who had lived in Dutch Recife and was brother to the notable philosopher Uriel da Costa (excommunicated from the Jewish community of Amsterdam for denying the immortality of the soul), was one of the Jews who came to New Amsterdam from Brazil, arriving via Holland. Da Costa left Brazil in January, 1654, travelling to Holland, where he was involved in setting up a trading company that would be responsible for transactions between Amsterdam and New Amsterdam.[205] Among the company's Christian shareholders was a Dutchman named Gillis Verbrugge, who owned 25% of shares. Gillis already knew the business well, having been involved in trading since 1640. The other shareholders were Jewish, including Mordechay Abendana, with a quarter of the shares, and David Cardozo Davillar, with a sixth. Gillis and Abendana chose José da Costa, a shareholder in the West India Company at the time, to be their agent in New Amsterdam. In return, Da Costa would receive 95% of profits from the trade over a period of four years.

This contract was signed in April, 1655, and Da Costa left immediately for New Amsterdam. In December of that year, he rented a house located at 27 Pearl Street, which became his

---

[204] As above.

[205] HERSHKOWITZ, Leo. New Amsterdam's Twenty-Three Jews; op. cit., p. 172. José da Costa was the brother of Uriel da Costa, a Marrano born in Portugal who had returned to Judaism upon arriving in Amsterdam with his family. He was excommunicated by the leaders of the Jewish community of Amsterdam, who considered him a danger to the preservation of Judaism. His ideas questioned resurrection and the immortality of the soul, as well as calling into doubt the authority of Jewish oral law. On Uriel da Costa, see RIVKIN, Ellis, In Iberia Judaica: roteiros da memória. In: NOVINSKY, Anita; KUPERMAN, Diane. *Ibéria judaica: roteiros da memória*. Rio de Janeiro: Expressão e Cultura, 1996. BODIAN, Miriam. *Hebrews of the Portuguese Nation: Conversos and Community in Early Modern Amsterdam*. Bloomington: Indiana University Press, 1997. OSIER, Jean Pierre. *De Uriel da Costa a Baruch Spinosa*. Paris: Berg International, 1983.

permanent address. David Ferera was Moses Silva's commercial representative and, years later, he moved to Amsterdam with his brother, Elias Silva, to manage the business more closely, ending up remaining in the colony.

Other Jews arrived in the Dutch colony of New Amsterdam between 1656 and 1670.[206] These included **Moses de Lucena**, Isaac Mesa, Manoel Roiz Lucena, Joseph Francis, **Mevrow Abraham de Lucena**, David Machero, Rabba Couty, **Jacob Lumbroso**, **Joseph Bueno de Mesquita**, David and Simon Valentine Vanderwilde, **Jacob Israel**, **David Abendana** and Joshua Servateyn.[207] (Names in bold indicate those who had lived in Brazil under Dutch rule.)

Many of these had relatives living in New Amsterdam. Jacob Lumbroso was a relative of Moses Lumbroso; Joseph Bueno de Mesquita was Benjamim Bueno de Mesquita's brother; Jacob Israel was Isaac Israel's brother; Simon Valentine Wanderwilde was Asser Levy's brother-in-law, and had a wife and children; the Lucena family was led by Rabbi Abraham de Lucena, and had all lived in Brazil.[208]

Moses de Lucena became Asser Levy's partner in the ownership of a slaughterhouse. He also worked alongside José da Costa on the translation of documents into Spanish, an indication of the difficulty some members of the Jewish community had with the Dutch language. Moses de Lucena had arrived accompanied by another relative, Jacob de Lucena, who would remain in the area after the English conquest.[209]

In the 17th century, members of the Da Costa, Lucena and Cardozo families could be found living in Rio de Janeiro. Whether these families arrived in Pernambuco alongside the Dutch, before heading to Rio de Janeiro, and whether they really were relatives, remains unknown, because there are no comprehensive genealogical

---

[206] HERSHKOWITZ, Leo. New Amsterdam's Twenty-Three Jews; op. cit., p. 183.

[207] GOLLMAN, Earl A. Dictionary of American Jewish Biography in the 17th Century. *American Jewish Archives*, 1950, Rosenbloom and Samuel Oppenheim Collection.

[208] His name appears on the contracts drawn up for the purchase of what would become the first Jewish cemetery. See SOLA POOL, David. *Portraits Etched in Stone: Early Jewish Settlers*. New York: Columbia University Press, 1953.

[209] OPPENHEIM, Samuel. The Early History of the Jews in New York, 1654-1664, op. cit., p. 24.

studies with which to verify these facts. According to Lina Gorenstein, the Da Costa and Lucena families both kept their marriages within the Jewish community, something that would be replicated in New Amsterdam.[210]

The story of the twenty-three Brazilian Jews – and a handful of Protestants – who arrived in New Amsterdam in the first week of September, 1654, was only just beginning.

---

[210] GORENSTEIN, Lina. A Inquisição contra as mulheres – Rio de Janeiro, séculos XVII e XVIII. São Paulo: Humanitas/Fapesp, 2005. p. 75-84.

13. A Difficult New Beginning

The Autumn of 1654 represents a landmark in the history of the Jewish colonization of North America. Days before the celebration of the Jewish New Year, the twenty-three refugees from Brazil reached the Dutch colony in North America. Yet they were not the first Jews to arrive on North American soil: these had been Joaquim Gaunsen, who, in 1585, had worked as a metallurgist and mining engineer in the English colony of Roanoke Island, where he conducted experiments on North Carolina's soil, before returning to England a year later; and Soloman Franco, an agent for Dutch-Jewish merchants, who travelled to Boston, on business, in 1649.[211]

The Jewish refugees from Brazil arrived without any means of subsistence and with no solid ground on which to live. They were looking for a new life, somewhere to build a home and raise their children and grandchildren. These Brazilians are considered pioneers in the development of New York, and sometimes referred to as the Jewish Pilgrim Fathers.

According to Jonathan Sarna, in contrast to the English Pilgrims, who had arrived voluntarily in Massachusetts, in 1620, looking for a place where they could live according to their religious principles, the Jews were forced to leave Recife, which had been reconquered by the Portuguese.

When the passengers of the *Saint Charles* disembarked on the Island of Manhattan, what they discovered was a small village. The center consisted of five shops, all built of stone, and a few dozen wooden houses. There was a wharf for the boats, a sail loft to provide sails for the ships, a bakery, a barracks, a church with the pastor's residence behind it, and a granary, on Pearl Street. On the roads leading off of the commercial street, pigs and chickens wandered freely among the inhabitants. A French Jesuit, Isaac Jogues, calculated the population at somewhere between 500 and

---

[211] SARNA, Jonathan. *American Judaism: A History*. Connecticut: Yale University Press, 2004. p. 1. Carolina was one of the thirteen English colonies in North America, and was later divided into two regions, creating the states of North and South Carolina.

600 inhabitants.[212] In the same report, the Jesuit claimed that as many as eighteen different languages could be heard within the colony, a result of the diversity of immigrants, which included English, Scots, French Huguenots, the Welsh and Germans, as well as other minorities and African slaves.

The town's administration consisted of a director-general, two assistant-prefects and a committee of judges, who, combined, formed a legislative body known as the magistrates' court, which was similar to the one in Holland and based upon Dutch-Roman law. The main difference between the colony and the metropolis was that the governor of the colony, Peter Stuyvesant, was able to restrict the power of the municipal government, preventing elections from being held, with directors instead being chosen upon his indication.[213] The system of burghs, widely used in Holland, was transferred to the colony in North America. Under this system there were burghers and grand burghers. The grand burghers were prominent merchants, who contributed to improvements in the settlement, and in return received the right to trade and participate actively in the political administration of the settlement. A burgher was a kind of minor shareholder, with the right to engage in politics at the Town Hall. All small tradesmen applied for this position, including cobblers, millers, bakers, tailors and milliners.[214] This system can be compared to the political model used in Colonial Brazil, which allowed "good men" to participate in the politics of the Town Hall.

New Amsterdam society was aristocratic, with an elite comprised of great patroons (landholders), with manorial rights to extensive territories; next, came the merchant burghers, the owners of ships which traded with Africa and Europe: they took over furs and rum and brought back ivory and slaves; in third place, came the

---

[212] JAMESON, J. Franklin. *Narratives of New Netherland, 1609-1664*. New York: Charles Scribner's Sons, 1909.

[213] Roman law arrived in Holland under the Holy Roman Empire, and dated back to the rule of the Caesars and the Justinian code. See WESSELS. Johannes Wilhelmus. *History of the Roman-Dutch Law*. Grahamstown, Cape Colony: African Book, 1908. SEYMANN, Jerrold. *Colonial Charters, Patents and Grants to the Communities Comprising the City of New York*. New York: New York Public Library.

[214] MAIKA, Dennis J. *Commerce and Community: Manhattan Merchants*. 1995. Thesis (PhD) – New York University, New York.

burghers; and finally, there was the great mass of the population, consisting of workers, shopkeepers, craftsmen and commercial agents.[215]

This was the situation which greeted the refugees from Recife. Waiting for them at the port when the frigate docked in Manhattan, were two Dutch Jews: Jacob Barsimson and Solomon Pietersen.[216]

It is interesting to note that these two Jews must have had some prior knowledge of the "Brazilians," since they were already waiting for them at the port. The reverend of New Amsterdam, John Megapolensis, wrote a letter to the Reformed Church of Amsterdam suggesting the two Jews must have been sent by the Jewish leaders of that city.[217] One of them, Jacob Barsimson (or Jacob Bar Simson), had lived in Brazil under Dutch rule (his presence is supported by a document from Recife from March 31, 1647).[218] Barsimson was probably in Manhattan investigating the possibility of establishing a Jewish colony in New Amsterdam,[219] increasing trade between the colony and Holland and assisting the Dutch government in strengthening its hold over North America.[220]

At that time, the Dutch were expanding their domain in the Americas. While Curaçao and Dutch Guiana were small territories, the region of New Amsterdam seemed to offer the possibility of a new way of life and the settlement was desperate for the arrival of

---

[215] ROOSEVELT, Theodore. Stuyvesant and the End of Dutch Rule: 1647-1664. *Publications of the American Jewish Historical Society*, New York, v. 45, 1956.

[216] WIZNITZER, Arnold. The Exodus from Brazil and Arrival in New Netherlands of the Jewish Pilgrim Fathers, 1654. *Publications of the American Jewish Historical Society*, Philadelphia, v. 44, 1954.

[217] On this topic, see OPPENHEIM, Samuel. A Contemporary Account of How the Jews Came to Arrive in New Netherland. *Publications of the American Jewish Historical Society*, Philadelphia, Oct. 1926. MARCUS, J. R. *The Colonial American Jew*. Detroit: Wayne State University Press, 1969. v. 1. 215-222. STERN, Malcolm. Portuguese Sephardim in the Americas. In: COHEN, Martin A.; PECK, Abraham J. (Eds.). *Sephardim in the Americas: Studies in Culture and History*. Tuscaloosa/London: American Jewish Archives/University of Alabama Press, 1993. p. 156-159.

[218] DAG NOTULE, 31 Mar. 1647. Algemeen Rijksarchief, the Hague, Holland, Oude West Indische Compagnie 71, collection of codices and scrolls.

[219] SILVA, Leonardo Dantas. Zur Israel, uma comunidade judaica no Brasil. In: HERKENHOFF, Paulo (Org.). *O Brasil e os holandeses*. Rio de Janeiro: Sextante Artes, 1999. p. 45-48.

[220] OPPENHEIM, Samuel. The Early History of the Jews in New York, 1654-1664. American Jewish Historical Quarterly, Philadelphia, v. 18. p. 3-4, 1909.

more colonizers.[221] With this aim in mind, the Dutch government spared no effort and, in June, 1654, the West India Company loaded two ships, the *Peterboom* and the *Gelderse Bloom*, with fifty orphans, intended to help grow the population of Manhattan Island. The ships docked in August, during the summer of 1654, and Barsimson and Pieteresen arrived along with the children – just a month later, they were able to offer a great deal of help to the Jews arriving from Brazil.[222]

No sooner had the "Brazilians" arrived, than a series of disagreements broke out between the frigate's captain, Jacques de La Motte, and the refugees concerning payment. Among the Jews unable to pay their debts were the widow Judite de Mereda (Mercado) and the merchant Abraham Israel, who were forced to auction off their belongings. However, the auction did not raise enough funds to cover all of their debts, and the captain again appealed to the assembly, which ruled that two other members of the group, David Israel and Moses Ambrosius (Lumbroso), should be arrested. Pietersen served as a representative for the two prisoners and, in October, the captain and his sailors agreed to wait for the money, which would be arriving from Amsterdam.[223]

The impasse was over, but the sorry state in which the refugees now found themselves led the governor of New Amsterdam, Peter Stuyvesant, and his advisers, Megapolensis and Drisius, to begin a campaign against the Brazilian group being allowed to remain in the colony.

The governor, an authoritarian Calvinist and an anti-Semite, had complete control over the small colony, which was far from the gaze of the West India Company. The colony's inhabitants found themselves isolated in the New World, surrounded by the English,[224] with the nearest Dutch settlement located north of the Hudson River. Stuyvesant's actions were directed more by the

---

[221] SILVA, Leonardo Dantas. Zur Israel, uma comunidade judaica no Brasil, op. cit., p. 45-48.

[222] SOLA POOL, David; SOLA POOL, Tamar de. *An Old Faith in the New World. Portrait of Shearith Israel, 1654-1954*. New York: Colombia University Press, 1955. p. 12.

[223] The assembly was a kind of colonial political council and chamber of deputies.

[224] KESSLER, Henry; RACHLIS, Eugene. *Peter Stuyvesant and his New York*. New York: Random House, 1959. p. 176-186.

motivations of his Calvinist faith than by the interests of the Dutch campaign. He believed that tolerance of diversity would threaten his rulership, which had already earned criticism from the local population even before the arrival of the Jews. On that occasion, a delegation from New Amsterdam and Long Island had led a protest against the arbitrariness of his government. The arrival of the Jews provided new impetus to resistance against the excesses of the local authorities and constituted a renewed threat to Peter Stuyvesant's restrictive policies.

Stuyvesant's official role was director-general, and he was granted the power to create and impose new laws. He relied upon a council of nine trusted men to assist him. This council, known as the "Nine Men," came into constant conflict with Stuyvesant while defending the rights of the population, and would send reports to the central government in Holland recounting the disagreements within the colonial government.

Whenever the disagreements reached the point of actual opposition, Peter Stuyvesant would treat his political adversaries and opponents with severity, imprisoning them without the right to a trial. The governor imposed a despotic rule over the Dutch colony in New Amsterdam, and used to refer to the population as his subjects.[225]

At the beginning of his career, Stuyvesant had served the West India Company on the island of Fernando de Noronha, 220 miles off the coast of Pernambuco. Later, he was transferred to Curaçao, in the capacity of commissary of stores, supervising suppliers, corsairs and merchants on the Manhattan-Curaçao route. He was an elegant man, who dressed himself in accordance with the fashions of the merchant aristocracy, and had been provided with a strict Calvinist education by his father, a minister of the Reformed Church. Stuyvesant lost a leg during a battle on the island of Saint Martin, in the Caribbean, meaning he wore a prosthetic wooden limb attached to his hip, which was ornamented with silver bands. He arrived in New Amsterdam shortly after its foundation, in 1647, and was given

---

[225] TUCKERMAN, Bayard. *Peter Stuyvesant, Director-General for the West India Company in New Netherland.* New York: Cornell University Library, 1893. KESSLER, Henry; RACHLIS, Eugene. *Peter Stuyvesant and his New York*, op. cit., p. 176-186.

the mission of moralizing the colony, waging war on drunkenness, gambling, street brawling and betting on fights.

Stuyvesant believe that the arrival of the Jews, who he regarded as "hateful enemies and blasphemers of the name of Christ," might threaten the existing order, and argued that, as they were not trustworthy citizens, they might "infect" the colony.[226]

These ideas were shared by Reverend John Megapolensis, chief minister of the Dutch Church, and by Cornelis van Tienhoven, the local *schout*, a Dutch title which combined the roles of sheriff and prosecutor. Van Tienhoven was well-known for the lack of scruples that had allowed him to progress in his career. He stated openly that he did not like Jews and that, if they insisted upon remaining within his territory, he would persecute them mercilessly. The *schout* believed that the prominence achieved by persecuting the Jews would boost his career.[227] One rumor that did the rounds at the times was that Van Tienhoven was capable of sitting down for negotiations with Native American leaders while at the same time sending his troops to massacre their tribe. His tragic end is shrouded in mystery, with his disappearance in 1656 coming after he became the center of a colonial scandal after being seen to disregard the moral standards and behaviors imposed by Stuyvesant. Van Tienhoven had appeared in public with his lover at a time when he stood accused of doctoring the West India Company's accounts ledgers. Just days after this event, his hat and cane were discovered floating just offshore.

Stuyvesant declared the disappearance "death by drowning" and the case was closed. Van Tienhoven's brother, who had also been involved in the accounting scandal, disappeared in the same year, reemerging a year later in Barbados.

Van Tienhoven, Stuyvesant and Megapolensis were not the first in the colony to practice discrimination. Stuyvesant's predecessor, Director-General Van Dincklagen, had already taken against

---

[226] TUCKERMAN, Bayard. *Peter Stuyvesant, Director-General for the West India Company in New Netherland*, op. cit., "That the deceitful race – such hateful enemies and blasphemers of the name of Christ – be not allowed to further infect and trouble this new colony." See appendix – letter from Stuyvesant appealing against the Jews being allowed to remain in the colony.

[227] HUNTER, Leon. *Asser Levy: A Noted Jewish Burgher of Amsterdam. Publications of the American Jewish Historical Society*, v. 8, p. 9-23, 1900.

foreigners, limiting their privileges at Fort Amsterdam in September, 1648, and describing them as "destroyers of trade." Intolerance was a mainstay of this society.[228]

Governor Stuyvesant wrote to the directors of the West India Company, requesting the extradition of the Jews. In an attempt to justify his prejudice, he alleged that the new-arrivals would end up dependent on charity from the local church in order to survive the coming winter. He added that if he condescended to the Jews, he would be required to make equal concessions to other groups.

Since Recife, the West India Company had always been in favor of showing tolerance towards the Jews. After all, the Jews had been their collaborators in Brazil, and would assume the same position in North America. The company, therefore, rejected the governor's arguments about the need for the Calvinist church to concern itself with the preservation of the Jews. It also reminded him of the damage caused to the Jewish community by the Dutch war for Brazilian territory. Jews were granted permission to disembark and remain in New Amsterdam, and Stuyvesant was forced to accept their presence.[229]

Ever since the arrival of the refugees from Brazil, there had been disputes and misunderstandings between the Jews and the local authorities. Discrimination extended from the area of religion into the social sector, and, during the ten years the Jews spent under Dutch rule in New Amsterdam, anti-Jewish sentiment was a common occurrence.

Since governor Stuyvesant had been unable to prevent the Jews from remaining on his lands, he adopted the strategy of making their lives difficult, denying any request presented by the community and placing obstacles in the way of their involvement in trade. The governor's attitude was designed to cause even more hardship for the Jews living in the settlement, despite being aware that,

---

[228] The so-called "foreigners" were the Scots, French and English, who practiced Lutheranism and Catholicism, as well as the newly-arrived Jews. See MARCUS, J. R. *The Colonial American Jew*. Detroit: Wayne State University Press, 1970. v. 2. p. 548-549.

[229] OPPENHEIM, Samuel. The Early History of the Jews in New York, 1654-1664, op. cit., p. 1-74.

occasionally, following appeals to the directors, he would be forced to overturn his decisions.[230]

Once the Jews had been granted the right to settle, the group began focusing its efforts on being accepted as citizens.

The buying of a property was another key area in which the Jews faced obstacles. Salvador de Andrade, one of the leaders of the Jewish community, spent years trying to obtain some land on which to build a house, but discovered there was always an impediment. In December, 1655, he acquired a property on the west side of the island (Broad Street), that he had been renting for some time off the town crier, Teunis Cray. The purchase was contested by the Colonial Administrative Council. Cray saw his profits affected, because, due to the contestation of the agreement, he was forced to put the house back on the market at a lower price than the one he had previously negotiated. Following his frustrated attempts to buy a home, Salvador de Andrade gathered arguments against Stuyvesant to present a formal complaint to the city council in Amsterdam. He believed that, under pressure from the city council, the governor would be forced to back down. This case had serious repercussions, because complaints, which had previously come only from the Jews, were now arriving from other inhabitants of Manhattan Island.[231]

Frustrated by the difficulties they faced when attempting to acquire a roof over their heads, the Jews made use of a range of arguments, reminding local authorities that they paid land tax, and also taxes used for the construction of public infrastructure, such as the fort which protected the town from Indian attacks. Consequently, they believed they should be allowed the right to acquire property.

The response from the Colonial Council was that the taxes were used for the benefit of all, and that the request of the Jews could, therefore, be denied. The case was then taken before the authorities in Amsterdam by two members of the group of "Brazilian" Jews, Abraham de Lucena and Salvador d'Andrada, who were well aware of their rights under Dutch law. The Jewish community of Amsterdam applied political pressure, and the case was settled in

---

[230] MARCUS, J. R. *The Colonial American Jew*, op. cit., v. 1, p. 229-230.

[231] Ibid, p. 224.

their favor.[232] Stuyvesant's superiors invoked the legal precept which stated that "all persons will enjoy religious freedom," and highlighted Jewish investment in the West India Company. An order was issued allowing the Jews to engage in trade and purchase property.[233]

There were certain restrictions that the West India Company deemed acceptable, such as the ban on opening shops, forming civic organizations and engaging in manufacturing, all prohibitions which were also imposed in Holland. The Jews were expected to conduct their business peacefully and practice their religion within the silence of their own homes, without drawing attention to themselves, as occurred in the mother-community.

In order to resolve the issue, the government proposed the construction of a Jewish neighborhood, in which Jews would manage their own affairs, as in mediaeval ghettos, and remain isolated from Calvinist society.[234] The neighborhood would be located near White Hall Street, on the very south of Manhattan Island, the financial district of today.

Following the first New Amsterdam census, on July 10, 1660, conducted by Sheriff Nicasius de Sille, it became apparent that this intention had not been carried out, since the Jewish merchant Abraham de Lucena rented a home from Rutger Jacobsen near Megapolensis' property on Slyck Street (Muddy Lane), which also neighbored another Dutchman, Jan Reyndersen. The remaining property on Slyck Street was a tavern owned by Adrien Vincent, a Welshman. There were no other Jews living on this street, indicating that the Sephardic Jews were living among the local population, and not in a separate neighborhood. There was, however, a Jewish quarter, where the "Brazilian" David Ferera had purchased a property that had belonged to the wife of Claus Jansen Ruyter, located on Pearl Street, between Marketfield Street and North River. Nearby, on the west side of Stone Street, was the home of José da

---

[232] Ibid, p. 223-228.

[233] Ibid, p. 235.

[234] DRUCKER, Erna. *Jewish Settlers in New Amsterdam and Early New York, 1654-1825: A Selected Annotated Guide to Source Materials.* New York: City College of New York, Master of Library Science Thesis at Queens College, 1984. p. 1-3, 75-76, 83, 94, 104-108. 117-120, 125-126, 151 and 164-168.

Costa, situated between Pearl and Beaver Street. Salvador de Andrade lived on the corner of Broad and Stone Street.[235] Mill Street, not far from the roads mentioned, became known as "*Jews' Alley*" due to the number of Jewish immigrants living there. In 1660, the Jews of New Amsterdam certainly did not find themselves confined within a European-style ghetto.[236]

The community of New Amsterdam was one in which the Protestant prejudices of the Calvinists dominated everything, from the way people thought, to their moral, economic and social behavior, leading to extreme discrimination, with even Christians who disagreed with aspects of the government or the church risking exposure to violence or forced marginalization.

The beginnings of Jewish life in North America were anything but peaceful. Stuyvesant's fierce persecution led some Jews to seek other territories where they might face less coldness and discrimination, ending up travelling to the Caribbean, Holland and England.

Another obstacle the Jews had to overcome was the taxes and tariffs aimed exclusively at the Jewish community. The first of these tariffs concerned the colony's army; as Jews were unable to fight in defense of Dutch lands, they were required to pay a tax of 65 stivers.[237] A year later, in 1656, Asser Levy took legal action against a measure preventing Jews from participating in the local militia and being required to pay a special tax instead.[238]

Since the Middle Ages, Jews had been forced to pay special taxes merely for being Jewish. Levy and Barsimson decided not to allow that discrimination to be perpetuated in America and refused to pay the tax, instead offering to perform military service, which

---

[235] OPPENHEIM, Samuel. The Early History of the Jews in New York, 1654-1664, op. cit., p. 54.

[236] SILLE, Nicassius de. "List of the Houses of New Amsterdam, July, 10, 1660," in *New Netherland Papers*, New York. New York Public Library (Manuscripts Division), 10 Jul. 1660.

[237] In July, 1655, the governor received an order to attack the Swedes, who were in Delaware, and there was doubt over whether or not to allow Jews to enlist. In August, 1655, the decision was made that they should not be allowed to enlist and, therefore, should pay a tax of 65 stivers.

[238] FERNOW, Berthold. *Documents Relating to the History of the Early Colonial Settlements.* Albany: Weed, Parson and Company, 1883. p. 16-27 and 238-259.

consisted of standing guard at the settlement's fort.[239] Joining the militia meant being accepted as a citizen, and exercising the same rights and duties.[240] The governor justified his veto by explaining that the men in the militia would be averse to serving alongside Jews.

Attacks by Native Americans were common in Manhattan, which is why the settlement required a militia, as well as the construction of new forts for its defense. One of the most famous Indian attacks, occurring during the territorial disputes, came in September, 1655, during what became known as the Peach Tree War. The war was sparked by the death of a young Native American woman, who had decided to pick a peach from a tree on Sheriff Van Dyck's property. Outraged by the "girl's insolence" in invading his land, the sheriff fired his riffle just as the woman climbed up into the peach tree. In retaliation, over three days, 500 furious Indian warriors attacked the region of Hoboken and Staten Island. As a result, more than 100 Dutch settlers were killed and their houses destroyed.

In October, 1655, inhabitants of New Amsterdam were required to pay a tax intended to raise funds for the construction of a new fort.[241] Two hundred and thirty people obliged, among them Asser Levy, who contributed alongside eight other Jews. Of the 6,305 guilders collected, 12% was paid by Jews – five of the eight Jews were merchants, and each contributed 100 guilders. Only five non-Jews contributed a larger amount – Stuyvesant and four ship's captains – while another ten Christians matched the contribution of

---

[239] See HÜHNER, Leon. *Asser Levy: A Noted Jewish Burgher of Amsterdam*, op. cit., p. 9-23; KOHLER, Max. Civil Status of the Jews in Colonial New York. *Publications of the American Jewish Historical Society*, v. 7, p. 81-85, 1897.

[240] Whenever the settlement was attacked by Indians, the Jews would donate 100 guilders, which was a lot of money, given that only four people could afford to donate that amount.

[241] SHORTO, Russel. *A ilha no centro do mundo*. Rio de Janeiro: Objetiva, 2004. p. 340. The Indians reached Manhattan Island from the south side, firing arrows in the streets. On Staten Island, they went as far as burning houses and killing people, in retaliation for an assault Stuyvesant had led on Swedish settlers, who had been trading partners of the Susquehannock Indians for seventeen years. The name given to the war is an attempt to explain the origin of the attack, linking it to an incident in which a Dutchman killed an Indian woman accused of stealing peaches.

100 guilders.[242] As well as the tax, the town council declared that, for reasons of safety, no one would be allowed to travel inland without a permit, and even permit holders were not supposed to travel alone. This resolution only added to the challenges of developing an internal market, a sector the Jews had become involved in.

What the new land offered was a simple colonial life, in a remote settlement with intolerant citizens. From the moment they arrived in New Amsterdam, the Jews began the struggle to achieve economic equality and religious tolerance.

The Jewish struggle for equality would continue throughout the ten years of Dutch rule in North America. In 1664, the English captured the settlement, which, by that point, contained 1,500 inhabitants, among them around 60 Jews. In the surrender agreement it was established that all inhabitants would enjoy freedom of religion. There was no alteration to the aristocracy, which consisted of the Dutch, the Huguenots and the English. The English had exerted a strong influence over Stuyvesant's Dutch government, due to the fact that one third of New Amsterdam's population was English, and, after surrender and the establishment of the English government, Dutch merchants were allowed similar participation in the administrative council.[243] Despite the change in rulership, hierarchies were maintained, and the aristocracy, composed of businessmen and merchants, received support from the new government. While the nomenclature changed, positions and their functions were preserved. New elements were added to the colonial society, and Presbyterians from Scotland, Puritans and the Irish, who were all staunch opposers of the Episcopal Church, joined the Jews at the head of a people's party in opposition to the colonial government.

It was at this point that New Amsterdam became New York, a settlement where, despite boasting a government influenced by

---

[242] O'CALLAGHAN, Edmund Bailey. History of New Netherland. In: *documents Relative to the Colonial History of the State of New York*. Albany: Weed, Parsons and Company, 1856, p. 576-577. v. 1.

[243] See ROOSEVELT, Theodore. New Amsterdam Becomes New York. The Beginnings of English Rule. 1664-1674. In: *A Sketch of the City's Social, Political and Commercial Progress from the First Dutch Settlement to Recent Time.* New York: Charles Scribner's Sons, 1909.

progressive ideas, the struggle of the Jews to achieve democracy and integration continued.

The restrictive policies applied to Jews under Dutch rule, and also at the beginning of the English administration, were comparable to the situation that had previously been face by Jewish communities in various parts of Europe.

During this period, Jews essentially remained a group of foreign immigrants in North America. Only after 1740, with the proclamation of the Naturalization Act, did this *status* begin to gradually alter, paving the way to unlimited economic opportunities for Jews in the American provinces and elsewhere in the British Empire.[244]

However, civil equality is not political equality. Jews did not have permission to participate in Parliament or in the province's executive council, nor could they hold public offices, either civilian or military.[245] In order to become naturalized, applicants were required to take an oath, which was to be made "on the true faith of a Christian." This excluded all Jews from the right to become citizens. In 1753, the Jewish community of London applied pressure on Parliament to enact a law releasing Jews from the need to include this phrase as part of their oath of allegiance. This law became known as the "Jew Bill," but was only in place for a year, due to widespread disapproval by Protestants. The way out presented to Jews was the *denization patent*, an official letter conferring limited rights upon the holder, such as the purchasing and transference of land. In terms of economics, the Jews had made great strides, but in terms of politics, restrictions remained. Only after the American War of Independence were Jews finally able to attain full citizenship. The United States constitution guaranteed the principles of equality and liberty to all, independent of religious creed.[246]

---

[244] MARCUS, J. R. *The Colonial American Jew*, op. cit., p. 593. The imperial naturalization act of 1740 granted all Protestants and other foreigners, with the exception of Catholics, the right to citizenship. This right was offered by England and its colonies. To acquire this right, it was necessary to pay a 2-shilling tax.

[245] See HÜHNER, Leon. *Asser Levy: A Noted Jewish Burgher of Amsterdam*, op. cit., p. 21. KOHLER, Max. *Civil Status of the Jews in Colonial New York*, op. cit., p. 81-85.

[246] See HÜHNER, Leon. *Asser Levy: A Noted Jewish Burgher of Amsterdam*, op. cit., p. 21.

When, in 1789, George Washington proclaimed November 26 Thanksgiving Day, there were commemorative parades all across the country, and, among the various tables of food on display, there was one offering kosher fare. The Jews were no longer a tolerated minority, but full American citizens. This was the first time in the history of the Jewish diaspora that they had been considered the equals of their non-Jewish counterparts. So began a new era in North America for the descendants of the Jews from Brazil.[247]

---

[247] ANGEL, Marc D. (Rabbi). *A Portrait of America's First Jewish Congregation –* *Shearith Israel*. New York: Riverside Company Books, 2004. p. 39.

14. Extracts from a Life: Asser Levy, the Pioneer

Asser Levy was among the twenty-three pioneers who disembarked the *Saint Charles* at the port of Manhattan, having sailed from Brazil in the Autumn of 1654. In Recife, Pernambuco, he had served in the Dutch militia that fought the Portuguese to keep hold of the territory. Sometimes he would add Van Swellen to his surname, since he was supposedly born in the town of Schwelm, Westphalia, in the future Germany. He also occasionally adopted the name Wilde, which some historians believe was a version of Wilna, putting his origins in Vilnius.[248]

Asser Levy arrived in New Amsterdam as a very young man with no financial means, and his story follows that of many American immigrants, who, after a period of time and much hard work, managed to attain a comfortable position in society. His success was achieved after an intense battle against discrimination, and he went on to become one of the greatest leaders of New Amsterdam's Jewish community.[249]

Within the first week of his arrival, on September 14, 1654, Asser Levy had already become involved in a lawsuit against Ricke Nunes, over a sum of money he had loaned her in Jamaica during the voyage to New Amsterdam. At the same time, he found himself being sued by the sailors of the *Saint Charles* over his debt for the journey. Levy ended up spending a couple of days in jail, before managing to reach an agreement with the ship's captain, who dropped the charges.

Upon establishing himself in New Amsterdam, Asser Levy specialized in preparing meat in accordance with Jewish dietary laws – he may have inherited this skill from his "supposed father,"

---

[248] Leo Hershkowitz claims that the only time Asser Levy added Swellen to the end of his name was when signing a document in Amsterdam, while preparing to travel to Germany. Hershkowitz believes Levy was born in Vilnius. The fact remains that most documents signed by Asser Levy include both names. HERSHKOWITZ, Leo. Asser Levy and the Inventories of Early New York Jews. *American Jewish History*, v. 80, n. 1, p. 23-37, 1990.

[249] HÜHNER, Leon. Asser Levy: A Noted Jewish Burgher of New Amsterdam. *Publications of the American Jewish Historical Society*, v. 8, p. 9-23, 1900.

Benjamin Levy, the *shohet* of the Dutch colony in Recife.[250] There is no proof that Asser Levy really was the son of Benjamin Levy of Dutch Recife, only that the younger man spent some years living in the Recife colony while doing military service for the West India Company.[251] What can be verified is that the role of *shohet*[252] was passed on from father to son, or from uncle to nephew, and that there is a high probability this would have been the case within the Levy family, just as, many years later, Asser Levy's nephew inherited his uncle's profession.

In 1660, Asser Levy obtained a rare butcher's license. He opened a slaughterhouse and inaugurated a butcher shop, located on what is now the west side of Wall Street, outside the walls of the settlement in accordance with a law from 1677, which stated that all butchering of animals should take place beyond the limits of the town.[253] The role of butcher was the only artisanal trade Jews were allowed to engage in.[254]

Levy diversified his businesses, becoming involved in the competitive fur trade of the Hudson River valley. He also became a

---

[250] Hershkowitz questions the veracity of the theory that Benjamin Levy was Asser Levy's father (a theory supported by Wiznitzer), stating there is no proof to support this claim, as well as suggesting that the younger man was born in Vilnius. In this book, I shall side with Wiznitzer, as Asser and Benjamin Levy shared the same profession, which was traditionally passed down from father to son or uncle to nephew. In Pernambuco, there was only one *shohet*: Benjamin. There is a high possibility that Asser Levy would have taken the family trade to New Amsterdam. For more on this, see LEVY, Asser. *The New York Genealogical and Biographical Record*, v. 2, p. 2, 1971. HERSHOWITZ, Leo. Asser Levy and the Inventories of Early New York Jews, op. cit., n. 1, p. 26. HERSHKOWITZ, Leo. New Amsterdam's Twenty-Three Jews – Myth or Reality? In: *Hebrew and the Bible in America: The First Two Centuries*. Hanover/London: Shalom Goldman/University Press of New England, 1993. p. 169-183. HÜHNER, Leon. *Asser Levy: A Noted Jewish Burgher in New Amsterdam*, op. cit., p.12.

[251] STRYKER-RODDA, Harriet (Mott). *Asser Levy in the New York Genealogical and Biographical Record*. New York: New York Genealogical and Biographical Society, 1971, v. 102 n. 3. p. 129-135.

[252] A *shohet* is a specialist at butchering animals in accordance with Jewish dietary laws.

[253] The slaughterhouse was on the southwest corner of Wall and Pearl Street, and the butcher's shop, on the northeast corner of Wall and Pearl Street. MARCUS, J. R. *The Colonial American Jew: 1492-1776*, Michigan: Wayne State University Press, 1969. p. 246.

[254] The role of butcher was the only trade permitted to Jews, to allow for their strict kosher diet. Kosher products are food that has been prepared in accordance with Jewish dietary laws.

commercial agent, establishing import and export relationships with the Dutch colonies in the Caribbean and, later, with the British colonies there.

In 1661, when Jews were granted the right to own property, Levy immediately acquired a building in Albany as an investment, and, in 1662, bought some land on South William Street. This was the same street where the first synagogue was eventually built, and historians studying the period suspect it may have been constructed on Levy's land.

Levy was often the figurehead of the struggle for civil rights. No other Jew appears to have been involved in as many lawsuits, always listed as the claimant. He was responsible for litigation over the right of Jews to stand guard at the settlement's fort and stop paying punitive taxes, their right to burgher *status* and their right to trade at Fort Orange. He sued Nicholas Bayard, a relative of Stuyvesant's and an important politician, and denounced Johannes La Montaigne, the colony's clerk. Once under English rule, he protested against the new colonial administration, which imposed a tax of 2 florins per week to support English troops. When we examine all the lawsuits Asser Levy was involved in, we are left with the image of a man with a defiant nature and a profound sense of social justice.

During the decade of the 1660s, Asser Levy was considered one of the richest inhabitants of the region, even loaning funds to the settlement for the reconstruction of walls and palisades. He was recognized for his great contribution to the community of New Amsterdam, becoming the first Jew in North America to receive the title of grand burgher.[255] For Asser Levy, earning this title was a sign of his integration into local society, and also presented certain economic advantages by freeing him from commercial restrictions.

In 1665, New Amsterdam changed its name to New York, following the territory's capture by the English. The size of the Jewish community shrunk to around 55 people, but Asser Levy's social influence and economic standing grew among Jews and Christians alike. Years before Leisler's Rebellion, the unfortunate leaders of that famous uprising – Johannes de Peyster and Jacob Leisler – sought out Levy to discuss England's colonial policies, the

---

[255] MARCUS, J. R. *The Colonial American Jew*, op. cit., p. 246.

consequences of the Navigation Acts on colonial trade and the tyranny of the Anglo-Dutch elected assembly.[256]

Under the British Crown, Levy expanded his businesses into the Westchester region, a county of the state of New York. By 1678, the value of his properties had reached approximately 2,500 florins. Among his various businesses, he owned a tavern on Pearl Street, in partnership with a Dutchman, Garret Janses Rose, an important figure in Protestant society. The tavern had previously belonged to another Dutchman, Daniel Litscho, a sergeant of the Dutch East India Company who had served in Brazil in 1646.[257]

Levy's relationships with his Christian neighbors became increasingly intimate, and in 1670 he was named guardian of the children of Wessel Evestsen, a Dutchman who, years earlier, had sold him a property at 59 Stone Street. This transaction gave rise to a close friendship. At the time, it was rumored that Wessel needed a guardian for his children because he was going through a financial crisis.

In 1671, Asser Levy loaned a considerable sum of money to the Lutherans for the construction of their first House of Prayer, and his honesty and integrity kept him on excellent terms with the Protestants. He also had many friends among the Jewish citizens, and his name appears as an executor on various Christian inventories. In the same year, Asser Levy was invited to be a member of a trial jury, an honor usually reserved for the Protestant elite, and in the next year, 1672, Levy received an even greater honor when he was named State Curator by Jan Copal, governor of New York.

Despite not having a diploma, Levy acted as a lawyer in legal matters, especially issues relating to mercantile activity, working in defense of other Jews, such as when Jacob de Lucena, who had

---

[256] Leisler's Rebellion defended the idea that the colony's submission was unnatural, and that the policies implemented by King James II went against the interests of the colony, especially the English Navigations Act. In 1689, the rebels took over the elected assembly, and the captain of the New York militia, Jacob Leisler, proclaimed himself governor. The leaders of the rebellion had the support of Dutch workers and craftsmen. Leisler's rule lasted from 1689 to 1691, when English troops recovered power and sentenced the leaders of the rebellion to the gallows. The Navigations Act had been instituted in 1651 by Oliver Cromwell and decreed that, from that date forward, trade with England could only be carried out using English ships.

[257] Today 125 Pearl and 65 Wall Street.

arrived in New Amsterdam in 1655, was arrested for refusing to open his commercial establishment on Saturdays. Levy interceded with the authorities, and Lucena was exempted from that obligation.[258] Abraham Cohen Henriques and José da Costa also made use of Asser Levy's legal skills. As well as being a lawyer, Levy was regarded as trustworthy by the local court, and was brought in during a dispute between Thomas Williams and Edward Smith, two Christians, over merchandise. Levy was the person chosen to store the disputed merchandise until the judge reached his verdict.

Asser Levy's name soon became respected in other Dutch and English colonies. However, the fact that he maintained good relations with Protestants did not prevent him from continuing his work within the Jewish community.

Asser Levy married Miriam Israel and had a son. The couple lived in a house on Mill Lane and Stone Street. They were admired for their elegance – Levy always wore a velvet coat and silver scabbard. Despite all citizens being prohibited from carrying weapons on their belts, upstanding gentlemen in society were allowed that freedom, and even the militias would turn a blind eye. Levy's wife wore golden jewelry and was permanently accompanied by an African slave boy, to attend to her needs.[259] The family also employed a governess, who was Aucke Jansen's daughter.[260] The house where the Levy family lived had four floors: the basement, containing the kitchen; the first floor, with a large space, serving as an office or a shop, and a backroom; the second floor, consisting of four rooms; and an attic, reached by a small staircase.

Levy's sister, Raquel, was married to a Dutch Jew, named Valentine Vanderwilde, and had two children. Simon Valentine

---

[258] MARCUS, J. R. *The Colonial American Jew*, op. cit., p. 230.

[259] HÜHNER, Leon. Asser Levy: A Noted Jewish Burgher of New Amsterdam, op. cit., p. 15.

[260] FERNOW, Berthold. *The Records of New Amsterdam from 1653 to 1674 Anno Domini*. Baltimore: Genealogical Publishing, 1976. p. 4: 173, 5:176-177, 183, 188 and 2, 226. SNYDER, Holly. English Markets, Jewish Merchants, and the Atlantic Endeavors. In: KAGAN, Richard L.; MORGAN, Philip D. (Eds.). *Atlantic Diasporas: Jews, Conversos and Crypto – Jews in the Age of Mercantilism, 1500-1800*. Baltimore: John Hopkinson University Press, 2009.

worked with his uncle, learning the role of *shohet*, or slaughterer, and in 1701 became a respected merchant in Charleston, South Carolina. Their daughter, Rebecca, married Asher Michaels, another Dutch Jew, and had four children: two girls and two boys. Her daughters, Raquel and Richea, married a pair of brothers, Samuel Levy and Moses Levy, who were prestigious Jewish merchants, recently arrived from England, and who would go on to found the Jewish community in Philadelphia. The Levy brothers maintained commercial relationships with their relatives in London and started up a trading agency. Richea and Moses Levy's daughter, Abigail, married Jacob Franks, who had been a member of the Jewish community in London, and together they formed the Levy-Franks clan. Through their descendants, it is possible to trace Asser Levy's family tree right up until the present day.[261] Jacob Franks was sent to New York to run the family business and form closer relationships with relatives in North America. By keeping marriages within the clan, the family were able to build a complex business network and amass a great fortune. Abigail Franks left a wonderful contribution to historians investigating the period in the form of correspondence with her sons, who were studying in England.[262]

Levy remained in New Amsterdam until his death, in 1682. Though his exact date of birth is still uncertain, evidence suggests he died young, at around 43, and it is believed his funeral was held at the first Jewish cemetery, the location of which is still unknown. He left a large fortune to his children and wife, who became responsible for managing his estate. Among other exquisite relics, the inventory of his possessions includes lamps, Shabbat wine glasses and liturgical books in Hebrew, objects which demonstrate he must have been a religious man and that he maintained a strong connection to his Jewish heritage.[263] There is an extensive description of his kitchen, including objects that were typical of the

---

[261] See STERN, Malcolm. *First American Jewish Families: 600 Genealogies, 1654-1988*. Baltimore: Ottenheimer Publishers, 1991.

[262] See MARCUS, J. R. *The Colonial American Jew*, op. cit., p. 279-280. HERSHKOWITZ, Leo. Dutch Notorial Records Pertaining to Asser Levy, 1659-1692. (Part Three: New Documents for the Study of American Jewish History). *American Jewish History*, 1 Sep. 2003.

[263] *Shabbat* is Saturday, the sacred day for Jews. Lamps or candles are lit on Friday before sunset, when a prayer is conducted, alongside bread and wine.

colonial period, such as a large number of dishes and gold and silver tableware, as well as bedroom features, like beds, pillows, blankets and furs. Also included in the inventory was a long list of debtors and creditors, in total around 440 people from New York and its surrounding areas – the Hudson Valley, Long Island and Albany – who owed Asher Levy money. In all, his assets were estimated at 550 pounds. At that time, only seven people possessed assets that could equal or exceed this amount.[264]

After his death, Levy's widow, Miriam, moved to Holland, where she married a 29-year-old with the same name as her former husband, Asser Levy, and who, according to historian Leo Hershkowitz, may have been a nephew or cousin to the Asser Levy of New York.[265]

On December 23, 1684, Levy's son, Samuel, married a young woman called Margaret. Asser Levy's grandson, Samuel's son, would inherit his grandfather's name, and, during the American War of Independence, was included on the list of soldiers who defended New Jersey.[266] Meanwhile, Levy's great-nephew, David Franks, was involved in the battle for the state of Pennsylvania.[267]

In 1955, young Asser Levy, who had left Recife to seek refuge and opportunity in New Amsterdam, had his pioneering spirit recognized by the political authorities of New York. He was honored on Manhattan Island, where two blocks of Avenue A were renamed Asser Levy Place. A nearby recreation center was also named after him.[268] Between 1820 and 1870, outbreaks of cholera and typhoid devastated New York. In order to combat these epidemics, a Jewish doctor named Simon Baruch (father of Bernard Baruch, financial adviser to the American government during both world wars), who had studied the curative powers of water, proposed the council build public baths. Thirty years later, the public swimming pool and community center were inaugurated in Asser

---

[264] HERSHOWITZ, Leo. Asser Levy and the Inventories of Early New York Jews, op. cit., p. 21-55.

[265] HERSHOWITZ, Leo. Dutch Notarial Records Pertaining to Asser Levy, op. cit.

[266] Records of Connecticut (1717-1725), p. 432, 488, 576 and 577

[267] MARCUS, J. R. *The Colonial American Jew*, op. cit., p. 602.

[268] ANGEL, Marc D. (Rabbi). Remnant of Israel: A Portrait of America's First Jewish Congregation – Shearith Israel. New York: Riverside Company Books, 2004.

Levy's name. Beside the recreation center, a small park was constructed for New York children with special needs, inaugurated in 1993 and also named after Asser Levy. This was New York's small display of recognition for the great contribution made to the building of the city by this beacon of the Jewish community.

15. Anti-Semitism at the Dawn of the USA

In the 17th century, New Amsterdam was a colony made up of immigrants with deep-rooted sentiments against Jews, a legacy of medieval anti-Judaism.

Discrimination against Jews had been a factor since the 2nd and 3rd centuries, and, with the consolidation of the Church's power, the Christian mentality was conditioned to regard Christianity as the only truth. The Jew was demonized and perceived as a symbol of evil.

Influenced by this mentality, the governors of New Amsterdam considered Jews to be inferior beings and second-class citizens.

In the 17th century, not even Holland, which conceded freedom of religion to its citizens, entertained the idea of allowing Jews absolute equality. Even in relatively liberal countries, Jews were excluded, and, in some cities, forced to contribute extra taxes.

Tolerance was imposed by the directors of the West India Company or the representatives of the States General. Prejudice and discrimination originated within the colonial government, mainly due to economic rivalries. Religion held a prominent position for the elite of the colonial society and served as an excellent pretext.

The word "Jew" was used as a pejorative term, a thesis confirmed by numerous lawsuits. In one of these lawsuits, a Christian, Gisbert von Imbrough, accused another Christian, Altjen Sybrants, of having called him a Jew. Sybrant's defense alleged that their client had only used the word in response to Von Imbrough calling him a "pile of dung."[269]

On another occasion, during a trial, Joannes Vervelen turned to José da Costa, who was present, before stating that "people of your kind are all swindlers." When Vervelan was fined for insulting José da Costa, he denied having made the statement.[270]

In Brazil, prejudice had stemmed mostly from Calvinist preachers, while the wider population did not share these

---

[269] MARCUS, J. R. *The Colonial American Jew: 1492-1796*. Detroit: Wayne State University Press, 1969. p. 230.

[270] Ibid, p. 230.

sentiments. In New Amsterdam, however, both the rulers and common people were hostile to Jews and would regularly offend them, calling them fools.

David Ferera fell victim to these kinds of accusations when he was tried for removing a trunk from an official's home without the official's permission. The tone of the trial became more serious because the defendant, who was not a fluent speaker of Dutch, used "inappropriate" language. The sheriff adjudged that Ferera, who had been imprisoned with no right to bail, should be sentenced to a fine, public lashing and expulsion from the colony. The first sentencing demanded the payment of a fine of 800 guilders. The defendant appealed this decision and asked for an interpreter, a service provided by José da Costa. The final decision was taken to a jury, which reduced Ferera's fine to 120 guilders, plus 50 guilders to cover the cost of the trial. In their closing statement, the jury made it clear that Jews were unwelcome in the colony and could leave whenever they liked. The original harsh sentence handed down by the sheriff had clearly been influenced by the fact that Ferera was a Jew.[271]

The colony had a series of laws called "the Lord's Statutes," which regulated religious behavior. The Sunday Law prohibited work, travel and recreational activities on Sundays. The Blasphemy Law made it illegal to deny the Holy Trinity or refuse to accept Jesus as the messiah. There were harsh penalties for anyone found breaking these laws – prison, flogging and even death. If, in explaining his faith to a Christian, a Jew denied the New Testament, he could be arrested.[272]

Economic exclusion disguised as religious restriction could be observed in another set of laws which had existed on the Iberian Peninsula since the 15th century, and prevented Jews from accessing military orders, the Catholic Church and public office. Blood or heritage divided society into the "pure" and the "impure," a classification that carried with it the notion that the "malignant nature" of the Jews was passed down through blood to future

---

[271] FIELDSTEIN, Stanley. *The Land that I Show You: Three Centuries of Jewish Life in America*. New York: Anchor Press/Doubleday, 1978. p. 9.

[272] Ibid, p. 9.

generations. Stereotypes that had been repeated for generations also discriminated and excluded Jews from economic activity.[273]

The case of the "Brazilian," Abraham de Lucena, serves as an example: he was tried for selling goods during the Sunday sermon. Van Tienhoven was the prosecutor and demanded the court apply a fine of 600 guilders, far greater than the fine stipulated for this crime, and also that Abraham de Lucena's commercial license be revoked. As Lucena was a recent arrival and had been unaware of the laws of the land, he was ultimately released with only a caution.[274]

An exception occurred with another "Brazilian," Jacob de Lucena, or Lumbroso, who was indicted for blasphemy, before being mysteriously absolved. Might Lucena have agreed to baptism? His name, in its English adaptation, appears on documents affording him privileges usually only granted to Christians. In September, 1663, during the period of Jacob Lumbroso's trial, a man named John Lumbrozo received indemnity following a lawsuit – which appears to have been the same trial – using his anglicized name. The next year, Lumbroso served on the jury of another trial, a privilege only granted to Christians.[275]

There were frequent conflicts between Christians and Jews concerning Saturdays, but, after three years, the burgomasters finally recognized the significance of this holy day to Jews. When Jacob Barsinsom failed to appear in court to respond to two lawsuits, there were no reprisals, because both summonses had fallen precisely on Saturdays.

Elias Silva was tried and imprisoned for having intimate relations with a slave belonging to another man, but the charges were later dropped and he was released.[276]

In a colony that was extremely restrictive when it came to its religious principles, all those who did not practice the same set of beliefs were regarded with mistrust. The population complained

---

[273] CARNEIRO, Maria Luiza Tucci. O sangue como metáfora. Do antissemitismo tradicional ao antissemitismo moderno. In: *Ensaios sobre a intolerância*. São Paulo: Humanitas, 2005. p. 344-347.

[274] MARCUS, J. R. *The Colonial American Jew*, op. cit., p. 230.

[275] FIELDSTEIN, Stanley. *The Land that I Show You*, op. cit., p. 10.

[276] MARCUS, J. R. *The Colonial American Jew*, op. cit., p. 1,123-1,148.

about the Jews on a daily basis, pointing to their involvement in commerce, which had previously been run solely by Christians, observing that Jewish shops were never open on Saturdays, and that Jews, after earning their rights, now stood guard at the town fort, along with other citizens.

The population feared the arrival of an increasing number of Jews, potential competitors for local trade. The Jews were already afforded more opportunities in international trade than the Christians, because they spoke a number of languages and had relatives in different parts of the world, which facilitated the creation of international trade networks.

Involvement in local politics was an area that was closed off to Jews. In order to have a career in this field, Jews were required to convert to Christianity, or face never reaching the position they desired.

In 1655, the number of Jews in New Amsterdam increased, with animosity against the Jewish population rising proportionately. Megapolensis wrote various letters to "Classis," warning of the risk that the Jews might build a synagogue. In one of those letters, he writes: "We would like to request your intercedence with the directors of the company so that 'those godless people,' who bring nothing of benefit to this country, and look only to their own profit, may be sent far from here."[277]

During that same month, Stuyvesant had written various letters claiming to have refused a number of requests from Jews in relation to the practicing of their "abominable" religion.

Under English rule, there was little change in the anti-Jewish sentiment. In 1752, there were targeted protests by the populations of New York, Virginia, Charleston and Philadelphia following a production of Shakespeare's *The Merchant of Venice*. Other plays addressing aspects of Jewish life were performed, particularly those exploring the theme of the "Jewish villain". *The Fashionable Lover*, by Richard Cumberland, returned to the figure of the "inhuman Jewish moneylender"; *The Belle's Stratagem*, by Hannah Cowley, revived the stereotype of the satanic Jew; *The Young Quaker*, whose Jewish character, Shadrach Boaz, was described as the most

---

[277] O'CALLAGHAN, Edmund Bailey. *Documents Relative to The Colonial History of the State of New York*, Albany: Weed Parsons and Company, 1858. v. 2. p. 23-47.

repugnant ever to tread the boards, explored the innocence of a young woman at a difficult moment in her life.[278]

Theater and literature contributed to the propagation of anti-Jewish stereotypes. An example of this representation can be found in a verse included in a letter written by John Malcolm in 1790, and addressed to General Horatio Gates. The verse read:

Tax on tax young Belcour cries
More imposts, and a new exercise,
A Public debt's, a public blessing
Which 'tis of course a crime to lessen.
Each day a fresh report he broaches,
That Spies and Jews may ride in coaches.
Soldiers and Farmes don't despair,
Untax'd as yet are Earth and Air.[279]

The years following these theatrical productions saw a resurgence of the stereotype of the "Satanic Jew." In 1668, a Jewish merchant sued the Dutchman Balthazar d'Haert for fraud. D'Haert defended himself before the jury by stating that the merchant was a satanic Jew, and the jury found the Dutchman innocent.[280]

Even the synagogue of Newport was often called the "satanic synagogue." In 1743, during a long funeral procession which had departed from the Shearith Israel synagogue in New York, a group of people attacked the cortège and the synagogue with stones and pieces of wood. In 1746, the cemetery in Philadelphia was invaded and tombs were destroyed. In the same year, Chatham Square, the Jewish cemetery in Manhattan, was attacked, and its walls and tombs damaged. The merchant and community leader Jacob Franks offered a reward to anyone providing information on those responsible for the attack. In 1751, the act of vandalism was repeated, and Nathan Levy, Jacob Franks' brother-in-law, placed an ad in Philadelphia's *Pennsylvania Gazette* asking marksmen to stop

---

[278] CUMBERLANDS, Richard. *The Fashionable Lover: A Comedy*. London: W. Griffin at Garrick's Head, 1772.

[279] See FIELDSTEIN, Stanley. *The Land that I Show You*, op. cit., p. 17.

[280] MARCUS, J. R. *The Colonial American Jew*, op. cit., v. 3. p. 1,127.

using the walls of the Jewish cemetery on Spruce Street for target practice, and threatening to take the matter to the authorities.[281]

There was a curious case involving members of the colonial aristocracy. Olivier de Lancey, brother to the Chief Justice, James de Lancey, had been the lover of Phila Franks, a Jew, with whom he had a child. Seven years after the end of the affair, Oliver de Lancey was accused of invading the home of a Jewish immigrant, breaking all the furniture and verbally assaulting the proprietors. He had enlisted the help of friends for the occasion, and these had all been drunk and wearing hoods. De Lancey later explained that he had been attempting to seduce the woman of the house, a Dutch Jew, because she bore a resemblance to the wife of his great enemy, Governor George Clinton. This was a clear attempt to provoke his adversary.[282]

By the middle of the 18th century, anti-Semitic demonstrations were commonplace, and, in 1773, on the eve of the Jewish New Year, the Newport synagogue was attacked, its windows smashed using sticks and stones.

Conflicts between Jewish and non-Jewish merchants were frequent. On one occasion, in 1752, two Spanish ships, the *Saint Joseph* and the *Saint Helena*, loaded with gold and silver, had anchored at the port of Connecticut for technical reasons. The captain of the ship requested assistance, first from the Englishman Andrew McKenzie, before becoming suspicious of the man's intentions and turning to Benjamim Cardozo, a Jew who acted as an interpreter. Furious, McKenzie wrote to Dom Joseph Miguel de St. Juan, the person responsible for the ship and its cargo, explaining how "he had been strung along by the captain and by the faithless Jews, who had sold God out for money and then crucified him. How could you believe that he, a Portuguese-Spanish Jew, would behave

---

[281] SOLA POOL, David. *Portraits Etched in Stone: Jewish Settlers.* New York: Columbia University Press, 1953. p. 58.

[282] O'CALLAGHAN, Edmund Bailey, *Documents Relative to the Colonial History of the State of New York.* Albany: Weed, Parsons and Company, 1858. v. 6. p. 471. BRIDENBAUGH, Carl. *Cities in Revolt, Urban Life in America, 1743-1776.* New York: Knopf, 1955. p. 117-141.

honestly towards you? Where is the one place in which none of his kind are tolerated?"[283]

Other minorities, such as Lutherans, Quakers and Catholics, were also regarded mistrustfully because the Dutch rulers were followers of the Reformed Church. From the period of Dutch governance, Governor Stuyvesant had worried as much about the Lutherans as he did the Jews, going as far as deporting a pastor to Holland simply for being a Lutheran. He drafted a law prohibiting public or private religious gatherings, but, following direct intervention from the central government in Holland, this law was never enacted. When the first Quakers arrived in the colony, they were imprisoned and interrogated. Under the English administration, Presbyterians lost their right to deliver sermons for a time. The same happened with the Baptists, who were not granted permission to build a place of gathering until 1715. At the end of the 17th and beginning of the 18th century, there were still few Catholics in the settlement, and, in 1700, a law was passed banning Jesuits and Roman Catholics. If these insisted on remaining, they could face imprisonment and even the death penalty. The presence of Jews in the colony helped to reinforce the struggle for the conquest of civil, political and religious rights for all of these groups.

In the years of the American War of Independence (1775-1783), Jews had an ally on the General Assembly of New Hampshire in the Christian Samuel Langdon, who, during the assembly's elections, gave a speech entitled "The Republic of the Israelites, an Example to the American states."[284] The speech called upon Americans to learn from the example of the Jewish Republic of the pre-monarchic era. His argument was founded upon the importance of prayer for the strengthening of a people, and on the hypothesis that the Americans had been blessed by God, who had protected the colonies from the vengeance of the English and provided them with Washington as a servant of the American people. Langdon ended by

---

[283] The author of the letter was referring to the fact that Spain did not allow the presence of Jews within its territory. "Collections of the Connecticut Historical Society XVI, 200 ff., 225". Apud MARCUS, J. R. *The Colonial American Jew*, op. cit., p. 1,128.

[284] The speech was entitled "The Republic of the Israelites: An Example to the American States". In: LUTZ, Donald; WARREN, Jack D. *A Covenanted People: The Religious Tradition and the Origins of American Constitutionalism.* Rhode Island: The John Brown Carter Library, 1987. p. 69.

suggesting that the 12 tribes of Israel could be compared to the 13 states of the North American colony. The prayers of the people should confirm the New Constitution, as only then would they be able to demonstrate their suitability to be governed as a republic. Langdon's sermon had the desired effect, and New Hampshire became the ninth state to ratify the Constitution, giving the new government power to act.

Despite the enthusiasm for Jewish history following the War of Independence, it would be a number of years before Jews achieved equal legal rights. During the war, New York had granted Jews the right to vote and hold public office, but the Constitution adopted by the ten other states guaranteed full rights only to Christians. Restrictions on civil rights were not eradicated in Connecticut until 1818, in Massachusetts until 1821, in Maryland until 1826, on Rhode Island until 1843, in North Carolina until 1868 and in New Hampshire until 1877.

Anti-Semitic sentiment in the United States would endure for decades. An example of this was the Grand Union Hotel, belonging to captain Hilton, in Saratoga, which stopped accepting Jewish guests and turned away members of a prominent Jewish family. The scandal took on huge proportions, reaching the press and drawing criticism even from non-Jewish communities. The owner justified his actions by explaining that he only turned away loud and extravagant Jews. The Jewish community organized a boycott of shops belonging to the hotel proprietor. Clubs frequented by the financial elites also refused Jews membership.[285]

The struggle against anti-Semitism was a long process. The Jewish community was required to make a concerted effort to overcome anti-Semitic stereotypes. Gradually, Jews broke down barriers to universities, clubs, hotels and, fundamentally, the world of business.

Two centuries before the Statue of Liberty was gifted to the United States by the French in Manhattan, in 1886, Jews had already opened up a path to a free America.[286]

---

[285] ANGEL, Marc D. (Rabbi). Remnants of Israel: A Portrait of America's First Jewish Congregation – Shearith Israel. New York: Riverside Company Books, 2004. p. 28-36.

[286] SOLA POOL, David. *Portraits Etched in Stone*, op. cit., 1955, p. 36.

16. The Start of the Diaspora's Largest Community

The first festival to be celebrated within the newly-created Jewish community of New Amsterdam was the New Year, or Rosh Hashanah, of 1654. A formal religious service was organized, which also included the two Jews who had already been on the island, allowing for the formation of a *minyan* (the minimum number of men over the age of 13 required for Jewish prayers). The ceremony could not have taken place without the Torah, which had been saved from the shipwreck during the journey.[287]

By the next year, there were more men than necessary for a *minyan*. The new members arriving from Holland brought with them another Torah scroll and an ark in which to keep it, gifts from the Hispano-Portuguese community in Amsterdam. From that point onwards, religious services took place regularly on Shabbat and on religious holidays, and were carried out in private homes.

As the months went by, the community leaders began to think about building a synagogue. They dreamed of having a place for gatherings and discussions, where the newly-arrived could be received. The synagogue would become the focus of community life – there would be teachers to initiate the young in the study of the Torah, and organizations charged with caring for the needy, a concern and an obligation, or *mitzvah*, that was never forgotten by the Jews.[288]

Stuyvesant became aware of the intentions of the Sephardim and wrote to the directors of the West India Company, alerting them to the dangers of allowing public (non-Protestant) religious services. If Jews were allowed to profess their religion publicly, it would be impossible to prevent Christian dissidents, like Baptists, Lutherans

---

[287] MARCUS, J. R. *The Colonial American Jew, 1492-1776.* Detroit: Wayne State University Press, 1969. p. 218.

[288] SOLA POOL, David; SOLA POOL, Tamar de. *An Old Faith in the New World. Portrait of Shearith Israel, 1654-1954.* New York: Columbia University Press, 1955. p. 7. SOLA POOL, David. *Portraits Etched in Stone: Early Jewish Settlers.* New York: Columbia University Press, 1953. p. 10. SOLA POOL, David; PATAI, Raphael; CARDOZO, Abraham Lopes. *The World of Sephardim.* New York: Herzl Press, 1960. p. 12.

and Catholics, from doing the same. The Jewish cause was also the cause of all non-Calvinist Christians.[289]

After much debate, it was agreed that the practicing of other religions would be permitted "in the silence of the home." It appears the Jews were not particularly troubled by the colonial government's ruling, to the extent that, in 1658, religious gatherings would take place at the home of Mordecai Campanall, where Shabbat and the Jewish holidays were celebrated, and where Masonic meetings were also held.[290] The religious service followed Sephardic rituals, and the officiants were always volunteers – unable to count upon the presence of a rabbi, a *hazzan* would lead the services instead.[291]

The Shearith Israel synagogue was officially established at the end of the 17th century. A map of the city from 1695, produced by John Miller, features a rented house on Beaver Street that functioned as a synagogue and where, for a period of five years, religious activities took place. A real estate document provides evidence of a change of address in 1700, when a residence located on Mill Street, now South William Street, was used as a synagogue by the Jews. This house belonged to John Harpendick, and the street became known popularly as "Jews' Alley." Attached to this rented house, the Shearith Israel synagogue was later constructed, and would remain at this address for many years, before being moved to Central Park West, where it has been located to this day. The official name of the congregation is Kahal Kadosh Shearith Israel, or Holy Congregation of the Remnant of Israel.[292] The synagogue's first leader of prayer was Saul Pardo Brown, while its first cantor was Moses Lopes da Fonseca, son of the rabbi of the synagogue of Curaçao.[293]

---

[289] MARCUS, J. R. *The Colonial American Jew*, op. cit., v. 1, p. 221.

[290] KEREM, Itzchak. Sephardic Settlement in the British Colonies of the Americas in the 17th and 18th Centuries. In: VIGNE, Randolph; LITTLETON, Charles (Ed.s). From Strangers to Citizens: The Integration of Immigrant Communities in Britain, Ireland And Colonial America, 1550-1750. Brighton: Sussex Academic Press, 2001. p. 291.

[291] *Hazzan* is a Hebrew word designating a synagogue's cantor and leader of prayer.

[292] SOLA POOL, David. *Portraits Etched in Stone*, op. cit., p. 10.

[293] ARBELL, Mordechai. Early Relations Between the Jewish Communities in the Caribbean and the Guianas and those of the Near East 17th to 19th century. Available at: <http://www.sefarad.org/publication>; Accessed: 24 Nov. 2017.

The rabbi responsible for the synagogue on Mill Street was Abraham de Lucena, who had arrived in New Amsterdam from Holland in 1655, carrying the Torah scroll wrapped in green velvet and a damask cloak from India, which had been loaned by the synagogue of Amsterdam.[294] Accompanying Lucena were six more Jewish families from Holland.

The synagogue oversaw all aspects of Jewish religious life, including religious services, control of dietary laws – including the baking of unleavened bread during the Easter period – the Jewish life cycle (birth, religious coming of age, marriage and death), education, philanthropy, contact with Jews in other parts of the world, the upkeep of the cemetery and ritual baths.

The official language of the synagogue was Portuguese, and reports and official documents were written in this language, honoring its tradition as the language of the founders, something the leaders of the congregation made a point of upholding. Prayers were written and recited in Portuguese, especially the passages directed towards the local government.[295] Community members also communicated with each other in Portuguese, and sometimes Spanish. Later, with the arrival of Jews from Eastern Europe, German and Yiddish began to be spoken, as well as English, which, over time, became the common language. Hebrew and Ladino were only used for certain prayers.

Weddings during the colonial period normally took place on Wednesdays, with the exception of those involving widows, which were celebrated on other days of the week. Weddings were not always officiated by a rabbi or *hazzan*, as this is not a condition stipulated within the Torah – instead, marriages were sometimes overseen by an older male member of the family. The bride's dowry was arranged in advance between the couple's parents during the engagement period, and was registered in the marriage contract, or *ketubah*, which also established the fine to be paid if the wedding were called off. These details can be observed in the template of a *ketubah* from 1738, which describes the stages to be carried out when filling in the contract. These instructions would be

---

[294] SOLA POOL, David. *Portraits Etched in Stone*, op. cit., p. 40.

[295] During the religious service of Shabbat, part of the prayer sequence is a prayer for protection directed towards the government under which the community resides.

unnecessary if the wedding were being officiated by a rabbi, but the document proves that the majority of men in the community were well acquainted with Hebrew and Aramaic, since the template includes many words in these languages, as well as Portuguese.[296] The majority of marriage ceremonies were held in the home of the bride or groom, as inviting people into the home was seen as synonymous with hospitality and elegance, while having a wedding in the congregation building was regarded as impersonal.

Marriage between Jews and Christians was forbidden, and religious conversion considered unacceptable, on pain of excommunication for the Jewish man or woman attempting to convert their partner. A Jewish woman who married outside the community was considered lost to Judaism, while men who did so often continued to attend the synagogue. The children of either type of union were almost always raised as Christians. This rule was imposed after 1663 and was influenced by Jews arriving from London, who proposed that the rules adopted by the London Jewish community should also be applied in New Amsterdam. There was no impediment to weddings between Jews and New Christians wishing to return to Judaism.

Circumcision ceremonies followed the same pattern as weddings. By the end of the 17th century, New York had a specialist in this role, a *mohel*, Abraham I. Abraham, who would travel to any part of the colony where he was required. The events of the Jewish life cycle were always an opportunity for the community to socialize. Even funerals presented opportunities for reunions, as the performance of the ritual of morning prayer, which lasted for one week, was an occasion when family and friends would be received and provided with meals in the home of the family that had lost a relative.

Jewish dietary laws began to be adhered to more strictly once Asser Levy obtained his butcher's license. At this point, any meat consumed would be prepared in accordance with the rituals outlined within the Jewish bible.

---

[296] *Ketubah* provided by a New Your antiquarian. Mr Goldman.

Saturdays were faithfully respected. Even the Dutch government of New Amsterdam and the local town hall respected this right.[297]

As with every place where Jews organized themselves into a community, in New Amsterdam there was also a concern with the neediest among them. Following the winter of 1654-1655, there were no further complaints from Protestant deacons about having to provide for impoverished Jews, despite all assistance in the colony being controlled by the Reformed Church and financed by the mercantile elite of Amsterdam.

In contrast to what had taken place in Recife, in New Amsterdam there are no signs of the existence of autonomous Jewish charitable organizations at the beginning of the colonial period. After the establishment of the synagogue, this work became part of the responsibilities of that institution. The synagogue received donations from the wealthier Jews within the community and from Jewish institutions in Amsterdam, and its role was to provide food, clothing, an education for needy children, financial assistance for orphans and widows, shelter for travelers, and dowries for impoverished women. Listed among the articles of the synagogue's constitution at the beginning of the 18th century, it is possible to find a rule allowing any traveler or immigrant requiring assistance from the synagogue a sum of 8 shillings a week, for up to twelve weeks.

In 1785, the Hebra Gemilut Hasadim, or Society of Deeds of Loving Kindness, was founded, with the aim of providing financial and medical assistance to the needy. This work included home visits and aid for the sick, as well as funds for funerals and social care.[298]

An epidemic of yellow fever hit the community in 1798, leading to many deaths. The reverend Gershon Mendes Seixas raised funds from among the members of the New York synagogue to help those affected and to provide funeral assistance for the families of the dead.[299]

---

[297] MARCUS, J. R. *The Colonial American Jew*. Michigan: Wayne State University Press, 1970. v. 2. P. 955.

[298] ANGEL, Marc D. (Rabbi). Remnant of Israel: A Portrait of America's First Jewish Congregation – Shearith Israel. New York: Riverside Company Books, 2004. p. 104.

[299] Gershon Mendes Seixas was the second *hazzan* of the Shearith Israel synagogue; the first was Saul Pardo, and before him religious ceremonies were officiated by members of the community. Seixas is described as "reverend" because he was not a rabbi. In the

In July 1655, during the early days of the colonization, a request was made for a license to purchase a plot of land intended for the construction of a cemetery. Why was this? Because, for the Jewish community, the building of a cemetery was seen as a sign that they had established themselves permanently. This request was denied, under the excuse that there had yet to be a single death within the Jewish community. The community leaders argued that in Recife and Holland Jews had been buried in different locations to Christians, and in accordance with religious laws that are as significant after death as they are in life. Following the death of a Jew, in 1677, the authorities granted the community a small piece of land beyond the walls of the settlement for the construction of a cemetery. Supposedly, it was there that the community leader, Asser Levy, was buried.[300]

In 1682, when already under English rule, the New Christian Joseph Bueno de Mesquita, who had lived in Dutch Brazil and arrived in New York from London around 1680, bought a plot of land from William Merret that was approximately 52 feet x 52 feet in size, and was intended for the construction of a Jewish graveyard. The plot lay east of Park Row Highway, below Chatham Square and Saint James Place, and beside a stream, where Chinatown is today. The graveyard still exists, but visitor access is restricted.

The first Jew to be buried in New York was a member of the Bueno de Mesquita family, Benjamin Bueno de Mesquita, who died in 1683. Benjamin had lived in Brazil during the Dutch occupation and his name is included in the Minute Book of the Zur Israel synagogue in Recife. Upon leaving Recife, Benjamin Bueno de Mesquita and his brother Joseph first tried living in Portugal as New Christians, before leaving the Iberian Peninsula years later to end their days in New Amsterdam.[301]

---

synagogue he was referred to as *hazzan* and outside the Jewish community it was "minister" or "reverend". Seixas was devoted to the spiritual life and also very active in public life. He was the founder of the New York Humane Society and one of the founders of Colombia College. SOLA POOL, David. *Portraits Etched in Stone*, op. cit., p. 46. ANGEL, Marc D. (Rabbi), op. cit., p. 34-39.

[300] COHEN, Martin A.; PECK, Abraham J. (Eds.) *Sephardim in the Americas: Studies in the Culture and History*. Tuscaloosa/London: American Jewish Archives/University of Alabama Press, 1993. p. 157.

[301] MARCUS, J. *The Colonial American Jew*, op. cit., v. 2, p. 1,019.

Figure 3. Main Streets with a Jewish Presence in Manhattan

The tombs in the Jewish graveyard are still intact. It is possible to identify the gravestones of Joseph Tores Nunes (1704), Samuel Levy (1719), Moses Levy (1728), Abraham Burgos (1723), Sarah Bueno de Mesquita (1708) and Sarah Rodrigues de Rivera (1727). This graveyard is currently the second oldest in New York and is preserved to this day – the oldest cemetery in the city belongs to the Protestants.[302]

Sarah Bueno de Mesquita was the wife of Benjamin Bueno de Mesquita; Moses Levy and Samuel Levy were brothers and prominent merchants who had arrived from London at the end of the 17th century. As for the other Jews identified in the graveyard, we have very little information about who they were.

The Chatham Square Cemetery was purchased in the name of a natural person. As with the Episcopalian and Lutheran churches, the Jewish community, as a juridical person, did not yet have the right to acquire property, which is why the contract needed to be signed in this way.

During the early years of establishing themselves, the Portuguese who had arrived from Pernambuco found themselves without a Jewish school, in contrast to what had taken place in Recife, where the community had had a fully functioning educational system. In New York, the first Jewish school was built in 1730. Children would receive their secular educations in schools run by the Protestant church, which incurred a tax. There were Jewish tutors, responsible for the religious education of children, especially in preparation for *bar mitzvah*, religious coming of age. Reading in Hebrew was taught through the study of the Pentateuch and through prayer. Children unable to pay either the school tax or for a private tutor had their costs covered by the community leaders. The tutors were generally men with little spending power, or those who were just starting out in business and in need of an extra source of income. They were knowns as rabbis, or ribbis. One of the first rabbis in the region, Jerachmeel (Valentijn) Falk, lived in the 17th century, and was better known as Valentine Vanderwilde, brother-in-law to the influential New Amsterdam community leader, Asser Levy. In 1716, at the beginning of the 18th century, Judah Monis, a merchant recently arrived from Holland via Jamaica, instructed

---

[302] SOLA POOL, David. *Portraits Etched in Stone*, op. cit., p. 11.

children within the community in Judaism and provided Hebrew classes for Christians. In 1728, the *shohet*, a Sephardic Jew named Benjamin Elias, was also a teacher of Hebrew, and received a salary from the Shearith Israel synagogue for this role.[303]

In 1731, the Jewish school in New York opened its doors definitively. The school had been built by Mendes da Costa, a prominent Sephardic Jew from London. During the first half of the century, classes were taught in Portuguese and Spanish, and after 1750, in English. Children attended the school for half the day, either in the morning or afternoon. The classes concerned religion, with an emphasis on Hebrew and the Torah. In 1755, there was a change in the curriculum, and secular studies were introduced.[304]

Access to books and libraries was limited during the colonial period. The few books that did exist in New Amsterdam were private property. Even wealthier Jews only owned a small number of books, normally related to Jewish liturgy. In Boston, Samuel Frazao, who had taught at the Jewish school in Recife, kept a small library, including books on Jewish philosophy and a Spanish copy of the Bible.[305] In Pennsylvania, one of the first Jewish colonizers of Portuguese origin, Isaac Miranda, owned a copy of Hayyim Vital's kabbalistic work *Sha'ar ha Gilgulim*, from 1683, as well as manuscripts in Spanish and Portuguese relating to controversies involving Judaism and Christianity. He also kept a manuscript in prose and verse authored by Isaac de Castro, the martyr of the Inquisition of Lisbon. The greatest Jewish library of the colonial period, containing works in Hebrew and tomes on philosophy, belonged to Nathan Levy, one of the founders of the Philadelphia community, and the son of Moses Levy. The teachers Benjamin Elias and Judah Samuel, from New York, were very learned men and the owners of various religious and secular works, among them a manuscript of the Talmudic tractate, the *Makkot*.

---

[303] MARCUS, J. R. *The Colonial American Jew*, op. cit., v. 2, p. 1,095-1,097.

[304] Ibid, p. 1,074-1,077.

[305] ANGEL, Marc D. (Rabbi). *A Portrait of America's First Jewish Congregation – Shearith Israel.* New York: Riverside Company Book, 2004. Samuel Frazao is registered in the book of minutes of the Zur Israel Synagogue of Recife under the name Semuel Frazao.

Judah Monis was the first Jew in the English colonies to receive an academic diploma. He enrolled at Harvard University in 1720, after spending some years in New York, and became the first specialist in Hebrew, upon graduating from Harvard, as well as being the author of the first Hebrew grammar published in North America.

The first Jewish woman to attend university was Richea Gratz, who studied at Franklin College. Richea belonged to a family of Philadelphia merchants from the end of the 17th century.[306]

During the first years of the colonization, there were no Jewish hospitals, but some widows within the community received a salary from the synagogue for caring for its sick members. Patients were lodged in the houses of these woman and were attended as though at a medical center. The widows performed the role of nurses and, when a death occurred, were responsible for making all provisions for the funeral.[307]

One of the great problems faced by the community in New York was the isolation of the region, which affected the relationships between Jews. Dispersed across the territory, some men married Christian women, with their children being raised as Christians. Many Jews exchanged their Portuguese or Spanish names for English ones (under English rule), which makes it difficult to identify their descendants. The Jewish elite was left stunned when the children of Abigail Levy Franks and Jacob Franks, David and Phila, each married Christians – David married Margaret Evans, from Philadelphia, and Phila, Oliver de Lancey, both members of distinguished families in Christian colonial society. When Naphtali Franks' daughter died, she left her inheritance to the cause of converting Jews to Christianity. Due to the large number of mixed marriages, there are no longer any Jews to be found among the Franks' descendants.[308]

---

[306] MARCUS. J. R. *American Jewish Woman, 1654-1980*. New York/Cincinnati: KTVA Publishing House/American Jewish Archives, 1981. p. 25.

[307] PUBLICATIONS of American Jewish Historical Society. XXI, 80, 87-88, 91, 106, 109, 115; XXII, 161; XXVII, 22. SOLA POOL, David, op. cit., 1953, p. 89. MARCUS, J. R. *American Jewish Woman, 1654-1980*, op. cit., v. 2, p. 1,040.

[308] Abigail was the daughter of Moses Levy, an important merchant from Philadelphia, and married Jacob Franks, an Ashkenazi Jew. Together they founded the Levy-Franks clan, an important Jewish family

There is speculation about the conversion of certain Jews to Christianity during the 17th century. Isaac Israel, one of the Sephardi pioneers from Brazil, established himself in South River, Delaware, in 1655. Eight years later, a man, also named Israel, became a member of the Dutch council and filled the vacancy of vice-director for South River County – he had been a merchant for some time in Passyunk, today part of Philadelphia. This Israel was Isaac, or one of the other Israels from New Amsterdam, and must have converted to Christianity, otherwise he would have been unable to attain this political position, since during this period Jews were still prohibited from holding a political position in the Dutch colonies.

Most Jews fought to retain their religion and traditions. In 1686 after the revocation of the Edict of Nantes, in France, the families of French Marranos began arriving in New York. Among them were the Robles, Gomez and Lopez families. The devotion of these families to Judaism is documented in their family mottos:

> Boundless as the fishes of the sea
> was honour and integrity of the Gomez family,
> supported by lion's strength did their faith uphold,
> nor would they change it for a crown of gold. [309]

These families were heavily involved in the Shearith Israel Congregation of New York.

The New Christian Aaron Lopez arrived in Newport directly from Portugal, in 1752, along with his wife, Abigail, his daughter, Sarah, and his brother, David. He was approximately 21 years old at the time. His wife had relatives in New York; the Gomez family provided support for all of them during their early days in the city. [310] The Lopez family were fugitives from the Portuguese Inquisition, which is why they quickly exchanged their Christian names for Jewish ones. New Christians fleeing from the Portuguese Inquisition were well-received by members of the Jewish community in New York. Some would submit to circumcision, like Aaron Lopez

---

[309] AMERICAN JEWISH ARCHIVES, XIV, 66; MARCUS J. R., American Jewish documents, I, 42 ff., 57-57.

[310] The Gomez family arrived in New York between 1685 and 1743. They left Curaçao accompanied by the Rivera family. There was intermarriage between these families, which reinforced the ties between them. After Abigail's death, Aaron Lopes married Sarah, the daughter of Jacob Rivera, who, as well as his father-in-law, became his business partner. See ARBELL, Mordechai, op. cit. MARCUS, J. R. op. cit. v. 2, p. 642.

himself in 1750, having been received by his cousin, Daniel Gomez. Daniel had remained by Aaron's side during the circumcision ceremony and had hailed him, stating that this was the manifestation of sacred law.[311]

Both the Lopez and Gomez families were great merchants and contributed to the economic and spiritual growth of the community, helping to retain its traditions and assisting with the upkeep of the synagogue.

A section of the Jews who left Dutch Recife had made for England upon leaving Brazil. Members of the Nunes and Machado families, who were related, endured the terrible experience of the inquisitorial prisons in Portugal and, in 1733, sought refuge in the Savannah region. The patriarch of the Nunes family, Moses, had lived in Dutch Brazil, and, in 1654, left for England. Years later, his son, Dr Samuel Nunes, already fifty years old and accompanied by his own son, Moses, a name inherited from his grandfather, arrived in Savannah. They became Jewish pioneers of the region, part of a group of approximately fifteen people.[312]

By the middle of the 17th century, the Jewish community in New York had begun to feel the need to translate the Hebrew prayers into English. In 1766, Isaac Pinto, *hazzan* of the Sephardic synagogue, published a prayer book in English that covered *Shabbat, Rosh Hashanah* and *Yom Kippur* – the prayers follow the Portuguese and Spanish ritual.[313]

The first Jewish sermon published in North America was written in 1773 by Rabbi Haim Isaac Carigal, a Palestinian Jew who had

---

[311] Aaron Lopez became the greatest businessman of his era. He engaged in commerce with the Gulf of Guinea, England and the West Indies. He had correspondents (associated offices) in the Mediterranean, the Iberian Peninsula, Holland, Germany and Scandinavia and became the owner of a fleet of thirty ships.

[312] Dr Samuel Nunes was born in Portugal, in Beira Alta. It appears his parents had returned to Portugal from London. The details of the events which took place between their leaving Brazil and their arrival in Savannah remain nebulous. See STERN, Malcolm. Portuguese Sephardim in the Americas. In: COHEN, Martin A; PECK, Abraham J. (eds.). *Sephardim in the Americas: Studies in Culture and History.* Tuscaloosa/London: American Jewish Archives/University of Alabama Press, 1993. MARCUS, J. R. *The American Colonial Jew*, op. cit., p. 355.

[313] *Shabbat* is the sacred day of the Jews. *Rosh Hashanah* is the Jewish New Year. *Yom Kippur* is the Jewish day of atonement, a day dedicated to prayer. A *hazzan* is a liturgical cantor.

spent five months travelling through Philadelphia, New York and Newport. During his visit to Rhode Island, he made friends with the minister of the local Christian congregation, Ezra Stiles, who would later become president of Yale University. Stiles helped Carigal publish his sermon, which was delivered in Spanish, interspersed with words in Hebrew, at the Rhode Island synagogue, Newport, on May 28, 1773, in commemoration of the Jewish feast of Shavuot.[314] The men became great friends and, after Carigal left, he and Stiles began exchanging correspondence, particularly in relation to Stiles's interest in the Hebrew language. The speech "The Salvation of Israel" was translated into English by a Sephardic Jew named Abraham Lopes, of Newport, becoming the first Jewish sermon to be published in North America.[315]

During the American War of Independence, the Shearith Israel synagogue represented the main center of support for the revolutionaries. The *hazzan* of the Manhattan Island synagogue was Gershon Mendes Seixas, who had been born in the United States, in New York. In August, 1776, when George Washington lost the Battle of Brooklyn Heights, Seixas fled the city with the Torah scroll hidden among his belongings and joined other patriots in New Port, Rhode Island and Connecticut.

On the eve of independence, there were eleven Jewish communities in the United States, all predominantly of Portuguese and Spanish origin. The largest concentration of Jews could be found in Charleston, numbering almost 400 people. The other communities were smaller, but played a fundamental role in the growth of Judaism in what would become the United States of America.

---

[314] The feast of *Shavuot* relates to the time when the Jews received the Tablets of the Law, the Ten Commandments, on Mount Sinai.

[315] Haim Isaac Carigal (1729-1777). A sermon preached at the synagogue, in Newport, Rhode Island, called "The Salvation of Israel" (28 May, 1773). Rhode Island: S. Southwick, Abraham Lopez (trad.), 1773. PESTANA, Carla Gardina. *Liberty of Conscience and the Growth of Religious Diversity in Early America*, 1637-1786. Rhode Island: The John Carter Brown Library, 1986. p. 64.

17. Businessmen

Portuguese Jews – businessmen from Holland – looked to take advantage of the new economic opportunities that were opening up in the Dutch colony in North America. Among their goals, there was also the project of securing a safe region in which unsettled Sephardic Jews could live. Many traveled with their families, or married Protestant or Jewish women from Amsterdam as soon as they reached the new land – these "brides" began arriving in the colony with their relatives after 1655.

In the 17th century, New Amsterdam was a trading post for the West India Company. The sheriff, Nicassius de Sille, described it as:

A village dependent on the fur trade between colonists and Indians, in which all the inhabitants are traders – wealth consists of plough horses, cows, sheep and goats. The rivers have fish in abundance, and strawberries and blackberries can be picked from the bushes.[316]

With the passing of years, trade developed, and the small village gradually transformed into a town. The rustic wooden houses were replaced by bricks-and-mortar constructions, the roads were paved, gardens were pruned and arranged symmetrically, animals were taken off the streets, and the small stream, which cut through the center of town, was widened to form a canal, its banks reinforced with staves. The modest taverns were refashioned into attractive cafés, where the townspeople could meet to exchange ideas, plan trading ventures and discuss the past and future.[317]

The diet of the future New Yorkers was based on cheese and butter, and these items were often used as exchangeable goods, meaning dairy cows were regarded as carrying important economic

---

[316] SOLA POOL, David; SOLA POOL, Tamar de. *An Old Faith in the New World. Portrait of Shearith Israel, 1654-1954*. New York: Columbia University Press, 1955. p. 19.

[317] See MAIKA, Dennis J. *Commerce and Community: Manhattan Merchants in the Seventeenth Century*. 1995. Thesis (PhD) – New York University, New York. JAMESON, J. Franklin. *Narratives of New Netherland, 1609-1664*. New York: Scribner, 1909.

value. The system of barter, moreover, was widely used. Agricultural products, such as wheat, oats, barley, corn, pork and beef, were treated as assets and could be used to pay taxes. Also considered currency were beaver skins, *wampum* (a kind of Native American shell-beaded belt) and Dutch florins. The use of *wampum* went into decline during the 1650s, when the trading of agricultural products intensified. The disadvantage of using cereals as a form of payment was related to the quality of harvests, and contracts would often stipulate the value of a transaction in guilders, which could later be converted into wheat or other products. The land was extremely fertile and, therefore, allowed for the production of a variety of foodstuffs.[318]

Nevertheless, agriculture became regarded as a low-income activity as trading in furs with the Indians began to prove far more profitable.

New Holland's society faced serious challenges in terms of survival, internal disputes and animosities, and trade still bore traces of mediaeval structures.[319]

Day laborers only began to be remunerated for their work after the arrival of the first Jews, in 1654, receiving two guilders per day in corn, beaver skins or *wampum*.[320]

The economic freedom conceded to the Jews, who faced discrimination, was limited to trade within the small group of refugees who had arrived from Brazil. Yet, despite these restrictions, which were also enforced in Amsterdam, the Dutch had no interest in losing the support of the Jewish immigrants at a time when Holland's main rival, England, was expanding its control over the Caribbean.

Economic leadership within the small Jewish community of New Amsterdam was initially centered on five merchants of Portuguese origin, who had arrived from Amsterdam after fleeing Brazil, in 1655: Abraham de Lucena, Salvador d'Andrada, Jacob Cohen Henriques, Joseph d'Acosta and David Ferera. These men would be called upon by the colonial rulers to sign important

---

[318] RINK, Oliver A. Holland on the Hudson: An Economic and Social History of Dutch New York. New York: Cornell, 1986, p. 25-92.

[319] New Amsterdam was only one part of the Dutch territory known as New Holland.

[320] RINK, Oliver A. op. cit., p. 27.

petitions, and wielded enough power in the European metropolis for their Jewish associates to be able to intercede with the West India Company and burgomasters in Amsterdam.[321]

As in Dutch Brazil, Jews served as interpreters, and were indispensable in commercial transactions or legal disputes with the Spanish colonies and those in the Caribbean. These were men who engaged in a variety of pursuits, from butchers and bakers to great merchants. In fact, the New Amsterdam merchant class challenged any attempt at categorization – even men of great social and economic standing were involved in basic day-to-day activities, like making bread, slaughtering animals or brewing beer.[322] Jacob Henriques Cohen, one of the twenty-three refugees from Brazil, serves as an example, having tried to obtain a license to make and sell bread, but seeing his request turned down. Cohen was not a humble baker, but rather a businessman who wanted to diversify his commercial activity and break into the monopoly of local bakers, as well as be able to make bread in accordance with Jewish dietary laws. In Dutch Brazil, he had been a prosperous merchant, a member of the directorship of the Jewish community in Recife, and his son, Abraham Cohen Henriques, or Francisco Vaz de Leon, was a shareholder in the West India Company, having lived in the Dutch colonies of Recife and New Amsterdam and set up businesses in both places. On one occasion, in 1659, he had sued a Dutchman, by the name of Cornelis Janss Plavier, for nonpayment on a loan of 1,625 guilders, which was supposed to have been covered by the sale of a shipment of beaver skins in Amsterdam during the previous Autumn. Asser Levy acted as legal representative in the trial over the fulfilment of the debt. The court ruled that the defendant should mortgage his residence in Manhattan, located on Heere Straat (today, Broadway Steet) and honor the debt.[323]

Jews were also involved in wholesaling and retailing, but on a modest scale. Some merchants imported products directly from

---

[321] Ibid, p. 54.

[322] MAIKA, Dennis J. *Commerce and Community*, op. cit. MIDDLETON, S. "Artisans and Trade Privileges in New Amsterdam". Norwich: University of East Anglia. Work presented during the Rensselaerswijck Seminar, New York, 2001.

[323] HERSHKOWITZ, Leo. Dutch Notarial Records Pertaining to Asser Levy, 1659-1692, op. cit.

Holland to be sold on in the colony, while others became involved in grander ventures, entering into partnerships with the Dutch and English.

On one occasion, Asser Levy, the dynamic immigrant from Brazil, purchased a shipment of Dutch manufactured wares and gave the owner 75% of the fee as an advance, offering the mortgage on his home in New Amsterdam as a guarantee to the supplier.

Gradually, the Jewish population began to occupy a position within the colony's social hierarchy, demonstrated by elegant furniture and household items purchased from tradesmen and sales agents. Small European luxuries began arriving in Manhattan, such as damasks, saffron, quality paper, sassafras, sarsaparille, medicines and medical equipment.[324]

Products imported from Europe were advertised in local newspaper. In an edition of the *New York Gazette* from March 3, 1729, a Jew named Luis Gomes announced the sale of a collection of fine bowls, decorated with a coat of arms.

Numerous Jews were able to expand their businesses to other regions, particularly the Caribbean. At the time, Curaçao and Surinam were the largest Jewish hubs in the Caribbean and, since they were great sugar-producing areas, they witnessed an intensification of this trade.[325] This connection can be traced in the documents of the Pisa family, who are listed as the responsible party on a number of inventories along the trade route between New York, Surinam and Barbados.

The economic ties between Sephardic Jews in Curaçao and New York were strengthened by marriages between young members of the middle-class families in the two regions. Esther Levy, of New York, for example, married Daniel Gomes, of Curaçao, an active merchant who shipped goods from Spanish America to New York.[326] This trade route was also used by Isaac de Mesa, of South

---

[324] ARBELL, Mordechai. Early Relations Between the Jewish Communities in the Caribbean and the Guianas and those of the Near East 17th to 19th century. p. 1-5. Available at: <http://www.sefarad.org/publication>; Accessed: 24 Nov. 2017.

[325] ARBELL, Mordechai. Early Relations Between the Jewish Communities in the Caribbean and the Guianas and

[326] Ibid.

River, whose name appears on commercial contracts in Surinam and Barbados, too.

It was customary for Dutch merchants from the Caribbean and New Amsterdam, including a number of Jews, to establish trade between these two colonies, which were both ruled under the same flag and government.

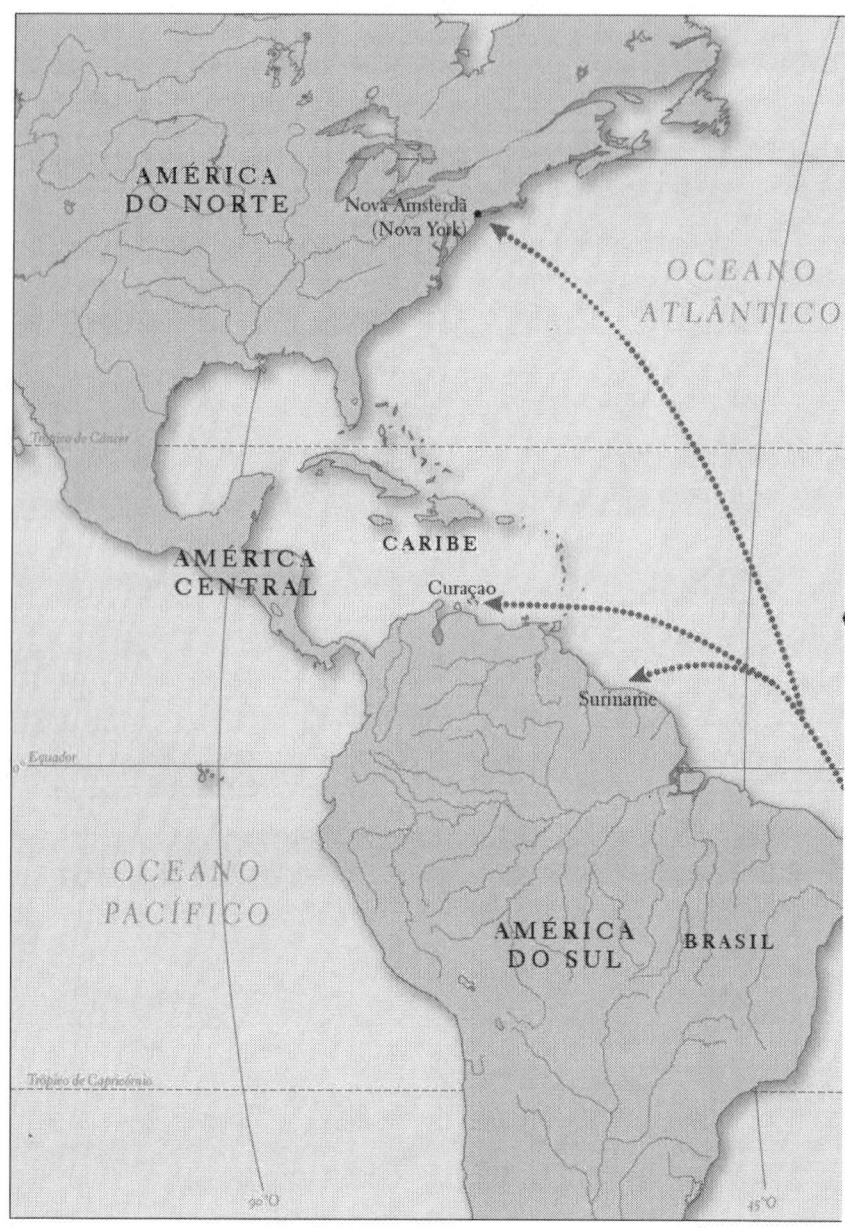

Figure 4. North America Trade Routes

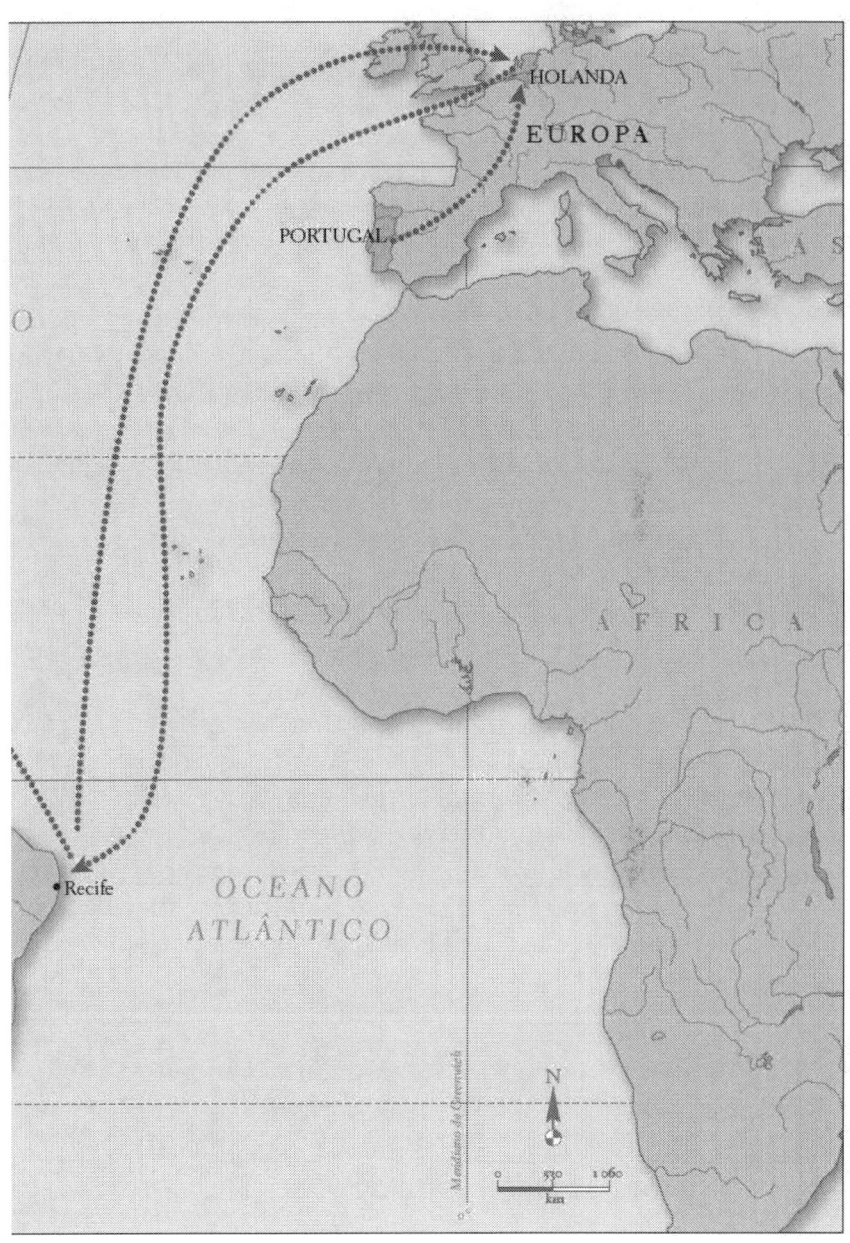

Figure 5. European Trade Routes

Peter Stuyvesant tried to prevent Jews from participating in the rapidly growing beaver skin trade at Fort Orange, located between the Hudson and Mohawk rivers. The region boasted a number of sawmills and brickyards, and these constructions quickly became a center for trade. The great urban expansion around Fort Orange and the arrival of an increasing number of immigrants led to the creation of a shelter, where people could stay while looking for work.[327] By 1660, Fort Orange was already the colony's second largest settlement, with a thousand inhabitants.

Jews were prohibited from trading with the Delaware Indians of the Hudson River, to the south.[328] Their leaders, Abraham de Lucena, Salvador d'Andrada and Jacob Cohen Henriques, appealed to the governor and his council, arguing that the West India Company had granted permission for all members of the community to trade within any region under Dutch jurisdiction. The appeal was rejected, although permission was granted for two men to travel south in order to investigate future commercial opportunities. The Jews, however, would only be able to act with complete freedom once the Dutch occupied the Swedish colonies in Delaware, in September, 1655.[329]

When it came to the frontier to the north of New Amsterdam, the situation was different: Jews were allowed to do business here from the start. It was a wild and difficult region to access, and those venturing northwards had to form alliances with the natives, who were generally hostile. The colonial government refused to offer any military assistance. The first Jews to become involved in this endeavor were Abraham de Lucena, Salvador d'Andrade and Jacob

---

[327] SHATTUCK, Martha. A Civil Society: Court and Community in Beverwijk, New Netherland, 1652-1654. 1993. Thesis (PhD) – Boston University, Boston.

[328] Fort Orange was a colonial trading post at the confluence of the Mohawk and Hudson rivers. See LAER, Van A. J. F. *New York Historical Manuscripts: Dutch.* Baltimore: Genealogical Publishing, 1974. v. 1. Register of Provincial Secretary, 1638-1642.

[329] Swedish colonizers arrived in the Delaware region in 1638 and founded the New Sweden colony. The Swedes had been sent by their country's government in order to build trade in the region. In 1655, the Dutch assembled a force with the intention of bringing the region under Dutch rule. The attack on the Delaware colonies was undertaken by six hundred men transported on seven ships. By the end of the battle, the Swedes were unable to hold out and surrendered the region.

Henriques Cohen, as well as Benjamin Cardozo and Isaac Israel, two young men who had recently arrived from Brazil, via Holland.[330]

By the spring of 1656, the Jewish businesses in South River had obtained licenses. They traded goods and drink with the Indians in exchange for skins and tobacco, which were sold on in Manhattan. José da Costa, a Jewish immigrant from Brazil, was a prominent figure at the time.[331] As an investor in the West India Company, he was sometimes confused with his nephew of the same name, who shipped merchandise from the same port.

Jews in the colony traded in furs, wheat, cattle, rams, butter, cheese, clothes and tools. Like other inhabitants, they also engaged in bartering, exchanging shoes for wheat or beer for tobacco.

The three commodities most often used in exchanges were liquor, tobacco and furs. According to Peter Stuyvesant's reports, liquor, in particular, was an important part of New Amsterdam's economy, to the extent that one in four houses in the town sold alcohol. Jewish merchants traded in hard liquor, beer and wine, with these drinks generally being imported from the Caribbean, though a small amount of alcohol was produced in the colony by local craftsmen.[332]

Tobacco was one of the main commercial crops, planted in large quantities and brought in from Maryland and Virginia. It was often traded for European products. Jacob Lumbroso, one of the twenty-three refugees from Brazil, cultivated tobacco in Maryland and sold it to Jewish merchants. By the end of 1650, tobacco harvests were being used as a currency, and Jews like Jacob Cohen Henriques, Abraham de Lucena and David Ferera were active participants in these transactions. Between 1656 and 1660, David Ferera bought and sold tobacco and other goods from Maryland, as well as transporting these products on his own ship, according to official records.[333] Abraham de Lucena formed a partnership with Luiz Gomez, a Marrano recently arrived from Portugal, and dedicated

---

[330] MARCUS, J. R. *The Colonial American Jew.* Detroit: Wayne State University Press, 1970. v. 2. p. 615-618.

[331] José da Costa was part of the directorship of the Jewish community in Recife.

[332] MAIKA, Dennis J. *Commerce and Community*, op. cit., p. 215. MARCUS, J. R. op. cit. v. 2, p. 569 and 583-588.

[333] MARCUS, J. R. op. cit., v. 2, p. 615-619.

himself to the exporting of large quantities of wheat to Lisbon and the importing of Portuguese wine.[334]

Despite signs of intense commercial activity, there was very little money in circulation. As a result, Jews followed the example of other merchants, paying rent for their commercial establishments in beaver skins, brandy and other goods agreed between parties. Only in 1680 was the use of silver coins introduced as a method of payment.[335]

The New Amsterdam economy gained momentum when members of Jewish family networks in England began emigrating to New York at the end of the 17th and beginning of the 18th century. Among these families were the Levys, Franks, Simsons, Nuneses, Pachecos, Machados and Seixases, who were all related in some way. These families brought with them new contacts that expanded trade, as well as introducing fresh currency in the form of loans and financing.

At the end of the 17th century, Jews still faced many restrictions to their businesses. Until 1690, they were prohibited from owning retail stores. In an attempt to overcome this restriction, they set up makeshift shops outside or at the back of their homes. Some were able to rely upon initial loans from relatives in London or Holland to start their businesses. This was the case with David Ferera in Maryland, who, among other commercial activities, owned a shop selling household items. Moses Levy and Jacob Franks, two of the most prominent businessmen of the 18th century in New York and Philadelphia, had begun their careers as shopkeepers and had been reliant upon financial backing from their London brothers, by means of partnerships. A trading arrangement was reached between businessmen and shopkeepers: merchants would provide products in bulk or on credit with deferred payment, and were responsible for importing and shipping them from London or the Caribbean ports, with the debt incurred only being repaid once products had been sold on to the end consumer.

The great shopkeepers offered their clients a wide variety of consumable goods. In 1745, the inventory of shopkeeper Isaac Levy,

---

[334] FELDSTEIN, Stanley. *The Land that I Show You: Three Centuries of Jewish Life in America.* New York: Anchor Press/Doubleday, 1978. p. 12-13.

[335] RINK, Oliver A. op. cit., 1986.

from New York, included tea, beeswax, pens, ink, clothing for women and children and even musical instruments, including 24 different kinds of harp.

Just as in Eastern and Central Europe, Jewish women also contributed to local commerce, having had a long history of participation in this sector, a tradition that was resumed in New Amsterdam. As shopkeepers or influential merchants, widows would often take over the businesses of their deceased husbands, and even single and married women who were allowed to manage small stores. One example of an influential merchant was Rachel Levy, sister of Asser Levy, who controlled the rum importation business for Boston and Rhode Island and sometimes brought in chocolate from Curaçao[336].

Retailing was generally considered a modest trade, dealing in small household goods, medicines and local newspapers. Frequently, the majority of sales were carried out door-to-door, heading directly to the consumer, with the shop serving only as a storeroom for merchandise. Sometimes, these salesmen could be confused with peddlers, a line of work in which Jews had little involvement. A small number of accounts of Jewish peddlers have been discovered, with some recorded in Connecticut and New York, but these date from a century after the Jewish colonization of North America. It is important to highlight the difference between the traveling salesman or tallyman and the peddler. The tallyman would concentrate on the outskirts of a city, primarily the suburbs. Sales were usually made in installments, and goods offered the vendor a financial return in the medium- to long-term. The objective was for the client to remain in debt: no sooner had the customer paid back what they owed, than they would find themselves set up with a new account from the purchase of further goods. The peddler was different: he would work principally in rural areas, in small towns and villages, travelling over large distances and visiting isolated settlements. The peddler carried goods that could offer him a

---

[336] Ibid, p. 217.

quicker return and were cheaper, because he usually took payment at sight.[337]

According to Werner Sombart, there was a class of Jewish merchant that provided a service for the less fortunate. These merchants sold clothes and personal items on installment plans, with the poorer sector of society as their target demographic.[338] In this case, Jews who were working in this area should be described as tallymen, and not peddlers.

In North America, the role of peddler and tallyman faced numerous obstacles, since it was rare to find good commercial routes, organized hubs in rural areas and safe roads. In an attempt to stave off competition, influential merchants and shopkeepers put up strong opposition to the peddlers, spreading numerous malicious lies about them. Defamatory stereotypes associated peddlers with swindlers, purveyors of stolen merchandise and even carriers of disease.

The provincial governments, swayed by the merchant classes, approved laws limiting the activities of peddlers and imposing expensive licenses, which were only valid for a short time. Prejudice against peddlers was stoked up for personal financial gain and, of course, did not only affect Jews, but also individuals of other faiths. There are records from 1660 of Jewish peddlers working in the Connecticut area, who traded cattle, horses and local produce with farms in the region. In 1680, there is a mention of a peddler named Isaac Gabai Faro, from New York, who had formed a partnership with Joseph Brown Pardo, a relative of the *hazzan* of New York, Saul Pardo Brown.[339]

For Jews, beginning work or starting a professional career in colonial America was difficult. Sometimes, a young man would be

---

[337] LEWIN, Helena. A economia errante: a inserção dos imigrantes judeus no processo produtivo brasileiro. In: AMACNIO, Moacir (Org.). *Ato de presença: hineni – homenagem a Rifka Berezin*. São Paulo: Humanitas, 2005, p. 308-310.

[338] SOMBART, Werner. *Les juifs et la vie économique*. Paris: Seoul, 1923. p. 201. LEWIN, Helena, op. cit., p. 308.

[339] Book F., (1707-1711) Emanuel Marques, Register of the province, S. C. Archives, Columbia, p. 97; *The South Carolina Historical and Geological Magazine*, XXIX, 273; Mordechai Nathan, Charleston, S. C., to Nathan Simsom, New York, Apr. 29, 1914, Simson Papers; in Publications of American Jewish Historical Society, XLIX, 36 ff. MARCUS, J. R. op. cit., v. 2, p. 552.

offered the opportunity to train with an experienced merchant. As an assistant and apprentice, following the model of a mediaeval guild, the young Jew would serve the merchant for five years and, in exchange, receive lessons in accounting and craftsmanship, as well as board, clothing and night schooling in the winter. After a given time, the merchant would be required to offer the apprentice ten tons of stock, in bulk, so that he could start his own business.

One of the Jews from New Amsterdam, Solomon Morache, founder of the Mikveh Israel synagogue in Philadelphia and a distant relative of Asser Levy, began his career in this way. His mother sent him to work for a Dutch Jew named Issac Hays, an important businessman in New York, when Morache was around fourteen years old. Morache learned his trade from Hays, but was unable to complete the five-year apprenticeship because his instructor decided to return to Holland. Morache became a shopkeeper and merchant, and, in 1760, formed a partnership with Hayman Levy, a businessman from the Levy family in London.[340]

Prejudice and discrimination against Jews extended to prohibitions on manufacturing. On June 14, 1656, Peter Stuyvesant received a letter from the West India Company instructing him to prohibit Jews, or Portuguese New Christians, from working as "mechanics" (manual laborers or artisans), in accordance with Dutch regulations. However, Jews did possess manual skills, which they had often inherited from their parents. As European Jews had become excluded from guilds, they had formed associations of their own, some of which were dedicated to industrial production. In Amsterdam, some manufacturing sectors did not exclude Jews, specifically those involved in the production of tobacco and chocolate, as well as in the cutting of diamonds.[341] These trades were passed down from father to son and, in New York, some Jews earned recognition within the fields of manufacturing and craftsmanship. In the New York city records there is a list of free men, on which Jews appear as soap manufacturers, clockmakers, jewelers, shoemakers, tailors and bakers, among other professions.

---

[340] MARCUS, J. R. op. cit., v. 2, p. 559. Hayman Levy was a relative of Morache's, a distant relative of Asser Levy and brother-in-law to the gold and silversmith Myer Myers.

[341] ISRAEL, Jonathan. Diasporas Within a Diaspora: Jews, Crypto-Jews and the World Maritime Empires (1540-1740). Leiden: Brill, 2002. p. 395.

The most famous Jewish craftsman of the 18th century was Myer Myers, born in New York and a distant relative of Asser Levy, who produced works in silver and gold. He was elected president of the Gold and Silver Smith's Society of New York, an organization that formed part of the General Society of Mechanics and Tradesmen.[342] He fashioned everything from fine homeware and jewelry to decorative ornaments for the scrolls of the Hebrew Bible at the synagogue of New York, where he was appointed president during the 1780s. Myers's brother made bells that could be seen on top of the penitentiary and at the New York Stock Exchange. Another fine craftsman was Levy Simons, who advertised his workshop in the city's newspaper, the *New York Journal*. Meanwhile, some decades earlier, Isaac Navarro had earned a reputation as a goldsmith in Recife and New Amsterdam, and was responsible for painting the synagogue in New York. Navarro later moved to Annapolis, in Maryland, where he switched to manufacturing chocolate.

Samuel de Lucena, a descendant of Jacob de Lucena, obtained a monopoly after building a potash plant, which covered an area of 32 kilometers in Norwalk, Connecticut. Potash had been manufactured by Jews on the island of Itamaracá, in Brazil, and had great commercial value in England, where it was often used to whiten fabrics. Other Jews obtained monopolies over the manufacture of bleach, such as Moses Lopez, in Newport and Boston; Barrack Hays, in Albany; and Joseph Simon and Dr Samuel Boude, in Pennsylvania. For Jews, this created new opportunities, since high consumption of these products meant they could be used as payment on imported English goods.[343]

In 1760, James Lucena obtained a ten-year monopoly over the manufacture of soap on Rhode Island. Mordecai Gomes produced tobacco and had Michael Asher and Isaac Simons, who owned a tobacco plantation, as business partners and suppliers.

The sale and production of soap appears to have been a common practice within the Jewish community. During the 1720s, Moses

---

[342] The General Society of Mechanics and Tradesmen was founded in 1785, with the slogan: *By hammer and hands all arts to stand*. For more on Myer Myers, see ROSENBAUM, Jeanette. *Myer Myers, Goldsmith 1723-1795*. Philadelphia: The Jewish Publication Society of America, 1964. BARQUIST, David. *Myer Myers: Jewish Silversmith* in Colonial New York. New York: Yale University Art Gallery, 2001.

[343] MARCUS, J. R. op. cit., v. 2, p. 681-682.

Levy imported soap from Barbados and Antigua to Philadelphia and Surinam. Years later, in partnership with Michael Moses and David Franks, he began manufacturing soap and candles in the south of Philadelphia.

Jews also stood out in the liberal professions. In Maryland, Jacob Lumbroso, who had arrived from Brazil on the *Saint Charles*, acted as a legal representative, as well as practicing other professions, such as doctor, farmer and merchant. There was high demand for professionals with legal expertise due to the volume of commercial lawsuits, and Jacob Lumbroso acted in many of these cases.

Despite not having a law degree, Lumbroso's aid was frequently solicited, particularly in relation to commercial disputes with the Caribbean colonies. Asser Levy also achieved prominence in this field, providing legal representation for many of his friends. On one occasion, he assisted José da Costa in resolving a legal dispute with a Dutchman which had begun in Recife. The case had already been tried in Brazil, and the Dutchman had only been able to default on his debt because of the Portuguese reconquest. Levy also represented Abraham Cohen, from Amsterdam, and received 1,620 guilders in payment.

In the 17th and 18th centuries, it was common for Jews to provide representation for merchants, despite not having academic qualifications, and intervene in legal disputes with the Caribbean.

In the 1760s, the son of David Franks, an important merchant, became the first Jew to earn the right to study at the University of Pennsylvania. After completing his studies, Moses Franks was accepted as a lawyer in London. He worked as an official legal representative, and later moved to the Bahamas, where he became chief justice.[344]

The Jews had always maintained the tradition of practicing medicine. In the inventory of the assets of Dr Jacob Lumbroso, who had worked as a doctor and a surgeon as well as a legal representative, there are payments related to his treatment of patients in Maryland during the 1760s.[345]

---

[344] PUBLICATIONS of American Jewish Historical Society, XVIII, p. 213; XIX, p. 107 and 120; XXII, p. 149-150.

[345] MARCUS, J. R. op. cit., v. 2, p. 545.

In 1738, Dr Isaac Abrahams, son of *mohel* Abraham Israel, who was also a teacher and merchant, became the first Jew to graduate in medicine from King's College, New York.[346]

In 1752, the German Jew, Jacob Isaac, placed an ad for his clinic in the New York Gazette, describing himself as an expert in venereal diseases. Nathan Levy and Andrew Judah, who were related and both descendants of New York's first Jewish families, also ran clinics in the city. Dr Siccary (probably Siqueira), a Portuguese-Jewish doctor, developed a theory about the health benefits of tomatoes which made a positive impression on Thomas Jefferson, with the study even described in the *American Medical Biography* by James Thacher in 1826.[347]

As a way of diversifying their businesses, Jews operated discreetly in the property market. The purchasing of immovable property as a form of investment was unusual among New Holland's Jewish community. Even after winning the right to own property, Jews continued predominantly to rent: during the first five years, there is no documentation relating to the purchasing of large commercial properties, a fact that contrasts with Brazil, where Jews had become the owners of large farms and sugarcane plantations.

In New Amsterdam, the first Jewish property was purchased by Asser Levy, in 1661. The property was in Beverwyck, now Albany, and was sold on a year later. Levy was never able to live in the property, which he had instead rented out.[348]

The system of burghs, adopted in New Amsterdam, incentivized inhabitants to offer mutual support to each other. When the arrival of imports at the port increased, everyone benefited. Yet even the implementation of this system could not combat port customs inspections. Commercial risk was common in pioneering communities, and New Amsterdam was no exception. In 1656, a ship sent by Isaac Israel to South River was destroyed in an accident, and, though part of the shipment was saved, 10 gallons of brandy

---

[346] Abraham Israel is a descendant of David Israel, one of the *Saint Charles* pioneers and a refugee from Brazil.

[347] AMERICA. To Wich is Prefixed a Succinct History in the United States from the First Settlement of the Country. Boston: Richardson & Lord, 1826. v. 1. p. 74.

[348] LEVY, Asser. The New York Genealogical and Biographical Record. v. 2, n. 3, Jul. 1971.

and 15 parcels of cheese were stolen during the rescue effort, leading Israel to begin a lawsuit against the colonial government for losses and damages. This was an era in which fraud and contraband were commonplace. The merchant Salvador d'Andrada, for example, was accused of purchasing a silver bowl which was stolen property. Sometimes, goods arriving in the colony would be separated out and end up in the hands of the authorities. When Moses da Silva, a Dutch-Jewish merchant, sent a shipment of brandy to New Amsterdam, the cargo was mistakenly delivered to Sheriff Cornelis van Tienhoven, who appropriated the goods.[349]

The rights won by Jews in New Amsterdam were not conceded voluntarily by the Dutch colonizers, but imposed by the authorities in the metropolis. However, the political support received from Holland should not be overestimated. Despite Dutch Jews having a certain influence that allowed them to apply pressure on the Dutch government to the benefit of their companions in the colonies, there were also other interests at play. There was, for example, the necessity of finding new regions to which Holland's poorer Jews could be sent, since the urban centers could no longer support the impoverished sectors of their populations, particularly the Jews, who were only allowed restricted access to manufacturing work. The solution settled upon was to redirect this population to the colonies that boasted strong agricultural sectors, such as New Zealand and the Caribbean, where Jews could become involved in opening up new markets, as well as in developing agricultural production.[350] Due to their hard-won experience in managing a variety of interests, New Holland's Sephardic Jews were able to achieve economic distinction in the North American colony.

---

[349] MARCUS, J. R. op. cit., v. 2.

[350] ISRAEL, Jonathan, op. cit., p. 316.

18. The Building of a Nation

During the first years of the 18th century, numerous Sephardic Jews, members of the Shearith Israel synagogue in New York, were elected as city police officers, until then an honor only afforded to Protestants. Among those elected were Nathan Simson and Samuel Levy, in 1718; Moses Levy, in 1719; Jacob Franks, in 1720; and Jacob Hays, in 1726.[351]

During the American War of Independence, many of the descendants of the first Sephardic Jews fought side by side for the liberty of the nation. The Jew Rodrigo Pacheco was one of the five leaders of the protest against the Molasses Act, imposed by British authorities in March, 1733. Under this act, all sugarcane molasses not transported by English ships was to be taxed, making it more expensive than molasses sold by the English. The Jews, who already had experience in the sugar trade, were greatly affected by this imposition. Christian merchants looked to Jews for support and organized a large protest, which culminated in a refusal to comply with the tax. Other Jews who took part in the protest were Mordecai and David Gomes, Bernard Hart and Solomon Simson.[352] The British act came off the back of a series of other taxes and duties which would eventually cause the population of the thirteen colonies to rebel against the English metropolis, demanding independence. Asser Levy's grandson was among the revolutionary troops in the battle for New Jersey. Other Jews were also involved in the conflict, both on the frontline and in a civilian capacity, and Robert Morris, the Superintendent for Finance of the colonial troops, had three Jewish associates: Haym Solomon, of Philadelphia, Jacob Hart, of Baltimore, and Isaac Levy, of New York, who would eventually rise to the rank of lieutenant colonel.

The descendants of the Levy family were intimately involved in the revolutionary cause. Moses Levy's daughter, Billah Abigail, married Jacob Franks, an important Jewish merchant from

---

[351] Idem.

[352] ANGEL, Marc D. (Rabbi). *A Portrait of America's First Jewish Congregation – Shearith Israel.* New York: Riverside Company Book, 2004. p. 210.

Philadelphia. Jacob Franks was secretary to Colonel Isaac Franks, an official in the Continental Army, who fought in the Battle of Long Island. Franks was also a relative of Lieutenant Colonel David Salisbury Franks, an official under Colonel George Washington's command. Moses Levy's other granddaughter, Phila, married General Oliver de Lancey, a Loyalist officer, who was later appointed Chaplain in Ordinary to King George III. Phila's brother-in-law, James de Lancey, was governor of the province of New York.[353]

Joseph Simon, Bernard Gratz and Aaron Levy, all Jewish merchants from Philadelphia, received supplies from Jews in the Caribbean colonies, especially the island of St. Eustatius, and provided weapons, food and clothing for troops and warships in Pennsylvania.[354] Isaac Levy and Myers Michaels financed the cause in Virginia, while Manuel Josephson, of New York, equipped the Continental Army with munitions.[355]

In 1790, as a sign of his gratitude for Jewish support during the military campaigns, President George Washington sent letters to the leaders of the Jewish community, assuring them that Jews would be treated as equal citizens.

The artisan and goldsmith Myer Myers, a Jew descended from the Amsterdam community, also fought in the American militia during the revolutionary period. Myers was the caretaker of the Portuguese synagogue in New York between 1759 and 1770. In 1784, he was a member of the committee that negotiated lands for the expansion of the city's Jewish cemetery. His craftsmanship was recognized in 2001, when the Yale University Art Gallery organized an exhibition of his work.

Isaac Moses, a Portuguese Jew, was one of the founders of the New York Chamber of Commerce, in 1768, and caretaker of the

---

[353] CARDOZO'S PAPERS. *Columbia University in the city of New York*. Microfilm. The Jewish National and University Library. Hebrew University of Jerusalem, Israel.

[354] KEREM, Itzchak. Sephardic Settlement in the British Colonies of the Americas in the 17th and 18th Centuries. In: VIGNE, Randolph; LITTLETON, Charles (Eds.). *From Strangers to Citizens – the Integration of Immigrant Communities in Britain, Ireland and Colonial America*, 1550-1750. Brighton: Sussex Academic Press, 2001., p. 293.

[355] FIELDSTEIN, Stanley. *The Land that I Show You: Three Centuries of Jewish Life in America*. New York: Anchor Press/Doubleday, 1978. p. 20-23.

city's Portuguese synagogue. He was also responsible for drafting the Chamber of Commerce's constitution.

In 1792, twenty-four stockbrokers assembled to organize the New York Stock Exchange and sign the Buttonwood Agreement, which established the rules and commitments of investors to the newly-inaugurated institution. Among these stockbrokers there were three Jews, the New York Sephardi Benjamin Nathan Mendes Seixas, son of Isaac Mendes Seixas and grandson of Gershom Mendes Seixas, a great religious leader of the Portuguese Shearith Israel synagogue, and Ashkenazi Jews Ephraim Hart and Alexander Zuntz.[356] Benjamin Mendes Seixas brought together two prestigious Sephardi families when he married Zipporah Levy, daughter of the businessman Hayman Levy and granddaughter of Moses Levy, a merchant and benefactor of the Jewish community in New York.[357]

Gershom Mendes Seixas is notable for having been the only Jew present in the group that founded Columbia University. Seixas was a member of the university's board of trustees between 1787 and 1815. His great-nephew, Benjamin Nathan Cardozo, was on the same board many years later, from 1928 to 1932.[358]

Benjamin Nathan Cardozo was a prominent Sephardic Jew within New York society who had studied Greek and Political Economy at Columbia University. He was a very popular jurist and became a Chief Judge of the New York Court of Appeals. Years later, in 1932, public opinion led the president of the United States, Herbert Hoover, to appoint Cardozo to the country's Supreme Court. On the day Cardozo took up his position, the *New York Times* claimed: "President Hoover's final determination to turn to the New York jurist was the best kind of politics. It's given the country the best kind of judge."[359]

---

[356] Ibid, p. 22.

[357] Gershom Mendes Seixas's grandson was named after Gershom's father, Isaac Mendes Seixas. Born in Lisbon, Isaac Mendes Seixas had arrived in New York in 1740. He married Raquel Levy, great-granddaughter of Asser Levy, forming the nucleus of one of the city's great Jewish families. See STERN, Malcolm. *First American Jewish Families: 600 Genealogies, 1654-1988*. Baltimore: Ottenheimer Publishers, 1991.

[358] Columbia University Press. Benjamin Nathan Cardozo. 89C, 90AM, '92, 'I5LLD. September 23, 1938. The Jewish National and University Library. Jerusalem, Israel.

[359] Ibid, p. 57.

In the 19th century, members of the Portuguese Shearith Israel synagogue inaugurated the first Jewish hospital in New York, located on 28th Street. Sampson Simson, Benjamin Nathan, Henry Hendricks and Theodore Seixas founded the hospital, which would become a point of reference for other hospitals and, in 1866, was renamed the Mount Sinai Hospital.

Years later, in 1884, members of the Portuguese synagogue, led by Dr Henry Pereira and concerned with attending to the highest number of disadvantaged people possible, set up another hospital, named the Montefiore. At the end of the 19th century, Dr Pereira, who was concerned at how children with special needs were being integrated into society, founded a school for children with hearing impairments.[360]

Also included among the founders of the Mount Sinai Hospital was Henry Hendricks, a businessman responsible for starting up the copper industry and for modernizing American shipbuilding. Hendricks was involved in financing Jewish welfare organizations, like the Hebrew Benevolent Society, which he helped create in 1833, alongside his brother-in-law, Benjamin Nathan. Other members of this family also attained recognition, such as Annie Nathan Myers, who was founder of Barnard College. The tenth generation of the Hendricks family still lives in New York. At 84, Ruth Hendricks Schulson collaborated with this book, speaking of her pride at being a descendant of the first Sephardic Jews of Manhattan Island. Her ancestor, Louis Moses Gomez, was the first Parnas of the Portuguese Shearith Israel synagogue.

At the end of the 19th century, New York received an influx of Ashkenazi Jews, who were fleeing the pogroms of Eastern Europe. The newly-arrived immigrants had to put up with miserable living conditions and an entirely different culture, but found a defender in Emma Lazarus, a member of one of the city's well-established Sephardic families. Emma was the daughter of Esther, sister to Benjamin Nathan Mendes Seixas and daughter of Gershom Mendes Seixas. Esther had married Moses Lazarus, with whom she had two daughters, Emma and Josephine. This family was renowned for its evident artistic streak. Moses Lazarus's brother, Jacob Lazarus, was

---

[360] FELDSTEIN, Stanley, op. cit., p. 69-71. ANGEL, Marc D. (Rabbi), op. cit., p. 250.

a famous 19th century painter, and New York's Metropolitan Museum of Art even named a collection in his honor: the Lazarus Collection.[361]

Emma Lazarus was the great defender of the new immigrants and expressed her empathy with their plight in numerous poems. Always involved in important causes, she sold some of her writings to raise funds for the construction of a pedestal for the Statue of Liberty. Her poem "The New Collosus" was attached to the base of the statue in 1903, and can still be visited today.

> Give me your tired, your poor
> Your Huddled masses yearning to breathe free,
> The Wretched refuse of your teeming shore
> Send these, the homeless, tempest-tost to me,
> I lift my lamp beside the golden door![362]

Within this poet's literary output, there is a preoccupation with the place of Jews in the world. In an article entitled "The Jewish Problem," Lazarus questioned whether America would be able to meet the needs of Jews in terms of safety, decency and opportunity. Contact with Ashkenazi Jews from Russia awakened Emma Lazarus to the problem of anti-Semitism and brought her closer to the ideas of Zionism.[363]

But this is only part of the contribution made by a small group of Jews and their descendants to the building of America.

---

[361] CARDOZO'S PAPERS, op. cit., p 55-60. ANGEL, Marc D. (Rabbi), op. cit., p. 280-320.

[362] See ANGEL, Marc D. (Rabbi), op. cit., p. 283.

[363] COHEN, Martin A.; PECK, Abraham J. (Eds.). *Sephardim in the Americas: Studies in Culture and History.* Tuscaloosa/London: American Jewish Archives/University of Alabama Press, 1993. p. 115-132.

19. Final Considerations

The Dutch invasion of Brazil's Northeast was driven by the West India Company's interest in gaining control over the Brazilian sugar trade. Spying an opportunity for economic growth, Jews within the Amsterdam community joined the Dutch in this endeavor.

In the Dutch colonies in America, Jews benefitted from relative tolerance. They were able to maintain their customs and traditions, as well as practice their religion behind closed doors. As administrators of the new colonies, the West India Company guaranteed this policy of tolerance in return for greater profits, although there were times when anti-Semitism reared its head, especially on the part of the clergy of the Reformed Church.

In Brazil, Jews looked to organize themselves and form a community in line with the Dutch model. They received religious and financial assistance from the Jewish Congregation of Amsterdam, which also established offshoots of its aid organizations, such as the "company for the adoption of orphans and poor maidens," which operated in Pernambuco and was represented and overseen by Moisés Navarro (1639-1641).[364]

Jews participated actively in Recife society, far more than they were able to in regions of Europe. Encouraged by Governor Maurice of Nassau, they attained prominence in fields such as engineering, botany, goldsmithing, medicine and poetry. With the arrival of rabbis from Amsterdam, philosophy and literature also gathered momentum.

Jews living in Brazil's Northeast were able to become involved in agriculture, something they were excluded from in Europe, as well as in the commerce of goods and financial services, and were present in both rural and urban areas. They served as a link between Jews and Christians, acting as intermediaries in trade relationships between Western Europe and Iberian America.

The Jews developed international trade networks and played a fundamental role in the Northeast of Brazil, introducing luxury

---

[364] RIBEMBOIM, José Alexandre. *Senhores de engenho: judeus em Pernambuco colonial 1542-1624.* Recife: 20-20 Comunicação e Editora, 1995. p. 95-99.

items previously unknown to the local population. Recife was transformed into a center of progress for 17th century Brazil.

Despite the religious tolerance guaranteed by the West India Company, Catholics and Calvinists, often led by priests and pastors who were resentful of the social and economic success of Sephardic Jews within the Pernambuco community, acted as agents of discrimination and violence against the Jews. Many letters of complaint and reclamation were addressed to the directors of the West India Company, in an attempt to exclude Jews from business and local society.

During the war for the reconquest of Brazil's Northeast, the Inquisition managed to resume its activities in the region and take advantage of the instability to send back to Lisbon New Christians captured by the Portuguese in towns and villages. It was during battles that the Inquisition were able to apprehend the greatest number of soldiers of New Christian origin.

The war for the Northeast of Brazil ended with an agreement providing the Dutch with a negotiated timeframe in which to leave the region. In a singular moment in modern history, Jews were treated with respect and dignity by the Portuguese government, which accepted the inclusion of a clause in the agreement negotiated with the Dutch stating that Jews should receive equal treatment at the end of the war. The position of the Portuguese government was due above all to the stance of the Portuguese general, Francisco Barreto, who was responsible for negotiating the withdrawal of Dutch troops from Recife.

According to Cabral de Mello, the departure of the Dutch and Jews from the Northeast of Brazil, as a result of negotiations between Portugal and Holland that extended into 1661, had diplomatic repercussions across the globe and ended up granting commercial advantages to Holland.[365]

The New Christians were forced into a fresh exodus, spreading themselves across the Dutch colonies in the Caribbean and North America (New Holland). The "tolerance" defended by the West India Company began to wane. After 1654, the Brazil-Holland-Portugal economic axis was replaced by trade between the

---

[365] MELLO, Evaldo Cabral de. O negócio do Brasil-Portugal, os Países Baixos e o Nordeste, 1641-1669. Rio de Janeiro: Topbooks, 2003. p. 12.

Caribbean, Amsterdam and Spain, at a time when England had supplanted Portugal in terms of colonial maritime trade. In the 1650s, the West India Company saw its commercial advantage threatened by new maritime laws imposed by the economic policies of Oliver Cromwell. In the context of the maritime dispute, Jews and New Christians, who had until then been seen as strong economic allies, became regarded by the company as competitors.

In the wake of these events, the Dutch Republic was reluctant to extend the benefits that had been offered to Recife's Jews to other Dutch colonies in America. Even in the colony in the Northeastern Brazil, there had been frequent opposition to Jewish involvement in trade on the part of some Protestant investors in the West India Company. This opposition only intensified following the Dutch defeat in Brazil and the subsequent financial losses.[366] The company then turned to encouraging Jewish settlement in colonies where New Christian agricultural skills and experience in sugarcane production were required.[367]

In the colony of New Amsterdam, this policy was embodied by the colonial governor, Peter Stuyvesant, who aimed to keep the Jews out of local trade within the colony, where Jews were only permitted to remain under rigid economic and religious restrictions.

During the entire period of Dutch governance of New Holland, these restrictions were challenged by the nascent Jewish community. Far from the cultural and artistic progress Jews had experienced in Recife, the small community became a milestone in the Jewish struggle for survival and for the rights of citizenship. The Jewish presence in New Amsterdam provided a new impetus in the battle against Peter Stuyvesant's xenophobic policies.

Amid all of the challenges faced by Jews in New Holland, there is one Jew who stands out for his spirit of leadership and diplomacy:

---

[366] ISRAEL, Jonathan. Diasporas Within a Diaspora: Jews, Crypto-Jews and the World Maritime Empire (1540-1740). Leiden: Brill, 2002.

[367] Settlement in the colonies of Curaçao, Barbados and the Antilles were encouraged so that sugarcane production would increase due to the experience of the Sephardic Jews. Holland began cultivating sugar in the Antilles and exporting it to Europe, offering competition to Brazilian sugar, which led to an international drop in the price of sugar and caused the ruin of many sugar plantation owners in Brazil. CANNABRAVA, Alice P. A influência do fabrico do açúcar nas Antilhas Francesa e Inglesa em meados do século XVII. *Anuário da Faculdade de Ciências Econômicas e Administrativas*, São Paulo, 1946.

Asser Levy. Levy was able to move with the same ease among Christians and Jews, and became one of the most respected men in colonial society, maintaining close ties to the Protestant community. For other minorities, such as the Presbyterians and Lutherans, by refusing to settle for living on the margins of society, Levy became a symbol of the struggle for civil rights.

At a time when Manhattan was beginning to change and develop its urban areas, the Jews, with great difficulty, acquired the right to become involved in the region's businesses, to have their own slaughterhouse and build a cemetery.

In 1660, the Dutch colony of New Amsterdam was captured by the English. The administration suffered no great alterations, and many involved in the colonial government remained in their posts as auxiliaries to the English. For Jews, restrictions, particularly in terms of political involvement, were retained, as were their hard-won rights.

Professionally, Jews achieved distinction in various fields, expanding their trade in the Caribbean, which had grown in significance at the time due to its sugarcane production. There was also an increase in social and economic exchange between the Jewish community in London and the one being established in New Amsterdam, principally as a result of the familial ties connecting their members.[368]

The establishment of a synagogue was only documented in 1700. However, records suggest that a synagogue had been functioning in private homes since 1656. Shearith Israel was the name chosen for the congregation which, in the 18th century, became the center for all communal activities, such as celebrations of birth, Jewish coming of age, marriage and death, as well as the ministration of diet, education and philanthropy. The spiritual leaders, supported by members of the congregation, participated actively in the struggle for the liberation of the colony from the oppression of the English metropolis.

With the passing of years, descendants of the Sephardic pioneers married Jews arriving from other regions, particularly England and the Caribbean, and their families achieved prominent positions

---

[368] The Jewish community in London was initially formed of Sephardic Jews and New Christians from Holland, Brazil, Venice and Livorno.

within the colonial elite. They built the most highly-esteemed hospitals, schools and libraries, became integrated into the world of academia, contributed actively to economic progress and occupied important roles in public office. Jewish life blossomed, leading to the largest community in the diaspora.

APPENDIX A. BIBLIOGRAPHY

HANDWRITTEN PRIMARY SOURCES
- National Archive of Torre do Tombo – Inquisition of Lisbon
  - First Trial of Mor Rodrigues n. 8,827
  - Trial of Diogo Henriques n. 1,770
  - Trial of Gabriel Mendes n. 11,362
  - Trial of Gonçalo Lopes Homem n. 8,543
  - Trial of João Nunes Velho n. 11,575
  - Trial of Miguel Frances n. 7,276
  - Second Trial of Mor Rodrigues n. 13,142

PRINTED PRIMARY SOURCES

AMERICAN JEWISH ARCHIVES. Jewish Complaints During Civil War.

New York Historical Records: early Colonial Settlements. Letters between Jews and the Dutch West India Company.

_____. The Mill Street Synagogue Reconsidered in American Jewish Quarterly, v. LIII, n. 4, Jun. 1964

_____. Dutch Notarial Records Pertaining to Asser Levy, 1659-1692. Part 3: New Documents for the Study of American Jewish History *American Jewish History*, 1 Sep. 2003.

AMERICA. To Which Is Prefixed a Succinct History in the United States from the First Settlement of the Country. Boston: Richardson & Lord, 1826. v. 1.

ASSER LEVY. The New York Genealogical and Biographical Record. v. 2. n. 3, Jul. 1971.

CARDOZO'S PAPERS. *Columbia University in the City of New York.* Microfilm. The Jewish National and University Library. Hebrew University of Jerusalem, Israel.

COLLECTIONS of Connecticut Historical Society XVI, 200 ff.

CONCIÇÃO, José Marianno (Frei). Alographia dos Alkales fixos vegetal ou potassa mineral ou soda e dos seus nitratos segundo as melhores memórias estrangeiras, que se tem escripto a este assumpto.

Debaixo dos auspícios e de ordem de sua alteza real o príncipe do Brasil. Lisbon: Officina de Simão Thaddeo Ferreira, 1798.

DAG NOTULE, 22 Jan. 1654 Algemeen Rijksarchief, Hague, Holland, Criminele Papieren, n. 22, 1624, Portefeuillevan.

DAG NOTULE, 21 Feb. 1654 Algemeen Rijksarchief, Hague, Holland, Oude West Indische Compagnie, collection of manuscripts (codices and scrolls), 75.

DRUCKER, Erna. Jewish Settlers in New Amsterdam and Early New York, 1654-1824. A Selected *Annotated Guide to Source Materials.* New York: City College of New York, 1984.

DUTCH BRAZIL: Seventeen Letters from Vicente Joaquim Soler 1636-1643. Rio de Janeiro: Index, 1999.

FERNOW, Berthold. Documents Relating to the History of the Early Colonial Settlements. Albany: Weed, Parson and Company, 1883.

_____. Documents Relating to the History of Early Colonial Settlements Principally on Long Island, With a Map of Its Western Parts, Made in 1666. Albany: Weed, Parson and Company, 1883.

_____. The Records of New Amsterdam from 1653 to 1674 Anno Domini. Baltimore: Genealogical Publishing, 1976.

GEHRING, Concil. *Minutes, 1652-1654*. New York: New York State Public Library (Manuscript Division).

HAIM, Isaac Karigal. A Sermon Preached at the Synagogue, in Newport, Rhode Island, Called "The *Salvation of Israel* (May 28, 1773). Newport, Rhode Island: S. Southwick, 1773 (Rare Book and Special Collection Division).

HERSHKOWITZ, Leo; MEYER, Isidores S. The Lee Max Friedman Collection of American Jewish Colonial *Correspondence*. Philadelphia: American Jewish Historical Society, 1968.

HERSHKOWITZ, Leo. Asser Levy and the Inventories of Early New York Jews. American Jewish History, v. 80, n. 1, 1990.

_____. Dutch Notarial Records Pertaining to Asser Levy, 1659-1692. (Part Three: New Documents for the Study of American Jewish History). *American Jewish History*, 1 Sep. 2003.

INVENTORIES of munitions left by the Dutch in Pernambuco and of buildings constructed or repaired up until 1654. Recife: Imprensa Oficial, 1940.

LAER, Van A. J. F. *New York Historical Manuscripts: Dutch.* Baltimore: Genealogical Publishing, 1974. v. 1. Register of Provincial Sercetary, 1638-1642.

MELO, Francisco Manoel. Termo de capitulação da guerra luso-holandesa. Restauração de Enáfora *triunfante e outros escritos.* Recife: Secretaria do Interior, 1944. p. 55-57.

NARRATIVES of New Netherland, 1609-1664. New York: Scribner, 1909.

NEW NETHERLANDS COUNCIL. *Minutes,* 10-18 Jan. 1654. New York: New York Public Library (Rare Books and Manuscripts Division).

O'CALLAGHAN, Edmund Bailey. History of New Netherland. In: *Documents Relative to the Colonial History of the State of New York.* Albany: Weed, Parsons and Company, 1856. v. 1.

O'CALLAGHAN, Edmund Bailey. Documents Relative to the Colonial History of the State of New York. Albany: Weed, Parsons and Company, 1858. v. 2.

_____. Documents Relative to the Colonial History of the State of New York. Albany: Weed, Parsons and Company, 1858. v. 6.

O'CALLOGAN'S. *Collection: New York Manuscripts.* New York: New York Public Library (Manuscripts Division).

_____. Papers Relating to the City of New York. Albany: [s.n.], 1849.

_____. Documents Relative to the Colonial History of the State of New York: Procured in Holland,
England and France by John Romeyn Brodhead. Albany: Weed, Parsons and Company, 1856. v. 1-3.

OPPENHEIM, Samuel. A Contemporary Account of How the Jews Came to Arrive in New Netherland.

            Publications of the American Jewish Historical Society. Philadelphia, Oct. 1926.

_____. The Early History of Jews in New York, 1654-1664. *American Jewish Historical Quarterly*, Philadelphia, v. 18, p. 1-74, 1909.

_____. Notulen van Brasilie dated April 8, 1654. Copy Furnished by R. Bijlsma in Letter of January 22, 1925. In: Samuel Oppenheim Papers, box 28 – Brazil and Surinam – Notulan van Brasilien, 1649-1654. Publications of the American Jewish Historical Society, Philadelphia.

_____. Archief Staten General Dated June 25, 1657. N. 7406 – Letter to the Estates General of Holland from Jewish Community in Amsterdam. In: Samuel Oppenheim Papers, box 29 – Brazil and Surinam – Notulen van Brasilien, 1649-1654. Publications of the American Jewish Historical Society, Philadelphia.

_____. Minutes of States General Dated November 14, 1654. In: Samuel Oppenheim Papers, box 29 – Brazil and Surinam – Notulen van Brasilien, 1649-1654. *Publications of the American Jewish* Historical Society, Philadelphia.

_____. Letter of Peter Stuyvesant to the Dutch West India Company Dated September 22, 1654. In: Samuel Oppenheim Papers, box 32 – Brazil and Surinam – Notulen van Brasilien, 1649-1654.
            Publications of the American Jewish Historical Society, Philadelphia.

_____. Letter of Johan Megapolensis to the Classis of Amsterdam Dated March 18, 1655. In:
            Samuel Oppenheim Papers, box 32 – Brazil and Surinam – Notulen van Brasilien, 1649-1654.
            Publications of the American Jewish Historical Society, Philadelphia.

_____. Administrative Minutes. New York, 1661-1662, in Dutch. In: Samuel Oppenheim Papers.
            Publications of the American Jewish Historical Society, Philadelphia.

_____. An Early Jewish Colony in West Guiana. In: Samuel Oppenheim Papers. Unpublished
            Manuscript and Variant readings of Published Articles. *Publications of the American Jewish* Historical Society, Philadelphia.

_____. Excerpts from the Story of the Jews of Brazil, 1626-1654. A Paper Read at the Meeting of American Jewish Historical Society, February 7-8, 1925. In: Samuel Oppenheim Papers. Unpublished Manuscripts and Varian readings of Published Articles. *Publications of the American Jewish* Historical Society, Philadelphia.

_____. Newport Early Jewish History: The First Arrivals, The Cemetery, the Vote for Protection in 1684 and the Early Freemasonry of Rhode Island – Some New Matter on the Subject. In: Samuel Oppenheim Papers. Unpublished Manuscripts and Variant readings of Published Articles.
            Publications of the American Jewish Historical Society, Philadelphia.

_____. Letter of Hendrick van Reede van Reenswoode to the States General, dated at Madrid, 1658, c. February 1. In: Samuel Oppenheim Papers. *Publications of the American Jewish Historical Society*, Philadelphia.

_____. Letter of Staten General to King of Spain and mutatis mutandis to Baron van Vatterville,

Governor of St. Sebastiaen. Rijksarchief, Staten General, n. 3,613, July 23, 1657. In: Samuel

Oppenheim Papers. Publications of the American Jewish Historical Society, Philadelphia.

_____. Resolutien van Staten Generaal Dated November 14, 1654. In: Samuel Oppenheim Papers.

Publications of the American Jewish Historical Society, Philadelphia.

_____. Resolutien Staten Generaal, Archive Staten General n. 82 Dated June 25, 1657. In: Samuel

Oppenheim Papers. Publications of the American Jewish Society, Philadelphia.

RECORDS of Connecticut (1717-1725). p. 423, 488 and 576-577.

SALOMON, H. P. Os primeiros portugueses de Amsterdão. Documents from the National Archive of Torre do Tombo: 1595-1606. Caminiana Revista de Cultura Histórica, Literária, Artística, Etnografia *e Numismática*, n. 8, Jun. 1983.

SEYMANN, Jerrold. Colonial Charters, Patents and Grants to the Communities Comprising the City of *New York*. New York: New York Public Library (Rare Books and Manuscripts Division).

SILLE, Nicassius de. List of the Houses of New Amsterdam. *New Netherland Papers*, New York, New York Public Library (Manuscripts Division), 10 Jul. 1660.

SOUZA COUTINHO, Francisco de. Diplomatic correspondence from Francisco de Souza Coutinho during his ambassadorship in Holland. Published by Edgar Prestage and Pedro Azevedo. v. 2, 1647-1648 (May). Coimbra: Imprensa da Universidade, 1926.

STRUCKER-RODDA, Harriet (Mott). Asser Levy in The New York Genealogical and Biographical Record.

New York: Genealogical and Biographical Society, 1971. v. 102. n. 3.

THE JEWS of New York City 1654-1926 – a Record of Cooperation and Service. New York: The Jewish Tribune, 1927.

TUCKERMAN, Bayard. Peter Stuyvesant, Director-General for the West India Company in New *Netherland*. New York: Dodd, Mead and Company, 1905.

WIZNITZER, Arnold. The minute book of the Jewish congregations of Zur Israel in Recife and Magen Abraham in Maurícia, Brazil. 1648-53. *Annals of the National Library*, Rio de Janeiro, v. 74, 1953.

_____. Publications of the American Jewish Historical Society, New York, v. 2, Mar.-Jun. 1953.

CHRONICLERS

BARLEUS, Gaspar. História dos feitos recentemente praticados durante oito anos no Brasil. Preface and notes by Mário G. Ferri. Belo Horizonte, Itatiaia and São Paulo: Edusp, 1982.

BARRIOS, Daniel Levi. Triumpho del gobierno popular en la casa de Jacob. Amsterdam, 1683. p. 455-456. Volume B at the Bibliotheca Rosenthaliana (9G12) 5, 9. p. 455-456.

CALADO, Frei Manuel. *O valoroso Lucideno e o triunfo da Liberdade*. Belo Horizonte, Itatiaia and São Paulo: Edusp, 1987. v. 1.

ERICEIRA, Conde. *História de Portugal restaurada.* Porto: Livraria Civilização, 1945-1946. 4 v.

MENDES, David Franco; J, Mendes dos Remédios. *Os judeos potugueses em Amsterdão.* Lisboa: Edições Távola Redonda, 1990.

MORTERA, Saul Levi. *Tratado de verdade da lei de Moisés.* Facsimile edition (1659), introduction and commentary by H. P. Salomon. Coimbra: Por Ordem da Universidade, 1988.

_____. Providência de Dios com Ysrael. 1662. Translation by Yehuda Machabeu. Published by David Franco Mendes in the Hebrew periodical, *Há-Measeph*, 1784.

OTHER SOURCES

ABENSOUR, Miguel. Au-delà de la fluctuatio animi marrane. Spinosa en quête de l'universel. In:
    Tumultes. Le Paria. Une figure de la modernité. Paris: Kimé, 2003. n. 22-23.

ANGEL, Marc D. (Rabbi). A Portrait of America's First Jewish Congregation – Shearith Israel. New York: Riverside Company Books, 2004.

_____. (Rabbi). Remnant of Israel a Portrait of America's First Jewish Congregation – Shearith *Israel.* New York: Riverside Company Book, 2004.

ARBELL, Mordechai. Early Relations Between the Jewish Communities in the Caribbean and the Guianas and those of the Near East 17th to 19th Century. Available at: <http://www.sefarad.org/publication>. Accessed: 24 Nov. 2017.

AZEVEDO, João Lúcio. *História dos cristãos-novos portugueses.* Lisboa: Clássica, 1921.

BARQUIST, David. Myer Myers: Jewish Silversmith in Colonial New York. New York: Yale University Art Gallery, 2001.

BEL BRAVO, Maria Antônia. *Diaspora sefardi.* Madrid: Mapfre, 1992.

BERNARDINI, Paolo; FIERING, Norman (Eds.). The Jews and the Expansion of Europe to the West, 1450 *to 1800* (European Expansion and Global Interaction, number 2). New York: Berghahn, 2001.

BODIAN, Miriam. Hebrews of the Portuguese Nation: Conversos and Community in Early Modern *Amsterdam.* Bloomington: Indiana University Press, 1997.

BOXER, Charles R. *Os holandeses no Brasil: 1624-1654.* São Paulo: Companhia Editora Nacional, 1961.

BRIDENBAUGH, Carl. Cities in Revolt. Urban life in America, 1743-1776. New York: Knopf, 1955.

CANNABRAVA, Alice P. A influência do fabrico do açúcar nas Antilhas Francesa e Inglesa em meados do século XVII. Anuário da Faculdade de Ciências Econômicas e Administrativas, São Paulo, 1946.

CARNEIRO, Maria Luiza Tucci. Preconceito racial em Portugal e Brasil Colônia: os cristão-novos e o mito *da pureza de sangue.* São Paulo: Perspectiva, 2005.

_____. O sangue como metáfora. Do antissemitismo ao antissemitismo moderno. In: *Ensaios sobre a intolerância.* São Paulo: Humanitas, 2005.

COHEN, Martin A; PECK, Abraham J. (Eds.) Sephardim in the Americas: Studies in Culture and History.
Tuscaloosa/London: American Jewish Archives/University of Alabama Press, 1993.
CORTESÃO, Jaime. *Raposo Tavares e a formação territorial do Brasil*. Rio de Janeiro: Ministério da Educação e Cultura – Documentation service, Departamento de Imprensa Nacional, 1958.
CUMBERLANDS, Richard. *The Fashionable Lover: A Comedy*. London: W. Griffin at Garrick's Head, 1772.
DAMASIO, Antonia. Looking for Spinoza: Joy, Sorrow and the Feeling Brain. Nova York: Harvest, 2003.
DAVIS, David Brion. The Slave Trade and the Jews. *The New York Review of Books*, 22 Dec. 1994.
DRESCHER, Seymour. Jews and New Christians in the Atlantic Slave Trade. In: BERNARDINI, Paolo; FIERING, Norman (Eds.). The Jews and the Expansion of Europe to the West, 1450 to 1800 (European Expansion and Global Interaction, number 2). New York: Berghan Books, 2001.
_____. From Slavery to Freedom: Comparative Studies in the Rise and Fall of Atlantic Slavery. New York: New York University Press, 1999.
DRUCKER, Erna. Jewish Settlers in New Amsterdam and Early New York, 1654-1825: A Selected Annotated Guide to Source Materials. New York: City College of New York, 1984.
ELLIS, Miriam. A presença de Raposo Tavares na expansão paulista, *Revista to Instituto de Estudos Brasileiros*, São Paulo, Universidade de São Paulo, p. 40-41, 1970.
EMMANUEL, Isaac S. Seventeenth Century Brazilian Jewry: A Critical Review. *American Jewish* Archives, Apr. 1962.
FELDSTEIN, Stanley. The And that I Show You: Three Centuries of Jewish Life in America. New York: Anchor Press/Doubleday, 1978.
GEBHARD, Carl. *Spinoza*. Buenos Aires: Losada, 1940.
GOLLMAN, Earl A. Dictionary of American Jewish Biography in the Seventeenth Century. *American Jewish Archives*, 1950 (Rosenbloom and Samuel Oppenheim Collection).
GORENSTEIN, Lina. A Inquisição contra as mulheres – Rio de Janeiro, séculos XVII and XVIII. São Paulo: Humanitas/Fapesp, 2005.
GRINBERG, Keila (Org.). Judeus no Brasil: Inquisição, imigração e identidade. Rio de Janeiro: Civilização Brasileira, 2005. p. 161-183. Apud BAUER, Yehuda. Anti-Semitism as European and World Problem.
In: *patterns of Prejudice*. London: Institute of Jewish Affairs, 1993. v. 2. p. 14-15.
HERSHKOWITZ, Leo. New Amsterdam's Twenty-Three Jews – Myth or Reality?. In: *Hebrew and the Bible in America: The First Two Centuries*. Hannover/London: Shalon Goldman/University Press of New England, 1993. p. 169-183.
HUHNER, Leon. Asser Levy: A Noted Jewish Burgher of Amsterdam. *Publications of the American* Jewish Historical Society, v. 8, p. 9-23, 1900.

_____. Whence Came the First Jewish Settlers of New York? *Publications of the American Jewish Historical Society*, Philadelphia, v. 9, p. 75-85, 1901.

ISRAEL, Jonathan. Diasporas Within a Diaspora: Jews, Crypto-Jews and the World Maritime Empires *(1540-1740)*, Leiden: Brill, 2002.

JAMESON, J. Franklin. *Narratives of New Netherland, 1609-1664*. New York: Charles Scribner's Sons, 1909.

KAGAN, Richard L.; MORGAN, Philip D. (Eds.). Atlantic Diasporas: Jews, Conversos and Crypto – Jews *in the Age of Mercantilism, 1500-1800*. Baltimore: John Hopkins University Press, 2009.

KAPLAN, Yoesf. Judios novos em Amsterdam: estúdio sobre la historia social e intelectual del judaísmo sefardí en el siglo XVII. Barcelona: Gedisa, 1996.

KAUFMAN, Tânia. Un cemitério em arrecife dos navios. *Revista Clio de Arqueologia*, Recife, UFPE, n. 28, 2013.

KAYSERLING, Meyer. Isaac Aboab, the First Jewish Author in America. *Publications of the American* Jewish Historical Society, Baltimore, v. 5, 1897.

_____. *A história dos judeus em Portugal*. São Paulo: Pioneira, 1971.

KEREM, Itzchak. Sephardic Settlement in the British Colonies of the Americas in the 17th and 18th centuries. In: VIGNE, Randolph; LITTLETON, Charles (Eds.). *From Strangers to Citizens: The* Integration of Immigrant Communities in Britain, Ireland and Colonial America, 1550-1750.
Brighton: Sussex Academic Press, 2001.

KESSLER, Henry; RACHLIS, Eugene. *Peter Stuyvesant and his New York*. New York: Random House, 1959.

KOHLER, Max Civil Status of the Jews in Colonial New York. *Publications of the American Jewish Historical Society*, v. 7, p. 81-85, 1897.

LEVY, Asser. The New York Genealogical and Biographical Record. v. 2, n. 3, Jul. 1971.

LEWIN, Helena. A economia errante: a inserção dos imigrantes judeus no processo produtivo brasileiro. In: AMANCIO, Moacir (Org.). *Ato de presença: hineni – homenagem a Rifka Berezin*. São Paulo: Humanitas, 2005.

LIPNER, Elias. Izaque de Castro, o mancebo que veio preso ao Brasil. Recife: Massangana/Fundação Joaquim Nabuco, 1992.

LUTZ, Donald; WARREN, Jack D. A Covenanted People: The Religious Tradition and the Origins of *American Constitutionalism*. Rhode Island: The John Brown Carter Library, 1987.

MAIKA, Dennis J. Merchants of New Amsterdam. *Gering Council Minutes, 1652-1654*.

_____. Commerce and Community: Manhattan Merchants in the Seventeenth Century. 1995. Thesis (PhD) – New York University, New York.

MARCUS, J. R. *The Colonial American Jew*. Detroit: Wayne State University Press, 1969-1970. v. 1 and 2.

_____. *The American Jewish Woman, 1654-1980*. New York/Cincinnati: KTVA Publishing House/American Jewish Archives, 1981.

MELLO, Evaldo Cabral de. O Brasil e os holandeses: 1630-1654. In: HERKENHOFF, Paulo. (Org.). O Brasil e os holandeses. Rio de Janeiro: Sextante Artes, 1999.

_____. O negócio do Brasil-Portugal, os Países Baixos e o Nordeste, 1641-1669. Rio de Janeiro: Topbooks, 2003.

MELLO, José Antônio Gonsalves de. *Gente da nação*. Recife: Massangana/Fundação Joaquim Nabuco, 1996.

MELO, Francisco Manoel de. Restauração de Pernambuco: enáfora triunfante e outros escritos. Recife: Secretaria do Interior, 1944.

MENDES, David Franco; REMÉDIOS, J. Mendes dos. *Os judeus portugueses em Amsterdão*. Lisbon: Edições Távola Redonda, 1990.

MENEZES, José Luís Mota. A cidade de Maurício: observações sobre a história urbana do Recife. In: *A presença holandesa no Brasil: memória e imaginário*. Rio de Janeiro: Museu Histórico Nacional, 2004.

MIDDLETON, S. Artisans and Trade Privileges in New Amsterdam. Norwich: East Anglia University. Work presented during the Rensselaerswijck Seminary. New York, 2001.

NOVINSKY, Anita. Antissemitismo, os marranos e a *fluctuactio animi*. In: CARNEIRO, Maria Luiza Tucci (Org.). *Antissemitismo nas Américas*. São Paulo: Edusp, 2007.

_____. Cristãos-novos na Bahia: a Inquisição no Brasil. 2. ed. São Paulo: Perspectiva, 1992.

_____. Historical Bias – the New Christian Collaboration with Dutch Invaders of Brazil. 5th Congress of Jewish Studies, Jerusalem, Aug. 1969.

_____. Inquisição: inventários de bens confiscados a cristãos-novos. Rio de Janeiro: Imprensa Nacional/Casa de Moeda/Livraria Camões, 1976.

_____. Avatar du marranisme au Brésil. In: Les marranismes: de la religiosité cachée à la societé *ouverte*. Paris: Demopolis, 2014.

_____. Sur le marranisme au Brésil et la *fluctuactio animi*. In: *Miroir de l'anthropologie historique*. Rennes: Press Universitaires de Rennes, 2013.

_____. Ser marrano em Minas colonial. *Revista Brasileira de História*, São Paulo, v. 21, n. 40, 2001.

_____. Avatars du marranisme au Brésil. In: Les marranismes: de la religiosité cachée à la societé *ouverte*. Paris: Demopolis, 2014.

_____. Marranos e a Inquisição: sobre a rota de ouro em Minas Gerais. In: Padre Antônio Vieira, a Inquisição e os judeus. *Revista Novos Estudos Cebrap*, São Paulo, n. 29, Mar. 1991.

_____. Uma devassa do bispo dom Pedro da Silva: 1635-1637. São Paulo: Paulista, 1968. n. XXII.

NOVINSKY, Anita; KUPERMAN, Diane. *Ibéria judaica: roteiros da memória*. Rio de Janeiro: Expressão e Cultura, 1996.

OSIER, Jean-Pierra, *De Uriel da Costa a Baruch Spinosa*. Paris: Berg International, 1983.

PESTANA, Carla Gardina. Liberty of Conscience and the Growth of Religious Diversity in Early America. *1636-1786*. Rhode Island: The John Carter Brown Library, 1986.

PETRAM, L. O. The World's First Stock Exchange, 1602-1700. How the Amsterdam Market for Dutch East India Company Shares Became a Modern Security Market. Groningen: Instituut voor Cultuur en Geschiedenis, 2011.

Portugal – Dicionário Histórico, Corográfico, Heráldico, Bibliográfico, Numismático E Artístico. Lisbon: João Romano Torres, 1904-1915. v. 1.

RAMOS, Frank dos Santos. O paradoxo da América católica: Kahel Sur Israel – a primeira comunidade judaica legal no Novo Mundo. In: ASSIS, Angelo A. Faria de et al. (Org.). *Desvelando o poder* – histórias da dominação: Estado, religião, sociedade. Rio de Janeiro: Vício de Leitura, 2007.

RIBEMBOIM, José Alexandre. Senhores de engenho: judeus em Pernambuco colonial, 1542-1624. Recife: 20-20 Comunicação e Editora, 1995.

RINK, Oliver A. Holland on the Hudson: An Economic and Social History of Dutch New York. New York: Cornell, 1986.

ROOSEVELT, Theodore. Stuyvesant and the End of Dutch Rule: 1647-1664. *Publications of the* American Jewish Society, New York, v. 45, 1956.

ROSA, J. S. Silva. Geschiedenis de Portugueesche joden te Amsterdam 1593-1925. Amsterdam: M. Hertzberger, 1925.

ROSENBAUM, Jeanette. *Myer Myers, Goldsmith 1723-1795.* Philadelphia: The Jewish Publication Society of America, 1964.

ROTH, Cecil. *Dona Gracia of the House of Nasi.* Philadelphia: The Jewish Publication Society of America, 1948.

SALVADOR, José Gonçalves. *Os magnatas do tráfico negreiro.* São Paulo: Pioneira/Edusp, 1981.

SANTOS, João Henrique. A Inquisição calvinista: o sínodo do Brasil e os judeus no Brasil holandês. In: ASSIS, Angelo A. Faria de et al. (Org.). Desvelando o poder – histórias de dominação: Estado, religião *e sociedade.* Rio de Janeiro: Vício de Leitura, 2007.

SARNA, Jonathan. *American Judaism: A History.* Connecticut: Yale University Press, 2004.

SCHAMA, Simon. O desconforto da riqueza: cultura holandesa na época do ouro. São Paulo: Companhia das Letras, 1992.

SHATTUCK, Martha. A Civil Society: Court and Community in Beverwijk, New Netherland: 1652-1654. 1993. Thesis (PhD – Boston University, Boston.

SHORTO, Russel. *A ilha no centro do mundo.* Rio de Janeiro: Objetiva, 2004.

SILVA, Leonardo Dantas. Zur Israel, uma comunidade judaica no Brasil. In: HERKENHOFF, Paulo (Org,). *O Brasil e os holandeses.* Rio de Janeiro: Sextante Artes, 1999.

SNYDER, Holly. English Markets, Jewish Merchants, and Atlantic Endeavours. In: KAGAN, Richard L.; MORGAN, Philip D. (Eds.). Atlantic Diasporas: Jews, Conversos and Crypto – Jews in the Age of *Mercantilism, 1500-1800.* Baltimore: John Hopkins University Press, 2009.

SOLA POOL, David; SOLA POOL, Tamar de. An Old Faith in the New World. Portrait of Shearith Israel, *1654-1954.* New York: Columbia University Press, 1955.

SOLA POOL, David; PATAI, Raphael; CARDOZO, Abraham Lopes. *The World of Sephardim*. New York: Herzl, 1960.

SOMBART, Werner. *Les juifs et la vie économique.* Paris: Seoul, 1923.

STERN, Malcolm. First American Jewish Families: 600 Genealogies, 1654-1988. Baltimore: Ottenheimer Publishers, 1991.

STERN, Malcolm. Portuguese Sephardim in the Americas. In: COHEN, Martin A.; PECK, Abraham J. (eds.) Sephardim in the Americas: Studies in Culture and History. Tuscaloosa/London: American Jewish Archives/University of Alabama Press, 1993.

TEIXEIRA, Dante Martins. O mito da natureza intocada: a história natural no Brasil holandês (1624-654) e sua contribuição para o conhecimento da história recente da fauna no Novo Mundo. In: *A presença holandesa no Brasil: memória e imaginário*. Rio de Janeiro: Museu Histórico Nacional, 2004.

TUCKERMAN, Bayard. Peter Stuyvesant, Director-General for the West India Company in New *Netherland.* New York: Cornell University Library, 1893.

VAINFAS, Ronaldo. Jerusalém colonial. Judeus portugueses no Brasil holandês. Rio de Janeiro: Civilização Brasileira, 2010.

_____. Inquisição e judeus novos no contexto das guerras holandesas. *Texto de História*, v. 14, n. 1/2, 2006. Available at: <periodicos.unb.br/índex.php/textos/article/download/6056/5014>. Accessed: 20 Nov. 2017.

VERÍSSIMO, Joaquim Serrão. O reinado de dom António prior do Crato: 1531-1595. 1956. Thesis (PhD in Literature, Historical Science) – University of Coimbra, Lisbon.

WÄTJEN, Hermann. O domínio colonial hollandez no Brasil: um capítulo da história colonial do século *XVIII*. São Paulo: Companhia Editora Nacional, 1938.

WEITMAN, David Y. (Rabbi) *Bandeirantes espirituais do Brasil: século XVII*. São Paulo: Maayanot, 2003.

WESSELS, Johannes Wilhelmus. *History of the Roman-Dutch Law.* Grahamstown, Cape Colony: African Books, 1908.

WIZNITZER, Arnold. *Os judeus no Brasil Colonial*. São Paulo: Pioneira, 1966.

_____. Jewish Soldier in Dutch Brazil (1630-1654). Baltimore: *Publications American Jewish* Historical Society, v. 46, 1956.

_____. The Exodus from Brazil and Arrival in New Netherland of the Jewish Pilgrim Fathers, 1654. Publications of the American Jewish Historical Society, Philadelphia, v. 44, 1954.

_____. The Members of the Brazilian Jewish Community (1648-1653). *Publications of the American* Jewish Historical Society, Philadelphia, v. 42, 1953.

WOLFF, Egon; WOLFF, Frieda. *A odisseia dos judeus do Recife*. São Paulo: Edusp, 1979.

WOLFF, Egon; WOLFF, Frieda. *Quantos judeus estiveram no Brasil holandês*. Rio de Janeiro: s/n, 1991.

APPENDIX B.   SIGNIFICANT PEOPLE AND PLACES

- **Letter from Vicente Joaquim Soler, Protestant pastor in Recife, to André Rivet, member of the States General in the Hague, on May 6, 1640 (the content is anti-Semitic)[1]**

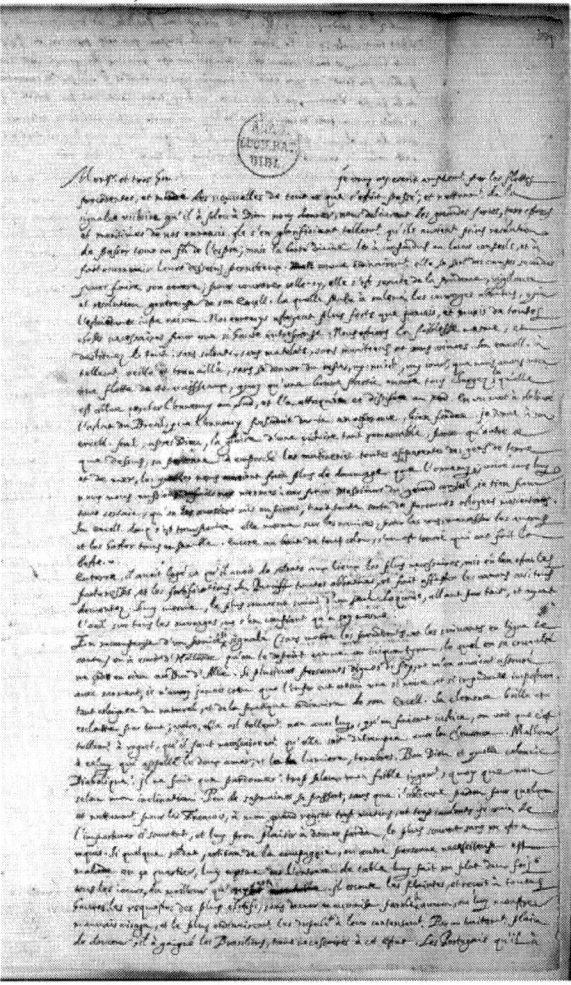

Figure 6. Letter from Vicente Joaquim Soler, Protestant pastor in Recife

o   The paragraph referring to the Jews **states**: "The Jews are multiplying, have great freedom and are holding their heads high more than ever. It is a truth as plain as day that they ruin trade, suck the blood of the people, frustrate and abuse the company. Nevertheless, they are supported and favored to

---

[1] Seventeen letters from Vicente Joaquim Soler, 1636-1643. Ed. Index. Organization B. N. Teensma. Rio de Janeiro, 1999. The letters were addressed to André Rivet – governor of Frederick Henry, Prince of Orange (future William II), in the Hague.

the detriment of Christian merchants; not by Your Excellency, who loathes the sight of them, but by those other gentlemen."

- **Jewish and New Christian sugar plantation owners in the Dutch Northeast (1630-1654)**[2]
  - **David Senior Coronel** (or **Duarte Saraiva**): a man of great standing within the Jewish community of Recife. He owned a property on the Jewish street, where ceremonies took place before the synagogue was founded. He was born in Portugal, in Amarante, around 1570. He was denounced by Izaque de Castro during his inquisitorial trial on January 28, 1647, when he was approaching 80 years old. He was the owner of the following sugar plantations: Bom Jesus; São João Salgado; the Novo plantation, in the Cabo de Santo Agostinho region; the Velho de Beberibe plantation, in Olinda; the Camaçari plantation, in Jaboatão; the Madalena plantation; and the Torre plantation.
  - **Diogo Dias Brandão**: bought the Pirapama plantation, in the Escada municipality, on June 23, 1637. Married a Catholic who converted to Judaism.
  - **Duarte Dias Henriques**: owner of the Nossa Senhora de Apresentação plantation. Attended the small synagogue of the Camaragibe plantation. On Saturdays, he would give his slaves the day off.
  - **Duarte Nunes**: acquired the Cucaú plantation, in Sirinhaém, in 1641.
  - **Fernão do Vale**: owner of the São Bartolomeu plantation, in 1637. A resident of Pernambuco from 1630, he was a prominent member of the local society. He was Baltazar da Fonseca's guarantor for the construction of the bridge linking Recife to the island of Antônio Vaz.
  - **Joseph d'Acosta**: owner of the Salgado plantation. He arrived in Brazil in 1644, and was a great merchant and businessman, as well as treasurer of the Tzur Israel Congregation in Recife.
  - **Moisés Navarro**: an important figure within Recife's Jewish community, he was representative and overseer of the Companhia de Dotar Órfãs e Donzelas Pobres de Amsterdã (Dotar) in Recife. Owner of the Juriçaca and Guararapes plantations, in the Muribeca parish.
  - **Moses Mendes**: lived on the Ubu plantation, in Igarassu, in around 1664, where he was a sugar farmer.
  - **Pedro Lopes de Vera**: owner of five sugar plantations in 1640: the Nossa Senhora do Rosário and São Brás plantations, in Sirinhaém; the Bom Jesus and São João plantations, both in Cabo de Santo Agostinho; and the Nossa Senhora da Palma plantation. He was nominated to the Câmara dos Escabinos (a kind of Town Hall) in Olinda, in 1637, but his name was vetoed due to his Jewish heritage. He fought alongside the Dutch to keep hold of the territory.
  - **Simão do Vale Fonseca**: born in Portugal, in 1602. He was a sugarcane farmer on the Jaboatão plantation belonging to Fernão do Vale. He was

---

[2] Taken from RIBEMBOIM, José Alexandre. *Senhores de engenho*: judeus em Pernambuco colonial 1542-1654. Recife: 20-20 Comunicação e Editora, 1995 p. 150-159.

already living in the region before the arrival of the Dutch, at which point he returned to Judaism and became circumcised. He also acted as an intermediary in the sale of slaves and as a tax collector, in 1643.

- o **Vicente Rodrigues Vila Real**: acquired the Guararapes plantation, from Moisés Navarro, in 1637. He was a Jewish proselytizer and, therefore, destroyed the plantation's chapel soon after completing the purchase. He died around 1642, due to an infection and hemorrhaging resulting from circumcision.

- **Letter from Peter Stuyvesant, governor of New Amsterdam, to the West India Company, on September 22, 1654,[3] attempting to prevent the permanency of the Jews from Brazil**
  - o In the letter, Stuyvesant asks for the company's permission to deport the Jewish refugees from Brazil. He insists that there are limited commercial opportunities in New Amsterdam and that the meagre trade should be reserved for Christian merchants, affirming, "now they have Jews round their necks who, doubtless, will infect and cause problems for the colony."

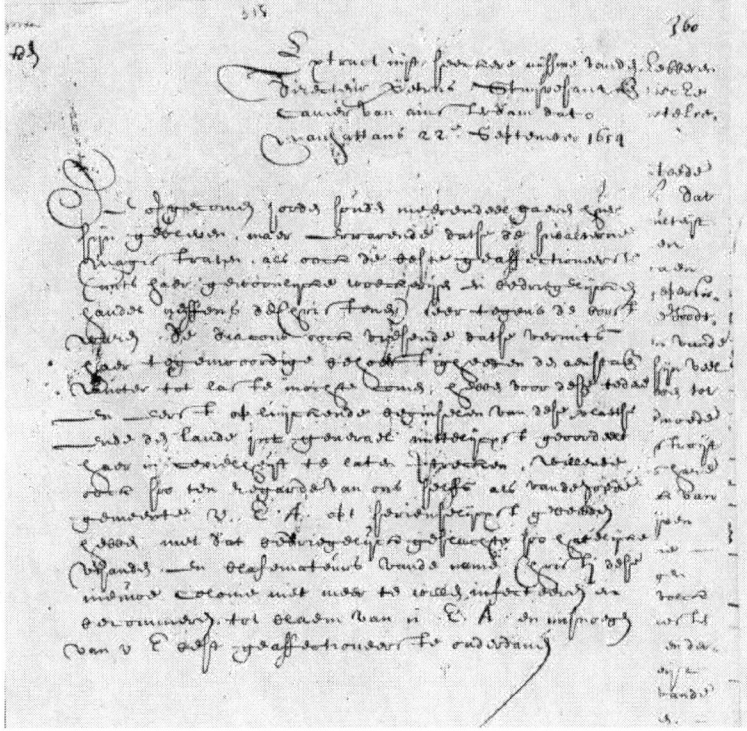

Figure 7. Letter from Peter Stuyvesant, governor of New Amsterdam

---

[3] STUYVESANT, Peter. "Letter to the Dutch West India Company dated September 22, 1654." In: *Samuel Oppenheim Papers* (Box 32 – Brazil and Suriname). American Jewish Historical Society, X, 147 ff.; XVIII, p. 4-5.

- **List of residences in New Amsterdam, from July 10, 1660, which was part of the census carried out by Nicasius de Sille.[4] The list proves that the Jews did not live in separate neighborhoods.**

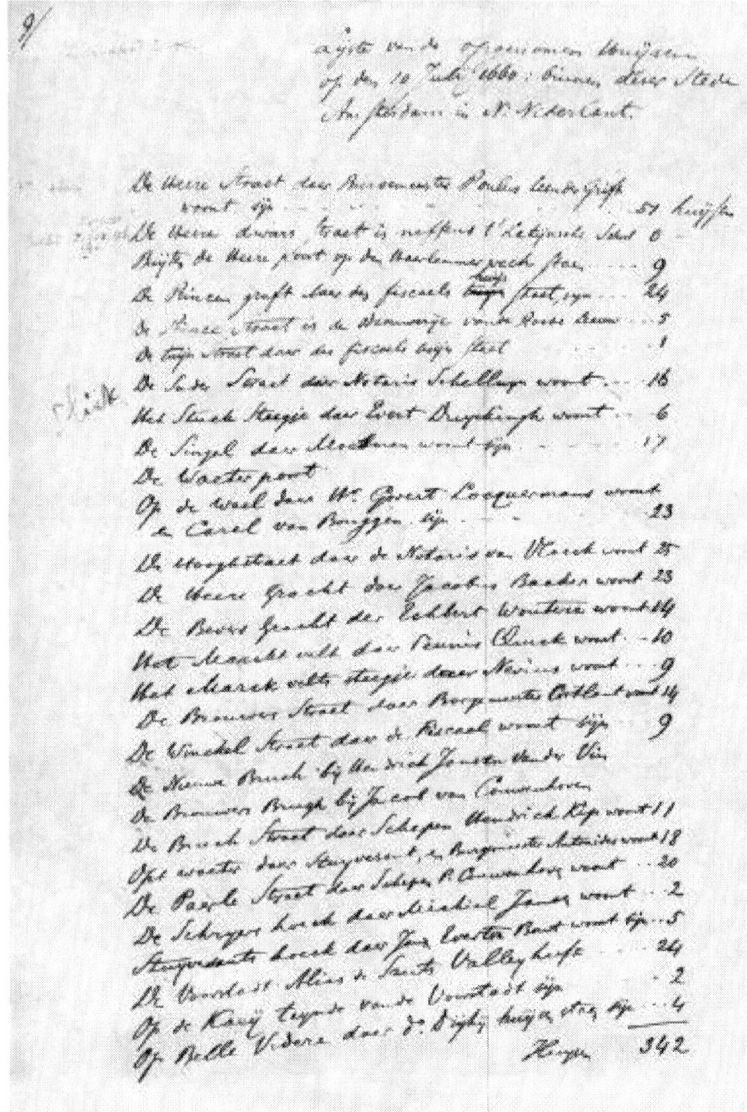

Figure 8. List of Residences in New Amsterdam, Part 1

---

[4] SILLE, Nicassius de. List of the Houses of New Amsterdam. *New Netherland Papers*, New York Public Library (Manuscript Division), 10 Jul. 1660.

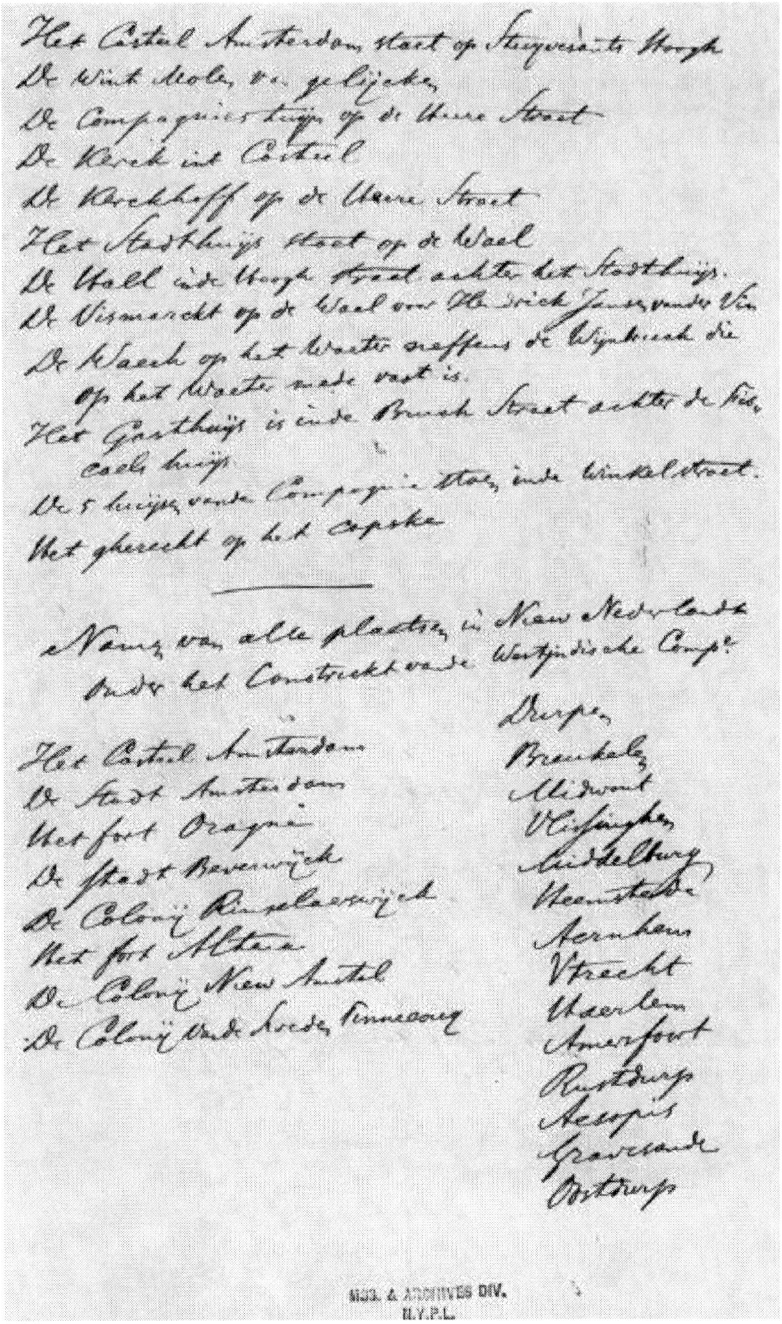

Het Castiel Amsterdam staet op Stuyvesants Hoogh
De Wint Molen van gelijcken
De Compagnies huys op de Heere Straet
De Kerck int Castiel
De Kerckhoff op de Heere Straet
Het Stadthuys staet op de Wael
De Wall inde Hooghe straet achter het Stadthuys.
De Vismarckt op de Wael van Hendrick Jansen vander Vin
De Waech op het Water neffens de Wijnkraen die
op het Water vast is.
Het Gasthuys is inde Brugh Straet achter de Fiscaels huys
De 5 huysen vande Compagnie staen inde Winkelstraet.
Het gherecht op het capske

Namen van alle plaetsen in New Nederlandt
onder het Constrickt vande Westjndische Compe.

Dorpen

Het Castiel Amsterdam
De Stadt Amsterdam
Het fort Orangie
De Stadt Beverwijck
De Colonie Rensselaerswijck
Het fort Altena
De Colonie New Amstel
De Colonie onder Loockers Pinnecorq

Breuckelen
Midwout
Vlissingen
Middelburg
Heemstede
Aernhem
Vtrecht
Haerlem
Amersfoort
Rustdorp
Aesopus
Gravesande
Oostdorp

Figure 9. List of Residences in New Amsterdam, Part 2

- **Template of a Ketubah (Jewish marriage contract), from the 16th century, with inscriptions in Portuguese and Hebrew, discovered in an antiques shop in Manhattan**

Figure 10. Jewish Marriage Contract, Part 1

Figure 11. Jewish Marriage Contract, Part 2

- **Members of the Tzur Israel Congregation of Recife in the 17th century**
  o   In 1953, Arnold Wiznitzer published the list of signatures included in the
      Minute Book of the Tzur Israel Congregation. Later, in 1955, I. S.
      Emmanuel corrected some of Wiznitzer's interpretations. In 1979, Egon
      and Frieda Wolff questioned the manner in which the names had been read,
      and proposed new transcriptions. In 1996, Gonçalves Melo performed
      another attempted reading, analyzing the Minute Book page by page. In
      2003, Rabbi David Weitman published a list of names alongside images of
      the signatures, so a comparison could be made.[5] What follows is a list based
      on the work of these historians:

Abraham Bueno Henriques	Binjamy Sarfatty
Abraham Cohen	Daniel Alvares de Torres
Abraham da Gama	Daniel Belmonte
Abraham de Azevedo	Daniel de Castro de Hamburgo
Abraham de Jeosua Aboab	Daniel Dormido
Abraham de Marchena	Davi Castiel
Abraham Drago	Davi Lopes
Abraham Faro	David Abendana
Abraham Mogo	David Aboaf
Abraham Querido	David Alvares
Abraham Querido Moro	David Alvares de Torres
Abraham Valverde	David Atias
Abraham Yisrael Diaz	David Burgos
Abraham Ysrael de Piza	David Cardoso
Abram Azuly	David Cohen Casseres
Abram Gabay Vila	David da Costa
Real Abran da Fonseca	David de Figueroa
Abrão Aboab Paiz	David Diaz
Abrão Decaserez	David Israel Faro
Abrão Glion	David Jesurun Coelho
Aharon Serfatti	David Judá Leão
Aram Jonas	David Levi Bomdia
Arao Burgos	David Loeb
Arom Levy Frezão	David Maestro
Aron de la Faya	David Mendes
Aron Dorta Depaz	David Senior Coronel
Aron Guabay	David Zuzarte
Beniamin Levy	Dr. Abraham de Mercado
Benjamy Barzilay	Eliau Nahmias
Benyamin Bueno de Mesquita	Eliau Pretto
Binjamin de Solis	Eliauh Veiga

---

[5] WIZNITZER, op. cit. p. 121-122. GONÇALVES, op. cit. p. 340-344. WEITMAN,
David Y. (Rabbi). *Bandeirantes espirituais do Brasil: século XVII.* São Paulo: Maayanot,
2003. p. 43-51.

Francisco de Faria
Isaac Aboab
Isaac Athyas
Isaiah Salom
Isaque Abendana
Isaque Baruh
Isaque Castanho
Isaque da Serra
Isaque da Silva
Isaque Gabai Side
Isaque Izarael
Isaque Levy
Isaque Montesinos
Isaque Pereira
Isaque Preto
Isaque R. Dez da Matos
Ishac Benhacar e Bomdia
Ishac Franco Drago
Ishac Franco Drago
Ishac Senior Coronel
Ishac Senior Coronel
Israel Abendana
Israel Levy Mendes
Izaia Preto
Izaque Canchess
Izaque Defontes
Izaque Feboff
Izaque Gabai
Izaque Isra Quelozo
Izaque Rison
Jaacob Henriques
Jaacob Senior
Jacob Abendana
Jacob Abendana
Jacob Cohen Henriques
Jacob de Lemos
Jacob Draco
Jacob Franco Mendes
Jacob Frazão
Jacob Fundão
Jacob Fundão
Jacob Gabai Correa
Jacob Gabbay de Morais
Jacob Gallas
Jacob Levy
Jacob Navarro

Jacob Zaccuto
Jahacob da Silva
Jahacob Mocata
Jahacob Valverde
Jehosuah Senior Coronel
Jehosuah Ys. de Avila
Jehudah Machabeu
Jeosua Velosino
Jeuda Bemvenista
Joseph da Costa
Joseph Francez
Joseph Francez
Joseph Jesurun Mendes
Joseph S. Alvares
Joseph Ysrael Belillos
Josseph Atias
Josseph Bueno Henriquez
Josseph Frazão Josua de Haro
Jozea (ilegível)
Manoel Levy
Matathathias Moreno
Mordechai Senior
Mordehay Machorro
Mose Lumbroso
Moseh Abendana
Moseh Aboab
Moseh Cohen Henriques
Moseh de Leão
Moseh de Mercado
Moseh Doliveyra
Moseh Henriques
Moseh Levy Rosso
Moseh Namiaz de Amburgo
Moseh Navarro
Moseh Netto
Moseh Nhemias Crastoz
Moseh Zacutto
Moshe Nunes
Moshe Peres
Mosse de Castro David Cera
Mosseh Cohen
Mosseh de Azevedo
Mosseh Nunez
Mosseh Rel d'Aguilar
Mosses Baruch Alvares
Salamão da Sylva

Salo Ysrael Mendes Diaz	Simeon Cardoso
Salomão Cardozo	Simson Guzdorff
Salomão Gabay	Yacob Mochoro
Samuel Barzilay	Yizhak Al Farin
Samuel da Veiga	Yosef Bemvenist
Semuel Frazão	Yshac Henriquez
Semuel Montesinos	Ysra Lemos Dormido

- **Members of the Portuguese synagogue of New York, Shearith Israel, in the 17th century. The following signatories were included on the list of members of the Shearith Israel Congregation at the end of the 17th century:**
  - David Machoro (relative of Mordechai and Jacob Machoro, who were in Dutch Brazil and were signatories of the list of the Tzur Israel Congregation in Recife)
  - David (1681) and Raphael Abendana (1694), members of the Recife congregation
  - ordecai Abendanon (died of chickenpox in 1690)
  - Moses Aboab, merchant (1684), from the Congregation of Recife
  - Isaac Asher
  - Simon Bonam (1687)
  - David Pardo (1684) and Joseph Pardo (1690)
  - Saul Brown Pardo (1685), rabbi of the Shearith Israel synagogue, and his wife Esther (1708)
  - Daniel Campanal (1697)
  - Isaac Coutinho (1676)
  - Raba Couty (1666-1674), an Italian Jew
  - Isaac da Costa (1686)
  - Benjamim e Esther de Casseres (1689)
  - Isaac Cohen de Lara (1699)
  - Benjamim Bueno de Mesquita, who lived in Dutch Recife and died in 1683
  - Joseph Bueno de Mesquita, brother of Benjamim Bueno de Mesquita (1682) and his wife Rachel Doval
  - Jacob de Robles, David e Benvenida de Robles, fugitives from the persecutions in France in 1687
  - Isaac Fernandes Dias
  - Jacob do Porto (1697)
  - Isaac Gabai Faro (1686), his wife Esther Bueno de Mesquita and his daughter Billah
  - Benjamin Franks, jeweler, arrived from Barbados in 1696
  - Bianca Henriques Granada, who died during a smallpox epidemic in 1690
  - Isaac Henriques, butcher (shohet), inhabitant of Dutch Brazil
  - Elijah Ilhoa, who died in 1699
  - Abraham Isaacs (1699)
  - Moses Levi (admitted as a free man in 1695)
  - Ansell Samuel Levy, butcher (shohet) and his wife Margarete, widow of leader Asser Levy

o   Moses Levy, who built the Mill Street synagogue and died in 1728; his
     wife Grace Mears Levy; his brother Samuel Levy and wife Rachel (1732)
o   Isaac (1695) and Rebecca Rodrigues Marques (1697)
o   Abraham de Sosa Mendes (1683)
o   Asher and Rebecca Michaels
o   Isaac and Sarah Naphtali
o   Joseph Tores Nunes, a young merchant who died at 30 in 1704
o   David D. Robles (1696)
o   David Valentine van der Wilde, Asser Levy's brother-in-law
- **Jews buried in Dutch Recife**
o   Below are the names of Jews who lived in Pernambuco during the Dutch
     occupation, and whose deaths took place between 1638 and 1654. They
     were buried in the Jewish cemetery in Recife.[1]

Name	Burial year
Manuel Mendes de Castro	1638
Benedictus Jacob	1641
Moisés Abendana	1642
Benjamin Pereira	1644
Moses Mendes	1645
Isaac Russon (ou Rusten)	1645 or 1646
Antonio Montesinos	1646 or 1647
David Henriques	1648
David Barassar	1648
Baltazar da Fonseca	before 1649
Jacob Delian	1649
David Senior Coronel	1651
Salomão Musaphia	1651
Simon Bar Mayer	1653 or 1654
Antonio da Costa Cortizes	–
Esposa do neto de David Senior Coronel	–

---

[1] RIBEBOIM, José Alexandre; MENEZES, José Luís Mota. O primeiro cemitério judeu das Américas: período da dominação holandesa em Pernambuco 1630-1654. Recife: Edições Bagaço, 2005. p. 25.

Made in United States
Troutdale, OR
10/09/2024